Fear to Freedom

From victim to victory

ROSEMARY TRIBLE

VMI Publishers
Sisters, Oregon

Fear to Freedom: From victim to victory
© 2009 by Rosemary Trible
All rights reserved. Published 2009.

Published by
VMI Publishers
Sisters, Oregon
www.vmipublishers.com

ISBN: 1-935265-09-1
ISBN 13: 978-1-935265-09-2
Library of Congress Control Number: 2009942972

Scripture taken from the HOLY BIBLE,
TODAY'S NEW INTERNATIONAL VERSION®.
Copyright © 2001, 2005 by International Bible Society®.
Used by permission of International Bible Society®.
All rights reserved worldwide.

Printed in the USA.

Rosemary Trible is available for interviews on talk shows,
radio or print media and can be scheduled for appearances
at speaking engagements, retreats and conferences.
For more information or scheduling visit feartofreedomjourney.com.

Cover and interior design by Juanita Dix

TABLE OF CONTENTS

What Others Are Saying About
Fear to Freedom

Ever since our early days in Congress together, Janet and I have cherished our deep friendship with Paul and Rosemary Trible. We've walked through some of life's deepest valleys together, as during the heartbreaking loss of our son Matt. Rosemary's passionate faith and unusual connection with God have challenged and strengthened my own relationship with Him. Read this book, and you'll find the same result in your own life!

—The Honorable Tony Hall,
U.S. Congressman from Ohio serving twenty-four years, retired;
Ambassador to the U.N. Food and
Agricultural Organization posted in Rome

This is a remarkable story from a remarkable woman that, nevertheless, helps the rest of us understand how to be more than conquerors over events in life that could easily destroy us. I give this book two thumbs-up!

—Tony Campolo, PhD,
Professor of Sociology, Eastern University;
pastor and motivational speaker

I've watched Rosemary touch lives on Capitol Hill and in impoverished villages in India. I've seen her boundless energy unleashed to help people in slums of Cuba, Cambodia, other developing nations, and in the inner city of Washington, D.C., Rosemary is a force of nature, powered by a supernatural relationship with God. She's been through deep valleys of pain and stood on mountaintops of joy. Her story is an inspiring example of what God can do with a life surrendered to Him. It is truly a blessing to see how God uses His people to open doors in so many arenas.

—Dois Rosser,
Founder, International Cooperating Ministries, businessman,
and author of *The God Who Hung On The Cross*

What Others Are Saying About *Fear to Freedom*

Every woman should run and buy two copies of this book—one for herself and one to give away—because each one of us experiences fear, and Rosemary's story will give you hope. Her book will make you laugh and cry but best of all she will lead you through fear to a pathway to freedom.

—**Susan Yates**,
Bestselling author of several books including
And Then I Had Teenagers, and *Barbara's and
Susan's Guide to the Empty Nest*

In the recovery rooms of hospitals in Gaza, Bolivia, and Columbia, I have seen Rosemary compassionately holding children after their Operation Smile surgery and then returning them to their families. I know her heart for those who are hurting and fearful, and I believe her story will help bring comfort to so many. Her joyful spirit always lights up a room, and I hope this joy encourages readers to find new hope and freedom in their lives.

—**Dr. Bill Magee**,
Plastic Surgeon, CEO & Co-Founder of Operation Smile,
an international charity treating facial deformities
such as cleft lips and cleft palates all around the world

"There is no fear in love; but perfect love casts out fear . . ." (1 John 4:18). In *Fear to Freedom*, Rosemary Trible shares a personal traumatic story that could have left her bitter, angry, and afraid; yet the love of Christ and the love of her husband brought her through this experience with joy and hope. This book will bring courage to families in crisis and transformational insights to caregivers.

—**Rev. Randel Everett**,
Executive Director of the Baptist
General Convention of Texas overseeing 5,600 churches
Former President of The John Leland
Center for Theological Studies

Choosing to heal takes an act of courage. Allowing others inside one's heart to see the process and the journey to wholeness requires uncommon valor. In this book Rosemary demonstrates both courage and uncommon valor.

—**Wintley A. Phipps**,
Gospel recording artist, motivational speaker,
and Founder/CEO U.S. Dream Academy, Inc.

Fear to Freedom

God often seems to work through paradox—in ways we'd least expect. Perhaps, only God would take a privileged Southern woman, married to a United States Senator, accustomed to the corridors of power, and use the tragedies of her upside-down life so she becomes a champion for real racial reconciliation and a force of hope for hurting women. Rosemary's story is surprising, powerful, and challenging.

—The Honorable John Ashcroft,
U.S. Attorney General 2001–2005, U.S. Senator 1995–2001
Governor of Missouri 1985–1993

Rosemary Trible's story will probably bring a tear to your eye. It will certainly bring joy to your heart. Rosemary writes with the authenticity of one who has suffered, thought profoundly about good and evil and the meaning of life, and has unshakeable confidence in His peace and joy. It's a wonderful book. I recommend it with enthusiasm.

—Senator William L. Armstrong,
President of Colorado Christian University,
Former U.S. Senator and Congressman from Colorado

Rosemary Trible is one of the most amazing people we have ever known. She is lovely, buoyant, energetic, wise, and deeply spiritual despite the fact that she has suffered a devastating tragedy in her life that she shares in this book. We believe her story will benefit many and we highly recommend *Fear to Freedom*.

—Denny Rydberg,
President of Young Life, and Marilyn, his wife and partner in ministry.
He is the author of ten books including *Beyond Graduation*,
How to Survive in College, and *Twentysomething*

In Christ we all know intellectually that we are free indeed. However, the journey from fear to freedom is often long and complex for each of us. Rosemary's journey serves to inspire and encourage us. I am thankful that she was willing to be so transparent, which will empower others to be set free.

—Kay Coles James,
President and Founder of the Gloucester Institute,
a leadership training center for young African Americans;
Director for the U.S. Office of Personnel Management 2001–2005;
Former Virginia Secretary of Health and Human Resources

What Others Are Saying About *Fear to Freedom*

In a world filled with so many things that are phony, Rosemary Trible has written a powerful and moving account of the most turbulent time of her life and how with God's and her husband's help, overcome it to experience healing and a new purpose. Every woman should read this book, whether they have been violated, or not. Every man should read it so they can better understand a woman's deepest fear.

—Cal Thomas,
Syndicated and *USA Today* Columnist/*Fox News* Contributor

My wife and I were up until the wee morning hours reading this amazing book! Most Christians who endure heartbreaking trials trust that God has allowed it so they can help others through a similar trial. Yet how many of us will risk becoming vulnerable enough to do so? Rosemary Trible did! An inspiration to us all, Rosemary shares the unspeakable heartaches she was forced to endure behind her seemingly "perfect" life as a senator's wife. When she and her husband turned to Jesus, He turned the ashes into something incredibly beautiful! From rape to redemption to a near-death experience that provides Rosemary with an amazing gift of forgiveness for the man who almost destroyed her life, this profound book will not only change lives, but it is bound for the screen!

—Ken Wales,
Producer of the movies
Amazing Grace (based on the life of William Wilberforce)
and *Revenge of the Pink Panther*,
Executive Producer, the CBS series *Christy*

Bill and I have known Rosemary and Paul since 1976 when he first went to Congress. Rosemary's story is witness to the promise that you too can end the cycle of fear and break free from the bondage of your past. This book is captivating and I highly recommend it to anyone looking for healing, forgiveness and restoration! I was also touched by the uplifting stories of college students who have overcome eating disorders, panic attacks or self worth issues. It brought joy to my heart to see how God's transforming power dramatically changed Rosemary's life as well as others. Read this and I believe you too will be inspired to join the journey from fear to freedom.

—Vonette Z. Bright
Co-Founder, Campus Crusade for Christ®

Fear to Freedom

After over eight decades as an advocate for equality, I am heartened by the covenant relationship between two women from totally different racial and cultural backgrounds, Rosemary Trible and Barbara Williams-Skinner. Their 15 years of walking in unconditional love and acceptance of one another described in this compelling book, affirms that true love is boundless and knows no color, political party or culture.

—Dr. Dorothy I. Height,
Chair Emerita, National Council of Negro Women

In 1994, immediately after Tom Skinner passed away at our temporary house in Virginia, Rosemary Trible was the first person to show up and offer support and encouragement through the most devastating experience I have ever had, the death of the love of my life. God is so amazing. Of all of the people He would send to walk through this most painful stage of my life would be a White, Southern, Republican sister to this Black, Progressive, Democrat. What I learned through my walk for over 15 years with Rosemary is that true love is boundless, knows no color, political party or culture. In *Fear to Freedom*, Rosemary bravely shares here her story of great loss that leads to fear that limits love. I am so grateful to have been a part of her story of healing as she has been such a vital part of mine.

—Dr. Barbara Williams-Skinner,
President, Skinner Leadership Institute
Former Executive Director, Congressional Black Caucus

ACKNOWLEDGMENTS

I am grateful to my husband, Paul, and my children Paul and Mary Katherine and her husband, Barrett, for their love, patience, and wonderful support of my own healing journey and in writing *Fear To Freedom*. Thank you for believing this book could help encourage those brokenhearted to experience new freedom and joy in their lives.

Without the assistance of many friends, especially Peggy Bowditch, René Bowditch, Linda Slattery, Margo Taylor and Ellen Vaughn this book would not have become a reality. My pastor, Rev. Carleton Bakkum, has been my constant mentor and friend. I am also devoted to my brother, Gene Dunaway, who has always come alongside and encouraged me to share my life story.

My thanks also to Susan Lohrer, my editor who was so gracious and patient with me as a new author, and to Lacey Hanes Ogle and Bill Carmichael at VMI publishers who walked with me every step of the way.

DEDICATION

This story was written for my
loving husband, Paul
and my children
Mary Katherine and Paul III.
Thank you for believing in me.
It is dedicated to my
"God children"
who are now with the Lord

Leland Bowditch

Jonathan Coe

Matt Hall

And also to:
all the young women
and students God
has brought into my life
who have been such a blessing.

PREFACE

My deepest desire is that my story will help someone else be less afraid. When we share deeply from our lives, we give something of ourselves to others. Undertake your own journey as a gift to yourself as you read this book (feartofreedomjourney.com).

This book is about getting set free. The Devotional Guide in the back of the book is a tool that will relate to each chapter and include a focus *Scripture*. It offers *Pause and Reflect* questions, and when appropriate, a *Practical Process* to explore.

You may choose to read through the book and then consider the devotional guide, or read one chapter at a time along with the *Pause and Reflect* questions to enhance your getting the most out of the book. The *Practical Processes* apply mostly to the last chapters, and will coach you as you move forward on your healing journey. Take your time as you answer the thought-provoking questions. These exercises will help you discover new techniques to finding deeper meaning and happiness in your life.

The guide will also work well with an accountability partner, small discussion group, or prayer group as a weekly guide. You might consider a twelve-week study covering two chapters a week or decide the best pace for your group. I want to help you envision what you want in your life, and I hope this book and Devotional Guide will inspire and empower you to be set free and find greater personal fulfillment and joy!

We sometimes believe outside circumstances or other people dictate our happiness, but the key is how we respond. I moved from victim to victory. My desire is you will come to understand that God loves you right where you are. As you find peace with your past, you can embrace new passion for life that brings love, purpose, and greater fulfillment. Some brokenness is inevitable. There will be obstacles—but *choose joy*.

Fear to Freedom

What if you did not
have to be so afraid?

CHAPTER 1

Will I Ever Dance Again?

My earliest fond memories are of my daddy holding me close in his arms when I was about three and waltzing me around the dance floor. I felt safe and happy. My hair flowed and my little feet flew as I tilted back my head and laughed as we twirled. As I grew a little older, Daddy put my sock feet on top of his so he could teach me the dance steps.

Throughout my life, on special occasions or just at home, Daddy would turn to me with a twinkle in his eye and ask, "May I have this dance?" My answer was always yes! On my wedding day, Dad, of course, had the first dance to "The Way You Look Tonight." At the end of the dance he kissed me, then led me over to my husband, Paul, and said, "Here's your new partner." I began life with such security and love from my dad.

Four years later, I learned what it is to live in great fear. In December of 1975, I was raped at gunpoint.

My world was shattered. My body was torn. My heart was crushed. My spirit was broken. My joy had been stolen. I thought I might never dance again. I was taken captive by fear that began to control me. I knew I could not live this way. It sent me searching for answers that began my journey from fear to faith to forgiveness to freedom, a journey from victim to victory.

What I came to realize is that fear can grip our lives and destroy our peace, or we can learn to surrender the fear and move toward a more fearless heart. Surrender does not mean giving in and putting up the white flag. It means letting go and depending on God's strength, not your own.

1

Fear to Freedom

Fear happens. This book addresses the question, "How do I turn my fear and mourning into joy?" Out of my own depth of grief comes this story of renewed hope for those caught in the grip of fear. God redeemed my stolen joy. Now I hope this transformation and the lessons I learned will help others begin their own healing journey.

Though this book includes moments of pain, it doesn't dwell on the dark side. It shows how people who have experienced great pain and darkness in their lives can move to the light. It's about sexual assault, terror, and healing. It is about reconciled hearts and finding forgiveness in fractured places. It's about big dreams, the death of dreams, and becoming bold enough to dream again. It's about growing out of cultural category boxes, moving into racial reconciliation, and building friendships that only God could make possible. It's about hope and healing. Although my trauma dealt with sexual abuse, I believe the healing process described here will be useful to anyone who has experienced immense suffering and loss. The cycle of fear can be broken, and lost joy can be found again.

Over the years of a very public life as the wife of a U.S. congressman, senator, and president of a university, my greatest fulfillment has been to walk alongside many women and young girls who have struggled with personal trials in so many forms: a sense of loneliness, rejection, or lack of self-worth. They may have dealt with eating disorders or physical or verbal abuse. I have come to know these women not only by name, but also to know where their hearts are breaking. I try to walk with them in their pain, and encourage them to overcome fear so they can lead a happy and fulfilling life. Together we begin a healing process using practical tools, many shared in this book, that help these young women keep fear from controlling their lives.

We cannot deny suffering. We live in a world where fear is part of our everyday lives and anxiety is all around us. There is fear of abandonment, inadequacy, or failure. There is fear of violence or abuse, both personally and in our world at large. There is fear during an economic crisis of losing homes or jobs or retirement savings. Then there is fear of death or even fear of fear. Our very culture seems to promote fear as moment by moment we are bombarded by pictures of economic dislocation, threats of terrorism, war, famine, or natural disasters. There are stories of pain, suffering, homelessness, and hunger throughout every newscast.

Will I Ever Dance Again?

Sometimes, however, fear can protect us from harm and warn us of danger. Fear can challenge us to do things we never thought possible, such as overcoming a fear of public speaking. To love deeply means we may fear the loss of someone we love. But we can also become so controlled and consumed by fear and anxiety that they destroy our hearts. Fear also can affect our relationships and sense of well-being.

Is there one of us who has not experienced some fear or anxiety in her life? Perhaps you have felt brokenhearted by the loss of a loved one, the disappointment in a career, or the death of a precious pet? There may be those who have felt trapped in a situation or bound by an addiction. Have you ever grieved over a child gone astray or friend who has been unfaithful?

It seems we are anxious about so many things. We question, "What if this or that might happen?" Yet most of these fears are imagined and will never come true. *Fear exists primarily in what isn't, not in what is.* Fear creeps into our lives every day and cloaks us in a feeling of uncertainty.

There may be deep-seated fears from our past that have never received healing and affect our sense of well-being. Some of these come from our belief about a situation or circumstance. These continue to trigger reactions to events and situations today like an echo from the past. We become trapped in a cycle of fear—overwhelmed by a sense of anxiety.

We tend to hide our fears. We put on that wonderful smile for all to see and respond, "Oh, I am fine. I'm just fine." Meanwhile the hurt grows deeper in our hearts if there has been no true healing. Fear, however, is like bacteria. If you keep bacteria in the dark, it continues to grow. But if you bring it into the light, it dies. It takes courage to recognize our fears and seek healing. Especially difficult are those wounds from our past that have been buried in the darkness of our hearts for a long time.

Sadly, women who have suffered from rape are often the ones hiding their pain and experiencing deep brokenness. The statistics of the Department of Justice as reported by RAINN (Rape, Abuse & Incest National Network) are devastating. One in eight women will get some kind of cancer in her life. However, "one in six women will be sexually assaulted sometime in her lifetime. College-age women are four times more likely to be assaulted and since 60% of sexual assaults are not reported to the police, the number

3

of victims is probably far greater. In 2007, there were 248,300 victims of rape, attempted rape, or sexual assault in the U.S."[1]

As I spoke with Scott Berkowitz, founder and president of RAINN, he said, "These statistics mean that every two minutes an American is sexually assaulted. We want to do everything we can to help these victims." (Free, confidential 24/7; National Sexual Assault Hotline for help 1-800 656-HOPE. Online Hotline; www.rainn.org).

Another major challenge is human trafficking that affects us both at home and internationally. Unfortunately, there is much smuggling across borders that involves sex rings of both children and adults. President George W. Bush's address to the U.N. General Assembly in 2003 stated, "Each year an estimated 800,000 – 900,000 human beings are bought, sold, or forced across the world's borders. Among them are hundreds of thousands of teenage girls and others as young as five, who fall victim to the sex trade. The victims of the sex trade see little of life before they see the very worst of life, an underground of brutality and lonely fear."[2]

Whatever pain may have wounded you—whatever has stolen your joy— take heart. How we respond to life's pain and challenges is what is important. If I had not traveled my own dark road of fear, I would not be able to challenge others to travel their own journeys of forgiveness, healing, and finding their purpose.

When you're a victim of fear, you believe your life is ruined and you'll never feel normal again. The natural question is often "Where was God when this happened to me?" This book doesn't give easy answers. There are none. Yet, as I struggled with pain and panic in the aftermath of the crime against me, I began to sense God in new ways. I began to embrace a new life of faith and forgiveness. I began to explore new possibilities and purpose for my life.

You can learn to dance again! I have come to love the Scripture "You turned my wailing into dancing . . . and clothed me with joy" (Ps. 30:11). This has been true in my life, and I believe it can be true for others who are suffering. There was no magic wand or instant cure. However, my spirit of despair and fear was indeed turned into everlasting joy. My life is now filled with healing, happiness, and hope.

Will I Ever Dance Again?

Fear to Freedom shares my own personal journey, and the Devotional Guide in the back of the book will serve to encourage those willing to begin their own path to healing.

What has stolen your joy? Are you ready to move from that feeling of being a victim to walking in victory in your life? This book points the reader toward receiving the grace only God can bring to the heart.

In addition to finding freedom from fear, another theme throughout the book is that of reconciliation and the importance of loving people out of our comfort zones. My African-American friend Barbara Williams-Skinner has become like a sister to me over the last twenty-five years. Our relationship has stretched me in countless ways, because we are so different in our backgrounds, cultures, and political persuasions. I will share the Ten Commandments of our Friendship to help others see they don't have to look alike or think alike to love one another.

My stolen joy was powerfully redeemed through a "near-life experience" fourteen years ago. Although similar in some ways to a near-death experience, I call it *near-life* because I felt fully embraced by the next life and the power of eternal love. This was a transformational moment in my life. It took away the fear of death forever and was a powerful lesson in forgiveness. Even though physically I could not move, speak, or open my eyes, I knew such intimacy with God and felt saturated by love. Though an evil act had crippled me, I found there could be new hope and new life both now and for eternity. God sees the larger picture and can use our suffering for a larger purpose. This book shares three themes that have been woven throughout my life. My desire to:

Walk intimately with God.

Love and forgive everyone.

Inspire and empower others to live free from fear.

I felt convicted to write this book at church one day when our pastor, Rev. David May, during his sermon asked two questions: First, "What if you did not have to be so afraid?" and second, "What if you could help someone else not have to be so afraid?" When I heard the second question, I felt God was calling me to step out in faith and share my life story, which I had kept hidden inside for so many years.

Fear to Freedom

Mother Teresa said, "I am a little pencil in the hand of a writing God, who is sending a love letter to the world." [3] I pray God will use me as his little pencil to write this story as his love letter to those suffering from fear. May the brokenhearted find hope that God's healing power is transformational, and that when we are free in him we are free, indeed. God's amazing grace has released me from the shackles of fear to begin a new dance of freedom. He has opened my eyes to the power of forgiveness and being reconciled to others. And he has drawn me to adore prayer and come into the presence of love as I live moment to moment. Truly I have been blessed.

Now watch yourself. I warn you that this book is also a love story. It's about my falling head over heels in love with the greatest lover of all times, Jesus. Do you remember what it is like to fall in love? You become vulnerable and have those butterflies in your stomach. Love can be a scary thing because it brings you close to the flame. As we fall into the arms of a living God, we are then called to give ourselves in return. *Falling in faith* is like falling in love. We were created for this love and to this love I hope each of us opens our hearts. Nothing on earth is more satisfying or exciting!

As we journey together through this book may you find new freedom, new forgiveness, and new freshness in your love relationship with Jesus. May you find peace in your life, joy in your heart, and new ways to dance again.

CHAPTER 2

Redeeming Love

In my life I have experienced the power of God's redeeming love in many ways. My journey began with my family where I grew up in Little Rock, Arkansas. My dad and mom were happily married for fifty-five years. They loved to ballroom dance and taught Gene, my brother, and me to dance at an early age. When Gene was eight and I was six, I remember dressing up and driving to Memphis, Tennessee, to the Peabody Hotel to go dancing for my birthday. My dad would glide my mom around the dance floor. To make the floor smoother, he would take a sugar packet out of his pocket and sprinkle it on the dance floor as he waltzed Mother in his arms.

Music was a part of our lives and I can always remember Mother whistling. She was even part of a whistling quartet in her younger years. On weekends we would drive to our farm, where I grew up riding horses, racing around the barrels at horse shows, and caring for all kinds of animals. Our whole family harmonized as we sang old songs driving back and forth to our farm, the D Down Dunaway Farm. My dad was an orthodontist, but his first love was horses.

We raised quarter horses, and I loved watching the new crop of foals being born and trained because there was such a transformation that took place. A young colt would go from great fear—terror of the unknown—to a relationship between horse and rider of deep friendship and a sense of oneness. The foal experienced freedom from fear as a wonderful bonding occurred, and the horse responded to a gentle touch of the reins or a whispered command.

I learned many lessons on our farm about trust and compassion, and I remember these as some of my most joyful days. When I graduated from high school, Dad decided to sell the farm and our hundred head of horses. That day when we left the barn for the last time, we both had tears in our eyes. We walked hand in hand knowing selling was the right thing to do, but our hearts were so sad. What treasured memories we had shared together throughout those early years.

My dad was the most compassionate and kind man I ever knew. He was always doing something for someone and never letting anyone know. Once he paid for a young woman's education after he heard her sing at Rotary Club. He saw her potential and knew she could never afford the kind of training she deserved. Dad lived by example as a man who put others first.

Another time at church Dad met Casey, a six-year-old girl with only one leg, who was visiting her grandmother. He offered to help financially with any necessary operations or future education, and a lifelong friendship developed.

St. Francis of Assisi said, "Preach the Gospel at all times and when necessary use words."[1] This was the way Dad lived his life. His philosophy was never to let the sun go down on his anger. As an orthodontist, he had to deal with emotional parents and upset kids who often broke their braces. When Dad got frustrated, he would go into his office and close the door. Out of his desk he would pull a little red flag on a toothpick stuck on a gumball.

He knew getting mad or saying something he might regret wasn't going to work. When that red flag was out, everybody in the office knew Dr. D, needed a little time to cool off. Then Dad would let go of the anger and put the flag away. He would say, "Sticks and stones may break your bones, but words will hurt you even more." Dad always carried this message in his wallet: "Water and words: easy to pour, impossible to recover."

Dad never wanted to hurt anyone. Learning from him, if I was hurt or upset with someone, I would write it on a piece of paper at night and put it in my nightstand. The next day I would tear it up and let it go.

Redeeming Love

My parents were strong in their faith, and for as long as I can remember we never missed a Sunday going to church. Dad was a staunch Baptist who had never danced until he met Mom. He asked his mother for permission to dance when he fell in love with Mom and then—well, they never stopped dancing. Mom was a Methodist so Dad agreed to become active in the First Methodist Church in downtown Little Rock.

Dad, however, believed I should not be baptized as a baby but should wait until I was old enough to make a decision about Jesus for myself. That moment of decision came for me one warm summer night in Little Rock when I was seven and we went to hear a man named Billy Graham.

We had to walk up pretty high to find seats in the War Memorial Stadium where the University of Arkansas Razorback football team played. I listened to this man's passionate talk about how you could have a personal relationship with this person named Jesus. At the end, he called people to come down, and I turned to my mom and said I wanted to go. I closed my eyes and said in childlike faith, "Jesus, I love you and I give my heart to you." That one moment made all the difference and was a turning point in my life.

We lived in the same white house on Colonial Court from the time I was two until Dad retired. It had rocking chairs on the big front porch and a beautiful side garden. I had always loved sitting on the steps that overlooked our azalea garden. I was drawn there often, and called this my "thinking spot."

Although I didn't really understand what it meant, I was drawn by a deep desire to be in silence. I would go to the steps outside our garden and there I would talk with a friend I could not see but whose presence I felt. Somehow, I was not alone. Somehow, I was understood. Our love grew as I shared my deepest secrets and discovered the adventure of just being together. That silent place, the beauty of the flowers, and this intimate friendship with Jesus are favorite childhood memories.

Several years later at ten years old, I was confirmed at our church. There were about twelve of us, but I was the only one that was also to be baptized in the service. Of course, I had seen lots of babies baptized, but here I stood alone at the altar rail as the pastor talked about this *living water*. Then he sprinkled water on top of my head and said, "I baptize you, Rosemary Dunaway, in the name of the Father and the Son and the Holy Spirit." I felt a special touch of the Spirit that has never left me.

Fear to Freedom

Overall my childhood was happy, but I confess my most challenging relationship was with my mom. I struggled as a child with the fear of inadequacy. My mom had a difficult childhood as her father died before she was born. She felt she always had to be the strong one; working to take care of everyone else, paying the bills, and keeping everything clean. In her early marriage, she was so particular that she used a stick covered with a cloth to get the dust out of the windowsills.

She was a beautiful, stylish woman, yet she always seemed anxious. Mom held so much inside, and it was hard for her to express her emotions. She had shut down her tears at an early age, and I don't recall ever seeing her cry until near the end of her life.

When I was sick, Mom would care for me and bring me soup but she would never come into the room for fear of getting sick. Sadly, even when I was well she would not kiss me, but would turn her head so I could kiss her cheek. (See photo at my wedding.)

I always felt I wasn't enough. Even though her strength was comforting, I longed as a child for her touch. She did not know how to be vulnerable, to laugh out loud, or ever dream of smiling when a photograph was taken.

I struggled to please Mom and felt I could never live up to her expectations or really win her love and affirmation. This probably propelled me into becoming more of a perfectionist in my schoolwork and extracurricular activities. When I became anxious, I always returned to my "thinking spot." There, I felt safe and loved. There, I would talk about my sadness to Jesus and feel comfort.

Mom would often compare me to my brother, Gene. She would shout at him, "You should work harder and be good like your sister." This would upset me because I adored my brother. I always wanted peace in the family and never was good at confrontation. When Mom said to me, "Rosemary, I am disappointed in you," it would break my heart.

It made me sad that I could not make her happy. I was afraid as a small child she might wag her finger at me and say, "Rosemary, you know better. You need to be a *big girl*." I did not want to be a big girl. I wanted to run and get dirty and roll in the grass. I wanted to play outside at the farm and smell like the animals. I wanted to laugh and act funny like a little girl. But Mother always wanted me to look clean and put together. I never really cared for the color pink, but she loved me to wear pink. I even had a pink poster bed that I never liked. She wanted me to be her big girl, but I longed to be myself.

She was rough on Gene, and this broke my heart. Gene always protected me. I remember how he cared for me when a plane crashed on our street a few houses from us. We slept in twin beds and awoke to what sounded like a freight train. Gene held me close as we huddled together on our bedroom floor and watched the shower of steel pass by our window. Later that morning when we went to the scene of the crash, where the pilot and our neighbor died, we saw the plane had destroyed her entire house.

I also tried to protect Gene and I took on the role as the peacemaker in the family. I shut down my anger as a child and took on things that were more than my responsibility to carry. I wanted to take care of everyone, and I somehow thought I could love everyone into being happy.

The pain in my early years was redeemed in a beautiful way before Mom died. Something truly healing came out of my deep need for her love and touch. Broken parts of my heart were restored during the last five years of Mom's life when she became ill with Alzheimer's.

Alzheimer's is terrible, but in Mom's case, a new freedom from anxiety came over her as she became more childlike. She endured constant pain from rheumatoid arthritis her last twenty years, yet she seldom complained. Mom had always worried, and now she could not remember anything long enough to worry about it, so she was set free. She had always been strong in her faith. But it wasn't until the last months of Mom's life that we experienced her intimacy with God. Now it seemed all she could talk about was Jesus. The shouting and frustration that characterized her earlier life gave way to her singing with great enthusiasm, "Hallelujah! To Thine be the Glory."

My mom and I spent the last eleven days of her life together. When I first arrived we visited for a while until I thought she was getting tired. As I arose to leave the bedroom, she pleaded, "Rosemary, don't leave me. It's dark out there. Come and lie here next to me on the bed." Tears flowed down my cheeks and joy filled my heart as a life's desire was fulfilled from this woman who seldom ever held me.

I lay down next to my mom, and we embraced each other as she drifted off to sleep. All those years, when I needed her touch so much, faded away into a precious contentment as I lay in her arms, and she rested completely in my embrace.

Mom's days and nights were mixed up so I stayed awake to keep her company in the middle of the night. I decided to write down on a little sticky note pad by the bed some of the things she said. Her words spoke of her sweet personal relationship with Jesus. With her memory all but gone, it was like God took her mind home before he came for her. She opened up like a flower that had been waiting to bloom. She'd wake up in the middle of the night and ask, "Do you know Jesus? He's the one with the big job. I want to see Jesus. He's a nice guy and he calms me down."

Another night she woke with a question. "Do you have some money? I don't know about heaven, and I've heard the streets are paved with gold. But I might just need some money up there." I took twenty dollars out of my purse, and she smiled as she tucked it away. I reassured her I thought God had everything under control in the way of finances. Mother has always balanced her checkbook down to the last penny, so she was just making sure she was covered.

Later she said, "He talks to me," and I asked, "What did he say"? She replied, "He said, Hi, Mary." She'd sing a verse from "Jesus Loves Me" or "The Old Rugged Cross," then she would fall back to sleep. She awakened again and sighed, "I'm so tired, I've been here such a long, long time. I want to go home." I told her I understood and for her to go to Jesus, whenever he called her home.

The last night, before she died, I lay beside her in the bed to comfort her, and I stroked her head lovingly. All those years of longing for her expressed affection faded away as our hearts were now one as mother and daughter. She drifted off to sleep, then awoke looking outward. She proclaimed with a smile on her face, "They're happy. They are so happy up there." It was followed by silence and then she whispered, "He's coming, He's coming for me!" Tears of joy filled my eyes. Those were the last words she spoke.

My brother, Gene, was flying home from Hong Kong where he had been on business. When he got to San Francisco, he was able to catch a red-eye flight so he could see her before she died. We had long ago forgiven Mom, and we both loved her deeply. Mother literally waited through the night to see her son one more time.

Redeeming Love

That afternoon I was with Mom quietly holding her hand when I thought of the bedtime prayer she had said with us long ago. I asked, "Do you remember, Mom, the prayer you taught us when we were children? It is the same prayer I taught my own children, and I would like to say it for you.

"Matthew, Mark, Luke, and John,

Bless the bed that I lie on.

Four corners to my bed,

Four angels around my head,

One to watch, one to pray

And two to bear my soul away."[2]

Mom in that very moment took her last breath. She had gone to be with Jesus. He had come for her as if the angels had borne her soul away, where every tear and all pain would be wiped away. I reached over and gently closed her eyes and then went to comfort Daddy.

One of my parents' favorite musicals was *The King and I*. They loved when the King turned to Anna and asked, "Shall we dance?" Kneeling beside Dad, I took his hand and gently said, "Dad you will always be Mom's dancing partner, but she's gone home. It's like Jesus came up to you and tagged you on that dance floor and said, 'May I have this dance with Mary?' One of your favorite love songs, "I'll Be Loving You Always," played as Jesus swept her gently into his arms and waltzed her into eternity."

Mom and Dad's lives were about loving God and serving others. Every family has some challenges, but my parents' love for each other is the greatest inheritance I could ever have. Our God is in the business of restoration and redemption, and I personally experienced this with my mom. He knew my heart needed that physical touch and expressed love I had longed for as a child. God restored to me that redeeming love in a special way as he answered my prayers of so many years before. After all, God's desire is to reconcile hearts and make broken things new if we will surrender them to him.

CHAPTER 3

A Reconciled Heart

A s I became a young adult I learned foundational lessons about reconciliation and love. One person who was a major influence in my early years was Willie Mae Smith, a wonderful African-American woman. She was like a second mother to me and was part of my family from the time I was two weeks old until I went to college. She always had a smile and a hug and she nurtured my brother, Gene, and me with awesome, faithful love.

I was like a little shadow that followed her everywhere whether she was making cookies, caring for my pet turtle, or doing the ironing. Willie loved Jesus. She would sing this wonderful spiritual, "He Touched Me," about how joy filled her heart when Jesus touched her and made her whole.

I remember laughing when Willie would cross her legs and let me sit on her foot as she bounced me up and down to her singing about how Jesus loves the little children—red, yellow, black, and white—all precious in his sight. Somehow I understood in a deep place in my heart that Willie loved me, and yes, this Jesus loved me too.

My brother and I were inseparable as children, and we felt safe talking to Willie about anything. I remember how she would tickle us until we cried for mercy and fell into each other's arms laughing.

Fear to Freedom

Then in later years my brother and I felt the impact of the upheaval in Little Rock over Central High School's integration. On September 23, 1957, nine black high school students faced an angry mob of white people protesting the integration. There was so much violence the police removed the nine, sometimes referred to as "the Little Rock Nine," from the building to protect them.

> One of the nine black students, Elizabeth Eckford, recalled, "they moved closer and closer." Somebody started yelling, "Lynch her! Lynch her!" I tried to see a friendly face somewhere in the crowd—someone who maybe could help. I looked into the face of an old woman and it seemed a kind face, but when I looked at her again, she spat on me. On September 25, President Eisenhower mobilized troops and federalized the National Guard who successfully escorted the students into Central High School. This was the first major test of the Supreme Court decision of Brown vs. The Board of Education.[1]

I was eight and Gene was eleven, and it helped to talk about this hatred with Willie and hear her point of view.

Fear rose in everyone as we watched the television reports of this historic moment. My heart broke and tears came to my eyes as I nestled next to Willie and together we watched people ridiculing these brave students as they walked into Central High School. The violence and unrest continued throughout the South and, during other demonstrations, the National Guard used dogs and turned hoses on people to contain them, all because of the color of their skin.

In 1960, when Gene was fourteen and I was eleven, a pivotal incident impacted our lives. First Methodist Church was our big downtown church, and Gene and I always sat in the balcony with our parents. During the service two black couples took seats in the balcony. Suddenly there was a hush and then great stirring among the congregation. The service went on but tension seethed in the air. At the close of church, the ushers quickly and firmly escorted the couples from the church.

Gene stormed out of our church that day, not to return until later in his adult life. Here sermons were preached about how we should love ev-

16

eryone. These now seemed like shallow words that did not apply to loving others despite the color of their skin.

Willie was a woman of God who had a tremendous impact on my faith as a child. I saw Jesus in everything she stood for: reconciliation, compassion, forgiveness, and unconditional love. I never saw her as different but experienced her as a sweet assurance of love that taught me to trust in God. Willie helped us understand the meaning of loving one another and God with all our heart, soul, mind, and strength.

Late in Willie's life, Gene and I were at her hospital bedside during her last hours. I stroked her forehead gently as she had lovingly done to me for many years as she put me to sleep. Willie was now blind, but as I caressed her tenderly and spoke of my love, tears fell down her cheeks and mine.

Gene and I spent the night reminiscing about Willie's extraordinary life, the lessons we had learned, and how blessed we were through her love. We thought of the sacrifice Willie had made being away from her family and daughter. Willie was a constant image of love and reconciliation. It stamped the lesson on my heart that we were to love and respect everyone, no matter what race, color, or background.

AMERICA'S JUNIOR MISS

Another early life lesson came when my mom suggested I enter and represent my high school in the local qualifying contest for the America's Junior Miss, a nationwide scholastic program. My first concern was what on earth my talent would be. I liked singing and dancing but was not prepared to perform either on stage.

I enjoyed public speaking, so my talent became a dramatic reading of "The Smile," a short story by Ray Bradbury about the smile of the Mona Lisa. My mom had me practice it till I knew it by heart. I went on to win the Arkansas competition. I could never have imagined how much this would change my life. I learned a lot about building confidence, responding to questions about our generation, and talking about leadership. This stretched me in public speaking and performing before a camera.

Next I went to Mobile, Alabama, for the national Junior Miss program that was televised nationwide. This was not a typical beauty pageant but focused on scholarship, interviews, youth fitness, and performance. Many funny things happened, such as the drizzly night we rode in convertible cars in a parade. Afterward, we were presented coming down a beautiful ballroom staircase at an historic Mobile hotel; but in the rain my long, flowing dress had stretched, and I caught my heel, taking a nice trip just as they called my name. After my hula hoop flew off the stage the next day in one of the practices, I laughed, relaxed, forgot about the judges, and just had a good time getting to know these great girls from each state. I enjoyed these new friendships more than anything.

At the conclusion of the televised show finals, they announced my name as America's Junior Miss. It was the greatest shock of my life. As I walked down the runway, it was as if I was in a dream that could not possibly be happening to me. In fact, Diane Sawyer had been selected as America's Junior Miss four years before me, and I had always greatly admired her. A flood of emotions filled my heart as the girls surrounded me with hugs and congratulations.

Immediately I was off to press conferences and speaking engagements. Those first few days were a whirlwind of interviews, meeting sponsors, and speaking to groups. I was introduced to Mrs. Mary Weatherby, the woman who would travel with me for that year that I served as America's Junior Miss. She had a peace about her throughout every situation, and I soon came to know her strength was from her love of Jesus.

I seldom share this demanding season of my life. However, I learned so much through dealing with the press and the challenges of facing public life at eighteen years old. I'll never forget my initial encounter with the press in New York.

Three days after the program finals, we had flown directly from Mobile to New York, and I stood before a national press core; open, vulnerable, trusting, and naive. The press conference was going well until a reporter asked me if there were any black contestants in the program. I answered honestly, "Not in the national finals or my state program in Arkansas, but I'm sure there must have been black contestants participating in some of the other states." The reporter probably had the story line already in mind when he asked the question, since there was so much in the news about the segregation issues in my hometown of Little Rock. The article in a New

A Reconciled Heart

York paper implied that an "all white" program had selected a Junior Miss from Little Rock, Arkansas.

I was completely devastated about the article and asked for forgiveness for any harm this may have caused. I was fearful that I had diminished what the program stood for. I was humiliated that I might have hurt any friends at home, especially Willie, who was like a mother to me. I was concerned I had been a disappointment to others. I was devastated that I could have hurt the feelings of other black contestants. I certainly did not mean to imply the program was showing any prejudice as the media suggested.

My own heart's desire was to show respect to everyone. The article was soon forgotten by all but me. We weathered the storm and I was grateful those in the program encouraged and supported me. It was a humbling experience, and a lesson in forgiveness and the challenges of being in the public eye. I promised myself I would always strive to be understanding of people from different races and cultures.

Overall my experience as America's Junior Miss was wonderful. Buddy Lauten, his nephew Steve, and Mary Weatherby traveled with me on our six weeks' American Heritage Tour across the country that summer. Other friends from the program met us at special events along the way, such as tea at the White House with President and Mrs. Johnson. Chevrolet was one of the national sponsors, so I was the spokesperson for the Detroit filming of the Driver's Education film that was used for years. Another national sponsor, the Breck Company, published my Junior Miss portrait as one of the "Breck Girls." You have to be pretty old to remember that!

In New York Bobby Vinton and I rode together in the Macy's Thanksgiving Day Parade, and he sang the whole parade route in the snow. Then later at the Rose Bowl Parade, I remember how Mason Bell, one of the vice presidents of Chevrolet, went into shock at the skimpy costume they selected for me to wear for the Chevrolet float. He said, "There is no way Rosemary is going to appear in that outfit!" Of course, Mary Weatherby agreed and a new costume was made and ready in a few hours for the next morning's parade.

There were wonderful adventures, speaking engagements, and positive articles. I will always treasure representing the America's Junior Miss program. This outstanding program has been an inspiration to many young women throughout the years. Often when I spoke, I talked about the importance of our generation being leaders who would be willing to serve others and go out and change the world for good.

While traveling a great deal that first year, I was also a freshman at Sweet Briar College in Virginia. It was difficult trying to keep up grades and be a normal college student while serving as America's Junior Miss. Mrs. Mary Weatherby always traveled with me, and her abiding faith strengthened me. We laughed when the schedule went crazy, fell exhausted after the end of a demanding day, and treated ourselves to chocolate sundaes. My own faith grew deeper as we would turn to prayer and found comfort in each other.

I actually came to enjoy the involvement with the media and especially the television interviews, even thinking I might want to pursue communication studies. But I had learned a difficult lesson from that first press conference. I saw how public life can be exciting, but have its challenges and be very demanding. At the end of that year it was great to pass this honor on to the next America's Junior Miss and go back again to being just Rosemary. A new season was about to begin.

FALLING IN LOVE

The first week of my sophomore year at Sweet Briar College, Paul Trible came into my life and changed everything. I got a call from one of my classmates asking if I would go out with this guy. At first I said, "No way." I'd had enough experiences with blind dates. But Paul got on the phone and convinced me in his charming way that we would just go out for a couple of hours, and he'd have me in by 10:00 p.m. sharp. We were having a wonderful time after dinner when Paul shocked me by announcing, "OK, let's go. I made a promise to have you in by ten."

We dated the next weekend and the next. I liked the fact that Paul had nothing to do with my Junior Miss year and seemed to care for me for who I was now. Soon we were seriously dating. Over that semester, I knew I was falling in love and was beginning to believe Paul would be the man I would marry. At the end of that year I was torn with a difficult decision to transfer from Sweet Briar and pursue a career in communications at the University of Texas. UT's Department of Radio, Television, and Film was one of the most outstanding in the country. But this would mean Paul and I would be dating long distance for two years which would be extremely difficult.

I could have lost the love of my life but thanks to lots of phone calls and Texas football—the Longhorns were #1 in the nation—we made it through. Paul made quite a few long road trips my way, and I returned to Virginia to see him whenever possible. We learned more about ourselves through our letters, and our faith in God and our love for each other deepened.

No matter where I lived, I always found what I had called as a child, my "thinking spot." More and more I was drawn to this time of silence and intimacy in prayer. I led a Bible study in my sorority, and my roommate both at Sweet Briar and Texas, René Roark, was my constant partner and forever friend.

At the end of my senior year, Paul was finishing his last year of law school at Washington and Lee University. We finally determined we could not afford not to get married, as we had so much invested in telephone calls and road trips.

However, Paul's growing interest in politics worried me. The idea of our marrying and my being in such a public life again raised new fears. I told him, "I will marry you if you don't go into politics, because it is just not for me." That very honest-looking young man I now have been married to for thirty-nine years responded, "Why, Rosemary, I'll never run for dogcatcher!" And he never has. I later realized I should have been more specific in my request.

I graduated from the University of Texas in May, and Paul and I were married October 9, 1971. We moved to northern Virginia where Paul clerked for U.S. District Court Judge Albert V. Bryan, Jr. Because of my uncertainly about a political life, when I interviewed for a job working for Senator John McClellan from Arkansas, I said I wanted to experience Capitol Hill to prove to myself that the fears I had about politics were unfounded. Over the next two years that I served as assistant press secretary for McClellan, I found out firsthand about the demands of the political life and the pressures on families. I would never have dreamed, however, what God had in store for us.

Paul next became an assistant U.S. attorney in Alexandria, Virginia, and was prosecuting criminal cases from day one. One morning he rolled over in bed and asked, "What would you think of my becoming Commonwealth's Attorney of Essex County?" The handwriting was on the wall and our public life started. We moved to the small, historic town of Tappahannock on the banks of the Rappahannock River, where Paul began his political career.

Paul was appointed as the criminal prosecutor by Judge Dixon Foster in April 1974. We immediately began campaigning because we had to stand for election in November. At twenty-seven Paul was elected to his first public office, winning more than eighty percent of all the votes. Paul may have kept his promise about not running for dogcatcher, but we were on our way to a life in politics. The most important thing was we were together, and I decided even then, "If you can't beat them, join them."

CHAPTER 4

Fear Steals My Joy

A s we stepped into this demanding life of politics, I wondered where I was going to find fulfillment in my communications career. I was learning how to trust that when one door is closed, God often opens a new window we might never have expected. "Trust in the Lord with all your heart, lean not on your own understanding, in all your ways acknowledge him, and he will guide your path" (Prov. 3:5–6). I began searching for a job in Richmond, which was about an hour away from Tappahannock. After several interviews and having to develop one live show, I was given a wonderful opportunity to host my own daily television talk show.

I would get up each weekday morning at six o'clock, gulp some coffee, kiss Paul good-bye, and drive an hour to the TV studio for the live show. The show on WTVR, Channel 6 was called *Rosemary's Guestbook*. It was a far cry from the Oprah era of today, but I adored the show and the excitement of meeting many wonderful people. I was responsible for just about everything. I appreciated my freedom to choose the theme for the shows, develop interview questions, select the guests, and welcome and prepare them for the show.

As the show began, the camera focused on a close-up of the guestbook, opened to the names of the guests written in calligraphy on the page. I set the tone with a thought for the day. Then I introduced the program and the live show began as the cameras rolled at 9:30 a.m. sharp four days a week.

We aired shows on everything from the political and cultural scene in Richmond to an on-location shoot of a personal tour through the Virginia governor's mansion with First Lady Catherine Godwin. I was honored she agreed to do the show, and our friendship grew close through her participation on *Rosemary's Guestbook*. My audience was primarily female, so I focused on subjects that were mostly relevant to women's lives.

Two weeks before Christmas 1975, I was twenty-five years old, married to Paul for four years, and was hosting *Rosemary's Guestbook* for my second year. My favorite shows were once a week when I tackled a more serious issue facing women. A week earlier I had aired a show on sexual assault—an issue that wasn't then commonly discussed on television, especially in conservative markets.

I wanted so much to help women who'd been violated. I felt that a program on this taboo topic could reach out to many women who lived daily with the fear and trauma of being raped, abused, or violated. My director, John Shand, agreed to the show even though it was a stretch for our station. I prepared carefully because I wanted this show to be helpful to those women who had experienced such a terrible event.

Two guests who had been raped agreed to share their stories, and we shadowed their faces to keep their identities protected. I gently questioned the women about their experiences and the aftermath of the crimes against them. A police officer and a district attorney also were guests. They provided support and valuable suggestions on prevention and dealing with such sexual assault crimes.

Afterward the studio was flooded with calls and mail as hundreds of women shared with me their painful experiences and the fear they had been hiding. For this moment, their grief had been heard and the victims acknowledged with sensitivity and compassion. I wept as I read the letters and listened to their stories. So many victims . . . so much pain.

A week after that show, I was going to stay in Richmond overnight to tape a few programs. My parents and brother were coming for Christmas, and I wanted to get some shows "in the can" so I could take time off to be with my family. A live show must go on whether it is Christmas or not! I checked into the hotel just across the street from the television studio. I planned to work on the shows so I would be well prepared for the next day.

About eleven o'clock that evening I was sitting at the desk in my hotel room working on the next day's scripts on my old Underwood typewriter. I was having trouble staying alert enough to finish my work, so I went downstairs to the hotel restaurant and got a cup of coffee. Then I hurried back to the room, unlocked my door, and returned to the desk. My back was to the windows.

I heard the curtains part.

A man grabbed me from behind. I felt the cold steel of a gun muzzle on my temple and his gloved hand around my neck.

He bent down and hissed in my ear. "OK, Miss Cute Talk Show Host. What do you do with a gun to your head?"

I struggled, fought, pled, and prayed as he held me in his stranglehold.

He raped me viciously.

I used all my strength and power to fight him off. I tried every bit of logic to combat his hold. I even tried to talk to him about God, pleading, "God cares about you. You don't have to do this." He had a ski mask pulled over his face and all I knew was that he was tall, black, muscular, and strong.

I repeated to myself the Lord's Prayer to try to keep my mind from going into shock. It was a night of sheer terror. My attacker never dropped the gun he held in his hand. I was completely horrified yet in a strange way I struggled to find God's presence.

"I will kill you if you tell. I know where you live," he whispered in my ear like a demon.

My heart cried out, "How can I live through this?"

Finally, pointing his gun to my head, he backed away, turned, and climbed out the window. This one floor of the hotel opens directly onto the roof of the parking garage. My attacker slipped away into the night.

Though he'd threatened to kill me if I told, I immediately called the hotel's front desk and told them what happened.

Security immediately responded, as did the police, but there was no trace of the rapist, nor any useful evidence.

Fear to Freedom

I trembled from head to toe as I called Paul, needing him more than ever before. "I've been raped," I sobbed on the phone. "I need you. Please come and hold me."

Then I huddled in a chair, clinging to my knees. I felt so filthy, so alone, so overwhelmed by fear. I cried out for God to be with me in my devastating pain. I felt frozen in fear.

A female officer burst into the room to question me, and I repeated every detail of the assault. It was 1:00 a.m., but thank God my new gynecologist, Dr. Crooks, mercifully agreed to meet me in the hospital emergency room. His gentleness and compassion made all the difference. After hosting the show I had great compassion for these women who had been rape victims and had called or written me about the show on sexual assault. Now I felt such a powerful connection with these women, for their pain had become my pain. Now, I had joined them, another statistic.

I never could have dreamed this would happen to me. My heart felt as though it were breaking in two. Later the officer did more debriefing, and I had to report the crime again in great detail even though my body and heart were exhausted and traumatized.

Paul, who had been two hours away visiting his parents, finally arrived about 2:30 a.m. As he held me gently, he was swallowing his own rage. As a trial lawyer he had prosecuted many hideous crimes but never imagined one would strike so close to home. He stroked me lovingly and protected me like a child, repeating, "I love you, sweetheart. It's going to be all right." Finally I fell into an exhausted sleep in his arms.

In just a few hours, I awoke and my fear grew in intensity. I called John Shand, the manager of the TV station, and told him what had happened. "John, I've got to appear on the show this morning," I said, my heart pounding. "Otherwise my attacker will know I told and I'm sure he'll be watching."

I dressed quickly, put on my best face, and with Paul close by my side, I walked across the street to the station. Like a robot, I did the live show. Then John said not to worry, he would take care of hosting the rest of the shows through Christmas week and give me some time to heal.

When I got home, I went to bed and slept fitfully. My body was bruised and aching and my heart completely broken. Something inside that had always made me a trusting and hugging person was crushed. Now, I felt anxious about being touched and nervous when a stranger looked at me. My rapist had done more than tear my body. He had stolen my joy. His rage filled me with fear and his hatred made me feel I could never be the same again.

I realized that regardless of the circumstances of a rape, the rapist wants to make his victim feel that whatever happens is her fault. She feels ashamed and broken even though he was the one who attacked her. And after all, I had done that show on rape, and that apparently prompted his anger toward me.

The next day my parents and brother arrived from Arkansas for the Christmas holidays and the community party we had planned. I confided in my brother but decided not to tell my parents about the rape because I wanted to protect them from the horror. "I can do this," I said to myself. I stuffed the pain and fear deep down inside and put on the old smile, even though I was devastated. After hosting a long-planned party for a hundred guests, I kept up the pretense through the holidays.

Yet at night I could not control my tears. My body shook as Paul held me close. He desired more than anything to take away my fear, but he could not.

Paul began to work with the police on the investigation to do everything they could to pursue my attacker. Aside from the physical markers and evidence from my abuse and rape, there seemed to be no real leads. I was sure the man who had raped me had done this many times before. He operated like a professional, and I was so afraid he would attack somebody else or find me again.

The Monday after Christmas, it was time to return to the television studio and host a new week of shows. My world had been shattered, and fear gripped my heart as I thought of going back to the station across from the scene of the crime. I got up, put on my makeup, drank coffee, and chatted with my brother, Gene, as I got ready to leave for Richmond.

Suddenly the fear became so strong, I needed to escape. I ran up to my bathroom as tears poured from my eyes. I questioned, "Will I ever find joy again? Will I ever be able to find a way out of this pain?"

I was so overwhelmed by terror and the thought of that cold gun pressed against my head, I passed out and awoke in my brother's arms.

Fear to Freedom

When I became conscious, Mom and Dad were at my side comforting me. Paul whispered gently, "It's all right. I've told them what happened. You don't need to hide it anymore."

John hosted a few more days of the show, which gave me a little more time to recover. When I returned to the show, a new fear arose. My period did not come; one month, then two.

I returned to Dr. Crooks, who encouraged me, "It's just the stress. Really, please don't worry. You are going to make it through this challenging time." Uncertainty brought anxiety, but I knew because of our deep love that Paul and I would work things out.

I continued the daily show on autopilot. On my commute home in the evenings I'd stop by the Rappahannock River Bridge. I would cry out to God with conflicting emotions of anger, deep sadness, and loneliness. After letting tears flow, I'd put on my makeup and drive home. I wanted to be there for Paul at this difficult time for he too was in pain. It broke his heart to see me so sad. He had been so incredibly gentle with me throughout the rape trauma. I wondered how we would learn to live and love in the present, without my being terrified from this memory that was still so raw.

Thankfully my period finally did come; I was not pregnant. It was a great relief yet fear still gripped me. Every day when I drove to and from work, I felt I could hear the same old tape of my attacker's voice saying, "I know where you live." I could hear his hateful taunt: "I will kill you if you tell anyone." I kept telling myself, "Rosemary, why can't you just get over this?" I tried to hide my emotions and push down the pain. Inside me, a powerful storm had hit my life, destroying my hope and stealing my joy.

The night of my rape had been a night of horror, but even more devastating was the fear my rapist had planted deep into my heart like a dagger. Fear took over my mind until the pain was unbearable. Fear trapped me. Fear held me captive. I could not get out.

Rape is not about the sexual act but about control and power over the victim. The attacker relishes the power he has over his victim; he feeds on his victim's helplessness.

After several months of living in fear, I resigned from the television show I loved. I told John, "This opportunity to host *Rosemary's Guestbook* has been wonderful. However, I can't find the joy anymore. I need to find the real Rosemary."

CHAPTER 5

Will I Ever Feel Normal Again?

I thought leaving my job at the television station would help release the pressure of the constant memory of the rape. I did not understand why fear continued to grip my soul and paralyze my mind. I kept telling myself, "It is over. It is time to move on." My heart and mind would not let it go. Healing was going to be a step-by-step, moment-by-moment process. I gave up the show I loved so I could be gentle with myself and give myself time to heal.

I found a good job nearby at St. Margaret's School working in fundraising to keep busy. It felt good to be doing something worthwhile, but when I left work, the tears would come again. I felt I was beginning to split into two people living disparate lives. One that managed well at work and put on a smile when I came home to Paul, and an interior life that was constantly tender and deeply grieving.

I felt like I would never find the real Rosemary again. Would I ever feel normal again? I had been a trusting person who saw the world as basically good. Would there always be this cloud over me? I felt like the Peanuts cartoon character Linus with his blanket snuggled close for comfort since trouble seemed to follow him everywhere. I had experienced such evil that the pain seemed unbearable. Strangely, although I greatly feared this man, I could not hate him.

Paul was wonderful and always comforting, but it was difficult for him to talk about my experience. I wanted so much for our lives to go back to normal and yet I wondered if they ever would. Months went by and Paul stayed in close communication with the police. There was no trace of the rapist. This was a great disappointment to Paul, especially since he too needed some closure for this crime. He wanted more than anything to see this man who had hurt his wife behind bars.

I struggled with the overwhelming feeling that there was no way out. I did not want to stop hoping and trusting, but I did not know how to get out from under the grip of fear my attacker had put over my life. It seemed I could not think of anything else even though I tried to live a normal life. It was like I was swinging on a trapeze as my emotions went up and down. I felt that if I let go, I would fly helplessly through the air, not knowing if anyone would be there to catch me.

I prayed, "God, take this fear away from me." I had been a confident, capable person. Now I was upset with myself because I did not seem to be healing like I thought I should. There was also a part of me still upset with God—questioning how he had deserted me. I was upset that I always felt a deep sense of loneliness. I kept trying to remind myself that faith is not a feeling. At times I had difficulty feeling God's presence, yet I knew I had to trust him with my terrible pain. There was nowhere else to turn. The Lord had never failed me, and what hope was there for healing except through his mercy?

Somehow I needed to break free from these horrible thoughts of the past pain that were ruining my life. These terrible thoughts were not only my memories of the abuse, but also thoughts of shame and worthlessness. I would tear up Paul's old T-shirts when a burst of fear would cause adrenalin to flow through my body. The sound of the ripping and the tearing physically helped me release the pressure and try to once again surrender my anger and pain.

How could I set my mind and believe what I knew to be true: that God would never fail me. Jesus, I believed, was trustworthy and would be there

Will I Ever Feel Normal Again?

to catch me when I felt I was falling. In those difficult months that followed, Jesus tenderly drew me near. Looking back I saw how the Lord never failed to take my hands as I reached out to him. I made a decision to trust God's grace to restore and renew what had been broken in my life. I began to realize:

Fear can lead to peace.

Death can lead to life.

Sadness can lead to joy.

Pain can lead to love.

Loss can lead to hope.

Grief can lead to grace.

Alienation can lead to healing.

Gratitude can lead to compassion.

Forgiveness can lead to freedom.

Henri Nouwen writes, "One of life's great questions centers not on what happens to us, but rather how we will live in and through whatever happens. Will I relate to life resentfully or gratefully?"[1]

I did not want to live with resentment and bitterness. I desperately desired God's presence so I turned to prayer and God's Word for comfort. I went through a Bible concordance and looked up every reference to the word *joy*. I began reading through these when I needed strength. The intimacy with the Spirit returned. It was so sweet that I began to call this special friend, the Holy Spirit, *Joy*. I was finally making some progress on my healing journey, but my heart was still so tender—not only for my brokenness, but for so many others who had been abused. There was a fellowship of suffering with these other women. I had no idea how God would use this pain in my future for his good.

Another woman, Debbie Smith, suffered from a devastating rape while her husband, who was a police officer, was asleep upstairs. Her attacker took her into the woods, used her own T-shirt to blindfold her, and threatened to kill her if she told anyone. She endured six years of suffering from her trauma till one day her husband got the news from the deputy chief of police, "They've got him!" Her attacker had been identified through DNA testing. Debbie used her pain to fight for abused women everywhere. Ultimately, Congress passed the Justice For All Act, most often known as the Debbie Smith bill, to expand DNA testing to fight crime, identify criminals, and help protect women from abuse.

She shares this advice for victims:

> I wish I could say that you are just going to get over this. You desperately want to feel normal again, but you have to find a "new" sense of normal for your life. This evil crime invaded my life, but I came to realize if I let this destroy me, he wins! I had to fight for who I am. Every day that I find joy in my life, I win.
>
> Sometimes girls that have been abused ask me, "How long is this going to take?" I tell them, "As long as it takes." In the midst of my pain I prayed every day, 'God, take this fear away.' Now I understand God loved me enough to allow me to go through this and use it for his glory. He could see the big picture on the other side.

I didn't have any idea how long it would take me to heal but I knew I could not let this man destroy my life and continue to control me with fear. I thought, "I can't let him win!" It was time to fight for my joy to return. I decided to write down every day something I was grateful for: I had a wonderful husband who loved me, and family and friends who cared.

Moments still came when I felt so broken I thought of myself as a cracked pot. Then I imagined the illustration of God reaching down with his hand and bringing the light into this cracked pot and asking, "Where does the light shine through?" I prayed God would use even this "cracked pot" for his glory and let his light shine through me to help others.

CHAPTER 6

Our Congressional Life Begins

I n the midst of my healing, a new and exciting opportunity opened up for
Paul. United States Congressman Tom Downing decided to retire. Paul
was a Republican, and the First District of Virginia had not been represented by a Republican since reconstruction. Virtually every office holder
was a Democrat. It would be a tough race, but Paul asked if I would be willing for him to run for Congress.

Campaigning would mean crisscrossing twenty-one counties and cities
in eastern Virginia, media coverage, and newspaper stories. I was excited
for Paul, as this was his life's dream, so of course I said yes. However, my
spirit was still tender with much fear. I could not imagine how I could handle
campaigning and meeting so many total strangers.

One of the most difficult things about my recovery was I had been an
open and vulnerable person. Now I had put up a wall to being touched,
especially by anyone I did not know. I found that when you are in the midst
of great pain, it is difficult to believe that you can and will survive and that
your heart will get better. I had to keep reminding myself that I was on a
journey to becoming whole once more. This journey moved slowly, but

Fear to Freedom

I drew hope from knowing I was growing stronger in my faith and I was beginning to trust again. A campaign still sounded overwhelming. I knew I needed some help.

I thought of my college roommate, René, who lived in Austin, Texas. We had been fast friends since our freshman year at Sweet Briar. Together we had transferred to the University of Texas, and there was a special song we loved by James Taylor, called "You've Got A Friend." We pledged to each other that if either of us really needed the other, all she had to do was call, and we'd be there for one another.

Having promised to be friends for life, I made the call and reminded René of our song. She said, "Absolutely yes! I'd love to come be with you and work on the campaign." She quit her job, left her house, and agreed to join me on the "Trible for Congress" campaign trail. I flew to Texas so we could drive back together to Virginia. We couldn't stop laughing because something quite odd was happening on the trip. My feet began to smell so bad that I wanted to put them out the window! I felt nauseated. I called my mom to tell her we made it safely and mentioned laughingly about my smelly feet to her on the phone. "You're pregnant!" Mom exclaimed happily. "When I was pregnant, I just could not get my feet far enough away from my nose!"

A few days later René and I slipped up to the local hospital to do a pregnancy test, although I thought it absolutely impossible I was pregnant. Well, Mom was right. I was pregnant with our first child, and I was thrilled. I called Paul and asked him to meet me on the courthouse steps. When I told Paul the news he literally swung me off my feet and around in a circle, he was so happy. Together we praised God for bringing good in a time of great pain. I felt once again the spark of the happiness that always used to be with me. I thanked God, for we were truly blessed by this news after months of struggle. Perhaps my joy would return with this new baby.

Still every once in a while I'd see a man about the size and shape of my attacker, and a burst of fear would flare inside. Yet like the woman with the alabaster jar that anointed Jesus, when something is broken something precious can also be released. I continued the healing process, drawing ever closer to God.

Discovering we were going to have this baby was a miracle for Paul and me. This child gave us hope that the anguish could subside, and we could be happy again. It gave us the courage to continue the campaign for Congress that also seemed like an impossible dream. It gave me hope that God was with me and I could trust his promise. I remembered a Scripture my dad shared with me when I was a child: "For I know the plans I have for you, declares the Lord, plans to prosper you and not to harm you, plans to give you hope and a future" (Jer. 29:11). Whatever the outcome of the race, we would be together as a family and that would make all the difference.

René was a great support during the campaign. She never left my side. Sometimes I would have a wave of sadness between political events, and she would just let me have a good cry. More often we shared a good wave of laughter. The campaign was demanding; when I was four months pregnant, I fainted campaigning door to door in August on a hundred-degree day. It was incredibly difficult being pregnant and keeping up the grueling schedule.

René suggested we consider a more limited schedule to care for my health and the health of the new baby, but there was just so much to do on the campaign trail. I became aware of things that triggered my fear. One of those was staying in hotels, so we spent the nights with supporters whenever possible. Our hard work was beginning to make a difference. I continued my healing process with some ups and downs. Paul was always loving and supportive, and because we were apart so much of the time, I was especially grateful for René's faithful friendship. It also worked out well for her, as at one political coffee she was pouring punch, and two single brothers flipped a coin to see which one would take her out. David, the brother who won the toss, ultimately became her husband.

Paul and I would have a good article and our spirits would soar, then a negative article or letter to the editor would throw us into a tailspin. Political campaigns are emotional roller coasters. We agreed we had to just give our best and trust God for the outcome.

One of our most challenging places to campaign was at the gates of the Newport News shipyard. Paul and I would join some volunteers at the gates at 6:00 a.m. to greet the workers as they arrived. Paul would pass out Trible campaign literature and shake as many hands as possible. At first there was little response. The shipyard workers threw away our brochures as soon as we handed them out. But as the weeks passed, the response became more and more positive. As we approached Election Day, we thought we just might win.

We spoke at hundreds of events, visited churches and nursing homes, and I had lots of coffees called Rosemary's Roundup. Our average contribution was $25 and we only had three $1,000 gifts, the maximum then allowed. Two of those contributions were from Paul's parents.

Paul had many debates with our opponent, who was a fine man and veteran state legislator. The candidates often debated at schools and colleges, where the students would afterward hold a mock election. We began winning these contests and receiving great publicity. We could sense the election turning in our direction, but we were afraid there was not enough time to win against this strong opponent.

On election night we waited for the results that seemed to take forever. Just before the 11:00 p.m. news our campaign manager said, "Paul, they are still counting votes in the rural areas but those results should put us over the top. Let's declare victory. It is better to be a congressman for an hour than never at all." We went down to an enthusiastic crowd of wonderful supporters and claimed victory. We won by less than 1,500 votes out of a total of 150,000 votes cast.

The outcome was an amazing upset. Paul was elected to Congress in 1976 at 29 years of age. The CBS commentator, Roger Mudd, announced around midnight that, "A nobody from nowhere was just elected as Congressman from the First District of Virginia." People in Tappahannock didn't care that Roger called Paul a nobody. But they were irate that he said that Tappahannock was nowhere. Many people wrote notes to CBS about their historic hometown.

At 4:00 a.m. we awoke to return to the gates of the shipyard to say thank you. No politician had ever come back to say thank you to the shipyard workers. It was a magical moment! Word spread like wildfire that Paul had returned as the First District congressman with his pregnant wife Rosemary. We will never forget the warmth of the workers' response. We had come from the depths of fear to the height of joy.

Yes, we had won a great victory, but now there was so much more to do. We had to hire a staff and organize a new congressional office. We had to prepare for the arrival of our first child. We had to find a place to live in the

Our Congressional Life Begins

Washington D.C., area and begin our new lives. The most exciting thing of course was our new baby. We took a three-day crash course on Lamaze and hoped like crazy that God had all this worked out.

Our baby was due December 29th—Paul's birthday. We thought this timing would be perfect. Dr. Crooks would deliver the baby in Richmond, before we moved to Washington. But our baby did not come on schedule. Our excitement grew as in January we moved into a quaint two-bedroom townhouse in Old Town, Alexandria.

I'll always remember my dad arriving from Arkansas in a truck with furniture we affectionately called *early attic*. He saved the day. Then I rode with Dad in this bumpy truck back down to our home in Tappahannock to get more of our personal belongings. I thought I might just have this baby any minute!

Ten days later Paul was sworn in as the U.S. Congressman from the First District of Virginia. It was one of the proudest days of our lives. I prayed the photographers would have mercy and take pictures that did not include my full width, because I literally felt I was five feet by four feet! When they suggested we climb the front steps of the capitol, I just started laughing and everyone joined in. Paul and his new colleagues were sworn into office in the ornate chamber of the House of Representatives. I sat with his parents and watched with great pride from the gallery above.

For me this was a time of new beginnings but also a challenging time. I had been pregnant throughout the congressional race, fainted campaigning door-to-door, completed a crash course in Lamaze, and made it through the swearing in. I was three weeks overdue yet these were some of the most exciting moments in our lives. I did not want to miss anything.

On January 12, 1977, I joined Paul to hear President Ford's farewell State of the Union address. I was so pregnant they let me sit on the floor of Congress instead of up in the balcony where most of the wives sit. René and our administrative assistant, Gus Edwards, joined us. Yes, you guessed it . . . I went into labor in the middle of President Ford's speech. Two congressmen, Caldwell Butler and Bill Whitehurst from Virginia, sitting behind us tapped Paul on the shoulder. They wanted to let us know they were taking bets as to whether we would make it through the night, or Paul would be the first congressman to become a father on the floor of Congress.

Fear to Freedom

René, our new press secretary, was thinking how wonderful the publicity would be in the event of an *event*. I sat on the aisle with Paul next to me, and René and Gus were to his right. Gus was the only one with a watch so when I had a contraction, I nudged Paul and then he nudged René. René then nudged Gus, who recorded the timing of my contractions on a little piece of paper. I prayed like crazy! At the end of the speech, the house doctor came rushing over to me and asked, "How close are your contractions?" I replied nervously, "Five minutes apart and regular!" He responded, "I'm a cardiologist. That's what most of these guys need." He nodded toward the congressmen as he said it. "You need to head for the hospital."

Looking back it sounds crazy but we drove two hours in a light January snow because Dr. Crooks, my gynecologist to whom I had grown so close through my ordeal, was in Richmond. René was doing the Lamaze breathing with me and Paul was driving as fast as he could. What an adventure!

Our precious Mary Katherine was born on January 13, 1977. When this ten-pound baby was delivered, Dr. Crooks said, "She has come into this world shaking hands and giving political speeches." Wow! That was all she had done for nine months plus three extra weeks. What a miracle to hold our precious little girl. How beautiful that God used Dr. Crooks to walk through the storm of earlier fear with me and now he delivered into our lives this incredible joy. My heart began to rejoice again.

Our new life had begun! Paul was engulfed in the excitement of being a new congressman, but in an amazing way God seemed to be reaching out to him. Now, no one believes you can go to Congress and have your faith deepened and intensified, but that is what happened to us. Paul and I had been active in our faith during our early life and our marriage; however, God deepened and transformed our spiritual life after Paul was elected to Congress. Paul had climbed a political mountaintop. He had succeeded in realizing his life's ambition at a very young age. But when he got to Congress he found something was lacking in his life.

Paul explains:

> It was not until my election to Congress that I came to realize that there was much more to the Christian experience. At twenty-nine I served in the greatest parliamentary body of the most powerful nation of the world. I had scaled

38

the mountaintop, but I soon recognized that there was something missing in my life. That missing something was an intense and personal relationship with the living God.

I came to realize that there is a loving, living God at work in this world, with whom we can walk and talk, on whom we can depend, and from whom we can derive great power, peace and purpose, now and forever. That recognition has changed my life. And only that recognition will change the life of this world.

Through the example of then Congressman Bill Armstrong from Colorado and other members, Paul was introduced to the importance of establishing a personal relationship with a living God in whom he can trust to provide the power to live each day so much more fully. In Bill, Paul saw a sense of peace in dealing with the challenges of political life that depended on the power that came through his faith in God. Although we had been active in our churches, Paul had seen Jesus more as someone he should follow, but not so much as someone with whom he could interact and who could impact and guide his life every day.

I was missing all the new congressional wives' activities and orientation, but it did not matter as I held Mary Katherine in my arms. In many ways she had saved my life, and my heart began to soar again with new life. I did wonder, at twenty-six years old with this new baby, how I would ever meet the demands of a public life I had always been afraid of living. However, the joy of Mary Katherine brought me such happiness that I tucked all my fears away.

CHAPTER 7

A Victim Again!

Then came the day our house was broken into. Mary Katherine was about six months old, and I'd taken her for a stroll. She was in my arms as I walked up the front porch to our home. Splinters of wood littered the step. The door had been forced open. When I cautiously pushed open the door and came inside, thankfully, there was no trace of the burglar. Everything was turned upside down. I gasped and my heart started pounding as I saw the television and VCR were gone. I quietly carried Mary Katherine to her room and gently tucked her in her crib. I didn't want her to be afraid and see me fall apart.

After shutting her door as though everything were normal, I returned to the living room and called the police and Paul. While waiting for them, I fell on my knees. The old storms of fear caused by my rape battered me with tremendous power. I was terrified by the thought that someone had been in my house, and I became a victim again. I felt violated. I cried out to God, "I can't live with this fear. Come hold me close. I need your presence more than anything. Lord, I surrender everything in my life to you."

Fear to Freedom

That moment was the great turning point of my life. I felt powerless to do anything except turn it all over to God. I knew I couldn't handle this on my own. My strength had to come from God. He was the only one who could set me free from fear. I had never experienced anything like what happened next. A warm covering settled gently over me like a comforter, protective yet light as feathers. I knew it was the Holy Spirit. "Do not fear," I heard in my heart. "I am here."

I pulled myself together and waited. Unlike the horrific waiting after the rape, an amazing peace flooded me. Finally I had faced and surrendered my tucked-away fear to the only one who could truly heal me. I knew I must live confidently by faith. I was experiencing just how wide and high and deep God's amazing love is.

People began to reach out to me during this trying time. I went to my first Congressional Wives' Prayer Group and enjoyed the special fellowship. Then a former congressional wife invited me to a luncheon at her home. Her husband, who was a former congressman, had left her for another woman. Later he went to prison for his part in the Abscam scandal. She had every reason to be bitter. Instead, she invited all the new congressional wives over for a discussion called "How to be married to a congressman? You do it not by your own strength, but through the strength of Jesus Christ."

Christian author Ann Kimmel and her sister, a marriage counselor, were the speakers that day. Because of our congressional campaign and with no hope of finding my attacker, I had kept everything about the rape private. Only a few close friends knew my pain. I felt that through these two women, God might open a door for me to share my story and perhaps be encouraged by their advice.

After the speech, I shared about my rape, the recent break-in of our house, and the peace I had received from my prayer. Ann gave me two things that have been dear to me: a card with a picture of God holding a little girl in his hand with the Scripture "I will not forget you. See, I have engraved you on the palms of my hands" (Isa. 49:15); and a black rock that had the word *first* on it. The rock, Ann said, was to remind me, "God is my rock, my strength and my stronghold and nothing can shake me from him." The word *first* was to remind me to keep Jesus first in my life. "It's not that you'll never have fear again," she told me, "but you know who to take it to. Take it to Jesus and keep him first."

Several days later, Paul and I went home after having dinner with Vonette and Bill Bright, the President of Campus Crusade, and a small group of congressmen and their spouses who had shared their faith and touched our hearts. That night when we arrived home we both got down on our knees and each of us recommitted our lives to Christ.

I recognized more than ever that God is not just about religion. He is about a relationship. I had wondered where God was when I was raped. I came to believe that Jesus was with me that terrible night. I knew he did not plan it. He hated its evil and despised its shame. I didn't understand why it had happened, but for the first time I knew God was with me in the midst of my pain. I would trust and claim the promise in Isaiah—that God would never leave me, nor forsake me. I was carved on the palm of his hand.

CHAPTER 8

Find Your Elephants!

Paul and I began to see the importance of having committed friend-ships in our lives. We met Doug Coe, whose compassion for others and devotion to Jesus is an inspiration, and we were introduced to the National Prayer Breakfast.

The National Prayer Breakfast hosted every year by the president and members of the House and Senate Prayer Groups brings together people from across the world in the Spirit of Jesus. The way Jesus lived, the way Jesus taught, the way Jesus prayed, the way Jesus loved his enemies, the way Jesus forgave, the way Jesus cared for the poor, the way Jesus uncondi-tionally loved—if only we could come together in that Spirit, this would be a better world. That Spirit is available today to guide, comfort, and unite our hearts so that we might overcome the differences that so often divide us.

Each February people gather in Washington from different nations representing many faiths, backgrounds, cultures, and politics. The Prayer Breakfast was first hosted by President Eisenhower in 1953, and is attended by the president, members of his cabinet, ambassadors, members of Con-gress, and other leaders and citizens of our country and nations around the world. Paul and I have been involved in this special breakfast since 1976 and have developed friendships from many nations. This experience helped me understand the importance of putting aside my fear and learning to embrace people from different cultures and backgrounds. Jesus began a revolution of love that is ongoing as we come together in his name today.

Paul became involved in the Congressional Prayer Groups that meet each week in the House of Representatives and in the Senate. Paul said of their weekly breakfast, "Republicans and Democrats, liberals and conservatives—we are too often divided by political philosophy and geography. By coming together in the Spirit of Jesus, praying, and sharing our lives we are able to know and respect each other. At the end of the hour we ask God to lead our lives and the life of this nation—powerful, tough, pragmatic men and women who recognize they are dependent on God's wisdom to lead this country."

He also was challenged to be in a small group meeting with three other congressmen: a Republican, Tom Evans of Delaware; and two Democrats, Bill Nelson from Florida and Don Bonker from the state of Washington. For the next eleven years these men would gather faithfully each week to pray and encourage one another.

Don Bonker was a liberal Democrat from the state of Washington, while Paul was a conservative Republican from Virginia. Don was from the West, Paul from the East. During the six years Paul and Don served together in the House of Representatives they probably canceled out each other's votes a thousand times, but they came to know and love each other. Paul said, "We may be from different political parties and cancel out each others votes in Congress, but our faith has allowed us to transcend those differences and work together to move this nation forward."

This was another lesson in the importance of being reconciled one to another despite differences. I began meeting weekly with their wives, Grace Nelson and Carolyn Bonker, and we committed ourselves to loving God and one another. This had a tremendous impact on my life, my healing from my past pain, and the strengthening of my faith. I was the only Republican, as Grace and Carolyn were both Democrats. We loved the Scripture: "Two are better than one . . . if one falls who will lift him up . . . a cord of three strands is not quickly broken" (Eccles. 4:9).

Find Your Elephants!

I used the example of the elephant to talk about our friendship. (I was the sole Republican after all!) I've heard the story when an elephant in Africa is wounded or ill and falls down, he will likely die because of his heavy weight. So two elephants will often come alongside the wounded one and literally hold him up for days until the elephant is strong enough to stand alone.

We desired to be that kind of friends and stand with each other in the good times and the bad—in the sorrows and joys of life. These women became my elephants, and we pledged to hold each other up through the challenges of our busy lives. Finally I had women with whom I could be honest about my past when at times the pain caused insecurities to come up in my life. I could be vulnerable and know that our conversation would be kept confidential. I was so grateful they were there to help strengthen me on my journey from being a victim to being stronger and more confident.

Over the years our group broadened to include Linda Slattery, wife of Congressman Jim Slattery of Kansas, and Janet Hall, wife of Congressman Tony Hall of Ohio. With these women, I always felt loved and safe to be myself. Though some of us are out of politics and some not, we remain sisters in Christ.

I believe Jesus was the greatest leader who ever lived. I have come to realize that the gospel *is* a person, Jesus; not information *about* this person. We can look at the leadership of Jesus and see how he poured his love and teachings into twelve disciples, who went out with this message of love to change the world for good. As couples we began to consider the impact and power of committed relationships, two or three gathered in Jesus' name. We also wanted to explore what a leadership led by God might look like, and how this might change a community, a state, or a nation.

We were inspired by the eighteenth-century British parliamentarian William Wilberforce and his committed group of friends. That included William Pitt, who became prime minister. Together they worked to bring an end to the slave trade and to reform society. After twenty years of disappointment, these friends saw Parliament vote to outlaw the slave trade in 1807.

Also Martin Luther King had a dedicated core of friends around him. They gave their lives to the vision of equality among people and their belief that people should not be judged by the color of their skin but by the content of their hearts and minds. Both of these leaders were men led by God; men surrounded by faithful friends; men who changed their societies and, yes, their nations for good.

For Paul and me, sharing our dreams, vision, and hopes for the future with this close-knit core of friends made all the difference. Little did I know that God would also use these friendships to stretch me to go into places that triggered old fear. I was about to enter deeper into the reality of my brokenness to learn a new step in healing. God was about to teach me a new lesson about trusting him in fearful situations and about the power of forgiveness.

CHAPTER 9

God, You Want Me To Go Where?

uring Paul's second year in Congress, I was invited to a meeting of inner-city pastors at Shiloh Baptist Church in Washington, D.C., to explore ways to help care for the needs of the poor. It sounded like a worthy idea, and our meeting was to be followed by dinner. The hope was to build friendships across racial and cultural differences by coming together around Jesus.

Grace was also invited, but when I found we couldn't go together, I began to panic. My old fear flooded my mind at the thought of going alone into the inner-city. I was scared and intimidated despite all the healing that had taken place. I would rather have gone anywhere in the world because the memory of the black man who had raped me brought up terrible thoughts of his violence. I was concerned about being safe as this was known to be a dangerous neighborhood.

I made a decision to push over my fear and not be controlled by my past. I locked my car door and headed for Shiloh Baptist Church. When I arrived, my heart was beating fast as I ran inside. Here I met Doug Coe, Grace Nelson, Congressman Tony Hall, and three African-American inner-city pastors: Tom Skinner, Sam Hines, and John Staggers. Little did I know the impact these pastors would have on my healing journey, and how Grace and I would grow even closer through our involvement in the inner city.

We all prayed that Washington, D.C., could become a City Set on a Hill for God. This Scripture inspired us: "You are the light of the world. A city set on a hill cannot be hidden. Neither do people light a lamp and put it under a bowl. Instead they put it on its stand, and it gives light to everyone in the house. In the same way, let your light so shine before men, that they see your good works and praise your Father in heaven" (Matt. 5:14–16).

At dinner that night twenty of us gathered at a long table. I became a little nervous when a big African-American man, Pat Patterson, came over and sat next to me. I asked him about himself and was amazed as he began to share his story. Pat had spent five years in the federal prison Alcatraz and seven years in Washington, D.C.'s Lorton Reformatory. Pat explained:

> John Staggers, the pastor sitting across from me, came to Lorton and shared the love of Jesus with me. After a year or so of John teaching me the Word, I prayed Jesus would be my Savior, and my sins would be forgiven. The Bible says when you ask in Jesus' name, you can be forgiven and your sins removed as far as the East is from the West! This is what set me free.

> When I got out of prison I came here. Now I work with John Staggers and inner-city kids who are heading down the wrong path. I tell them about Jesus and about the love of God. I show them there's another way to live. They listen because they know I've been there.

My heart started pounding. People didn't serve time in federal prison for minor offenses. This guy could well have raped or killed someone. Then I thought of the Scripture "Therefore, if anyone is in Christ, he is a new creation, the old has gone, the new has come" (2 Cor. 5:17). This man next to me was my brother. Pat was a new creature. He'd received forgiveness and he was set free.

I went to the bathroom, closed my eyes, and found myself praying. I thought of Pat, a man whose physical appearance and past life of crime terrified me. But, no matter what he had done, Pat had come to Christ and been forgiven. Now, I realized the only way I could be truly set free was to forgive my own offender.

In this cramped bathroom I dropped to my knees and prayed, "Lord, I forgive the man who raped me. And I will pray every day for the rest of my life that someone will tell him about Jesus and that I'll spend eternity with him." Somehow, meeting Pat allowed me to forgive and finally release my attacker to God. God was the only one who could transform this man who had done such evil into a new creature like Pat Patterson.

I know that it was through Jesus' strength, not my own, that I was able to say this prayer of forgiveness. Tears rolled from my eyes as I hoped the man who raped me would somehow come to know the power of forgiveness. I let go of a lot of the pain and fear. I prayed God would by the miracle of grace forgive the man that attacked me, because he had come to know Jesus as Savior.

A huge burden lifted as this act of forgiveness set me free. A flood of peace flowed over me, washing away much of the remaining fear that had filled me. When I returned to the table, John Staggers asked that everyone stand and take one another by the hand. I reached for Pat's hand without flinching. As I held it firmly, we sang together, "Jesus Loves Me."

Forgiveness, I came to believe, is the greatest power on earth next to love. Perhaps in forgiving this terrible evil, its stronghold over me would be broken in a new and powerful way. It was time to press in and face my past fear head-on. Only God knows, but I began to trust and believe that God could answer my prayer and this man would be forgiven and I would spend eternity with the man who had raped me.

My courage grew and during the years Paul served in Congress, I spent much of my time in the inner city. I was amazed to find that great joy can be found in broken places. I learned about the power of building bridges of love through reconciliation. We experienced reconciliation firsthand through a number of work projects.

One such project was on R Street, where seven children had been molested and drug deals were commonplace. John Staggers wanted to help these children live and play in a safer environment. We set out to build a playground at a community center where kids could gather after school until their parents returned from work. There were over three hundred latchkey children who otherwise roamed the streets in this rough area and often lived in fear.

I will never forget arriving early to meet the garbage trucks that were to dispose of the massive heap of filthy debris we had picked up to prepare for the new fence and playground equipment. I felt a little nervous because the other volunteers had not arrived and the people who worked in the center were strangers. I was looking anxiously out the front door when two police cars pulled up and the officers drew their guns. They shouted for me to go inside as they ran through the side yard.

I stood shaking in the kitchen, my palms sweaty and my heart pounding, as I watched the officer apprehend a man and put him in their police car. I struggled to press down the fear that wanted to overwhelm me and prayed, "Lord, you brought me here. Now protect me from this violence and my terror." Soon the other volunteers arrived, and I felt comforted to learn later that the police had succeeded in a major drug bust that morning. I realized that by going alone to the center, I had put myself in a situation that could trigger my fear, and I had not guarded my heart. I set my mind that fear would not overtake me again. My heart cried out for these children that live in this kind of corruption every day.

Later that day Al, a rough contractor from the suburbs, operated the bulldozer to prepare for the fence and playground equipment. The children from the neighborhood played around us and were excited about their new basketball court. Al lowered the front of the bulldozer and started taking the laughing children on a ride up and down in his equipment. Everyone wanted a turn. The kids were having a ball.

A precious little boy named Jeremy, with jet-black curly hair and beautiful eyes, came over to me and put his arms up. "Up, up," he said. I lifted him up onto the bulldozer next to Al. Jeremy immediately threw his little arms around Al, gave him a big hug, and said, "Thank you, this is the best day ever!" Tears rolled down Al's face and I knew he would never be the same. A little child had taught him about love and reconciliation.

Every Tuesday Grace and I met at Shiloh Baptist Church at 8:00 a.m. for a time of prayer for the city. Congressman Tony Hall hosted the gathering

God, You Want Me To Go Where?

while Pastor John Staggers and Rev. Sam Hines led our worship. I learned so much about the Bible, worship, and the celebration of life on those mornings. Here we would gather, Tony, Grace and some other congressional wives, with the homeless and those who worked in the inner city of Washington from all walks of life. We praised God, worshiped together and deep friendships were formed.

Music was an important part of our mornings and often Pat Barnes's voice would explode with praise as she sang "How Great Thou Art." Sometimes Wintley Phipps, who became a world-renowned vocal artist, would sing "Amazing Grace" in a way that brought tears to my eyes. Wintley founded the U.S. Dream Academy, which focuses on giving hope to at-risk kids, especially those who have a family member behind bars. At the end of our time, John would close us in prayer. Then we would all join hands and sing "Jesus Loves Me." As I looked around this circle, I realized my healing had come a long way from that terrible night.

John and Sam were reconcilers who had marched with Martin Luther King during that transformational time in our nation's history. They also traveled to South Africa during the time of apartheid and were key to bringing clashing parties together to pray for a peaceful solution. They devoted their lives to bringing black and white together.

Sam and John gave big hugs and under their wings I was being mentored and inspired. Their strong faith and great compassion deeply influenced my life. I had real affection for my African-American brothers and sisters. A deeper healing was taking place in my heart, allowing me to further let go of the pain of my past.

I had come to Washington with little understanding of the inner-city culture and the desperate needs of the city. These incredible men opened my eyes to see the poverty and brokenness all around me. I was compelled to become involved in the despair of Washington and not just celebrate the city's beauty and power. For many, the city is full of fear and helplessness. One of my favorite poems that Sam Hines shared touched my heart about the needs of the poor. I can still hear Sam's powerful voice telling us how easy it is to be blind to the pain around us. (Poem adapted in his sermon):

Fear to Freedom

I Was Hungry

I was hungry and you formed a humanities club.
Thank you.
I was imprisoned and you crept off quietly to pray for my release.
Nice.

I was naked and in your mind, you debated the morality of
my appearance.
What good did that do?

I was sick and you knelt and thanked God for your health,
But I needed you.

I was homeless and you preached to me of the shelter of the love of God.
I wish you had taken me home.

I was lonely and you left me alone to pray for me.
Why didn't you stay?

You seem so holy, so close to God,
But I'm still very hungry, lonely and cold and I'm still in pain.
Does it matter?

—Anonymous[1]

My friendship with Pat Patterson grew, and I admired how Pat went to court with troubled kids and brought families together. He worked tirelessly in the schools to get kids off drugs. He shared with them how Jesus loved them right where they were. I never asked Pat about his crime, but one day I told him about my rape. He was so furious I thought he might explode. He said, "I would never let anyone hurt you!" It made me feel so secure that this man who had done some terrible things wanted to make me feel safe.

One day when we were leaving our worship time, I realized I had locked my keys in the car. I had learned to avoid situations wherever possible that might trigger my fear, so I asked Pat if he would walk me to my car parked

God, You Want Me To Go Where?

in that troubled neighborhood. When we arrived, Pat whistled to a fellow across the street and asked if he could help me get into my car. It took that man only seconds to unlock the door. I could not believe my eyes—in a flash my car was opened!

I thanked him gratefully and offered him some money for his trouble. He smiled, said no, and left. Pat said, "Rosemary, don't worry about it. You see, he does this for a living." I now could laugh and give my friend Pat a hug. His African-American buddy held no fear over my life, and I realized how much I had grown from my experiences in the inner city and in our political life.

CHAPTER 10

A Door Opens To The Senate

A nother reelection campaign for the House of Representatives rolled around with great excitement as our son, Paul Trible III, was born September 26, 1980. Life is crazy during an election, so it was wonderful that Paul's birth came between two of his dad's speaking engagements. After Paul was reelected, I would often take the children into the restaurant in the Capitol to have dinner with their dad as late-night sessions were commonplace. It was a balancing act, but we loved our family and Paul was devoted to public service.

It was only a short time before we were on the campaign trail again as Senator Harry Byrd's retirement presented an opportunity for Paul to run for the Senate. The children went with us to fish fries, political rallies, and parades. I think they thought normal families lived this way. It was a challenging campaign but we were victorious. It was November 1982 and I remember holding then two-year-old Paul III on my hip as Mary Katherine looked up lovingly at her dad giving his acceptance speech. I adored my husband and was so very proud of what he had accomplished. Inside, however, I wondered what new challenges were in store for our family.

Fear to Freedom

The night before Paul's Senate swearing-in ceremony in January 1983, hundreds of our friends and supporters joined us for a service at Christ Episcopal Church in Old Town Alexandria. It was a dedication of our lives and Paul's service to God. There is no way we could have made it this far through the difficult healing process of my pain, the grueling campaigns and the challenges of political life without the comfort of Jesus, the guidance of God, and the help of friends. We were grateful for God's wonderful faithfulness. We were also thankful for our amazing congressional friends who celebrated our new election. Even though Paul would now be in the Senate, the other three congressmen promised to keep meeting with Paul to support each other in their pubic and private lives.

During our first year in the Senate, a young man named Jonathan Coe came to Paul's office to share a vision to bring leaders and young people together to explore the importance of faith and values and talk about Jesus as a leader. Jonathan challenged Paul, saying, "Leaders talk about caring about the next generation and how they are the hope for our future, but leaders never spend time just hanging out with them. Would you and Rosemary be willing to give a weekend to be with college students around Virginia?"

Paul and I became excited to join Jonathan and a group of dynamic young men and women to develop in Virginia a program for a gathering where government and community leaders would invest in young people. Out of these friendships was launched the Student Leadership Forum on Faith and Values, which spread from Virginia to many other states and countries.

In 1990 Vice President Dan Quayle, U.S. Senator Pete Domenici (R-NM), U.S. Representative Jim Slattery (D-KS), and Missouri Governor John Ashcroft joined Paul and me in convening a group of university student leaders from across the country for the first National Student Leadership Forum, which continues to this day. Linda and Jim Slattery have continued to provide great leadership throughout the years with other congressional hosts.

The hope is to challenge and inspire college students, as the future of our nation depends upon their leadership, character, and values. At the heart of National Student Leadership lies the dream that leaders, young and old, can exchange their thoughts on Jesus' teaching and be encouraged to live lives of significance.

God also opened this wonderful opportunity for me to be with students. Often I would get a nudge when I met a young woman that she was troubled.

A Door Opens To the Senate

We would spend time together where I would hear her story and comfort her in her pain. God quietly was using my past abuse to minister to others enduring trials, whether it was rape or other brokenness they were facing. I was experiencing on a deeper level this power of love to transform lives.

In an amazing way God merged my involvement in the needs of Washington D.C., with my passion for students. We would have a work project each forum to illustrate the importance of compassion for others. It might be cleaning an inner-city schoolyard, serving at a soup kitchen, painting a shelter for battered women, or gleaning the fields in a Harvest of Hope Program that provides produce to the hungry.[2]

I remember the first time we went gleaning on a farm around the D.C. area with a group from a housing project. A wonderful African-American woman Mildred and I were picking spinach in the rain when she remarked with a smile, "You know no one can look down on anyone else when we're on our knees together."

The student leaders were enthusiastic about the service projects, and many took these activities back to their colleges. They also heard members of Congress speak, both Democrats and Republicans, about the power of love through a relationship with Jesus rather than being caught up in the love of power.

People, especially in Washington, get caught up in power. Dick Halverson, chaplain of the Senate, once said, "You have to think of yourself as a zero." (That's very hard for senators to do!) "If you string zeroes together, what do you have? Zero. But, if you put a one in front of those zeros, then you've got something: one hundred, one thousand, one million. Jesus Christ is the one, and if we will just put him first in our lives, great things will happen." As prayer group couples, we committed to love Jesus, to love each other, and to keep the main thing the main thing: keeping Jesus number one.

I was reminded of the rock I still carried with the word *first* on it given to me by Ann Kemmel when I shared with her about the rape. It was turning to Jesus and surrendering my pain that had helped me on my healing journey. Now I understood, more than ever, how sharing your life with a few people you can trust and rely on as accountability sisters makes all the difference in living free from fear and in keeping Jesus first.

CHAPTER 11

Soul Sisters

One of the remarkable relationships I developed in Washington, D.C., was with a woman named Barbara Williams-Skinner. I had become good friends with her husband, Tom Skinner, a powerful evangelist who took God's message of hope and reconciliation around the world. He was chaplain for the Washington Redskins, deeply concerned for the needs of the poor, and got involved with me in National Student Leadership through his desire to equip a new generation of technically and spiritually excellent leaders.

Tom was gregarious and easy to know. Barbara, however, was another matter. Something drew me to reach out to Barbara. But we were so different that I wondered if I could ever become her friend. The fact we are black and white was the least of our differences.

Barbara grew up as one of eight children raised by her mother in a San Francisco housing project. She disliked Southern white women and sought the power of education and politics to set her free from her past. In fact, at ten years old, Barbara wrote a letter to her deeply religious mother, saying

61

she was having nothing further to do with God and this faith thing. She questioned, "Why should I believe in a God that can't even put food on the table? From now on I am not going to church, and I am not going to believe in this God of yours." Barbara used to say, "We weren't poor, we were 'po,' we could only afford one o."

I wanted not just to talk about reconciliation, but also to walk it with someone so I prayed God would send me a covenant sister. Be careful what you pray for because God sent me someone definitely out of my comfort zone! Barbara, I felt, had me in this category box labeled: "white, conservative, Southern Republican."

I was from Little Rock, Arkansas. Barbara grew up in Richmond, California, near San Francisco and lived in Los Angeles. I went to Sweet Briar College in Virginia as America's Junior Miss and graduated from the University of Texas, while Barbara was involved with the Black Panthers at the University of California at Berkeley. I was married to a conservative Republican Congressman, while Barbara was a Democrat and the first Director of the Congressional Black Caucus made up of all of the African-American members of Congress. I'm sentimental, known to cry at a good movie, and am definitely a hugger, while Barbara is brilliant, strong, and hardly ever cries. I'll stay up all night to have a good conversation; Barbara is ready for bed at 9:30 p.m. and she's up praying before dawn.

Sometimes we get caught up protecting ourselves and become afraid of building a relationship with anyone different. We judge and hold onto what we see as right from our perspective. We are often closed to new perspectives. To be truly reconciled, we must begin a journey of healing through love, dignity, and respect regardless of race, color, or beliefs.

I confess that at first, I was afraid to reach out to Barbara because I feared I would be rejected. I was right. When I approached her, saying, "I would like to get to know you better and become your friend," she looked at me as though I had some agenda. I had no agenda. God kept Barbara on my heart, and I couldn't walk away from that. After a tough beginning, finally Barbara opened up and we began a friendly relationship, but her guard was always up. As Barbara loves to say, "I had no choice. Rosemary just wouldn't go away!"

However, it wasn't until Tom became ill that we became committed sisters. Tom had been so strong and energetic but after a speaking engagement he became terribly ill and Barbara rushed him to the hospital. They discovered Tom had advanced leukemia, and he chose not to undergo chemotherapy. He wanted to live life to the fullest and to treasure every day with Barbara and his two daughters, Lauren and Kyla. Tom, Barbara, and his daughters moved down to an apartment next to the hospital where an expert doctor in alternative medicine and health nutrition with cancer patients could care for him. Tom lived out his last days close to the Lord and his beloved family.

I would go over a couple of times a week and take Tom and Barbara groceries from our local health food store. It was a wonderful opportunity for me to come to know them in a more personal way. One Friday I had picked up all their supplies and was headed across the bridge when a major accident blocked traffic. I called Tom to say I could not make it. In his jovial manner he laughed. "That's OK, Rosemary, I'll get to see you on Monday. We surely won't starve till then!" That's the last time I heard his wonderful voice.

At 2:00 a.m. on Saturday I got the call that Tom had died. I got in my car and drove to their apartment to see how I could help. I sat on the steps watching the sunrise until I heard stirring inside. Several friends arrived, and Kay James and I began packing all of Tom's belongings. Barbara and the girls talked about the necessary arrangements to follow. Words were few, but our hearts were both heavy and hopeful, for we knew Tom was rejoicing with the Lord.

During this process I saw strength and beauty in Barbara that could only have come from the Lord. I came to know what a beautiful vessel of God's love Barbara is. I love her boldness, her love of the Word, and her uncompromising, beautiful relationship with the Holy Spirit that carried her through this time of grief and loss.

Tom's home-going service was a beautiful tribute. It reflected a tapestry of a life dedicated to reconciliation. As Tom and Barbara had taken the message of God's love around the world, friends from near and far came to celebrate his life. Like the reality of Washington, D.C., Tom's home-going service, had the powerful and the powerless sitting side by side. A Catholic priest sat next to a Baptist minister. Members of Congress sat next to the homeless. Community leaders sat next to people just out of prison. Tom had lived an inspired life focused on the invisible rather than the visible—on faith instead of fear.

Tom's daughter read a poem, "To Those I Love," that I had shared with her.

I looked at Barbara on the first pew and realized the time had come for me to stop talking about racial reconciliation and take Barbara by the hand and start simply walking together. If our walk and our talk aren't the same, people don't care what we are talking about.

Alienation seems to be our greatest problem. God's answer is reconciliation. Tom's home-going service looked like how I envision the heavenly kingdom. It was a celebration of the diversity of life. I didn't know what it would take to begin building this bridge with Barbara, but I was willing to commit my friendship to her and submit to what God had in store. To build an honest friendship it would be necessary for us to move beyond our old prejudices and ways of thinking and work together to build trust and discern God's purpose—a vision for our being together.

This was one more step on my journey from fear to faith. God is calling us to love one another, and we must build that bridge one person at a time. Our friendship has stretched us both, but from that day on Barbara and I have been walking down the road together. When we first began our friendship it was a real risk. Our faith had drawn us to each other, but the first time we went to speak together was a disaster and we realized we had a long ways to go.

We flew to Boston, where we had been invited to speak about reconciliation and our relationship to the students at Boston College. We arrived in the pouring rain, and the president of the student body picked us up and took us for an informal dinner. We learned about the college and the challenges of students separated over racial and cultural differences. They had high hopes for this forum that new understanding and unity might come. Barbara and I almost blew the whole thing.

As we left the restaurant, the three of us were sharing one umbrella in the rain. Then I laughingly said, "Oh no, my naturally curly hair is really going to get fuzzy in this rain. Barbara, it's a good thing that yours doesn't move!" Well you would have thought I had set off an earthquake in Barbara. "What do you mean mine doesn't move," she shouted. "When did you become an expert on black hair? I have to work hard on my hair. You can just speak tomorrow all by yourself." I had pushed her button and she was hot! I stood dumbfounded, my heart pounding with fear. Had I destroyed this relationship with one innocent comment?

Later after Barbara cooled down, we talked about what went terribly wrong. Now this is Barbara's favorite story to tell and of course, the laugh is on me. We began to realize when we use words or experiences from our different cultures, misunderstandings can lead to hurt and further divide us. I expressed how some people are actually too intimidated to talk openly, because they are afraid they will insult or anger someone of a different race by their comments. For instance, some people are unsure when it's appropriate to use the term *African-American* versus *black.*

I honestly told Barbara, "Look, I am going to make some mistakes in our relationship. If I have to be perfect, then we might as well forget it. It will mean we need to give and take and have honest dialogue to create a safe place to learn how each of us feels and respect how each of us thinks." I confessed to her that I did not do well with confrontation, and we needed to learn how to communicate our differences in a spirit of love.

Barbara has a wonderful illustration of how our minds are like a bank. A large percentage of what we think is directed by our subconscious that has been formed since early childhood. The subconscious mind, like this bank, holds deposits, which have been made throughout the years in our brain. Some of those are negative deposits of fear of certain people, or prejudice toward others. It will take many positive deposits to offset the old way of thinking. We must begin this new way of thinking, especially for the sake of this next generation, and begin to communicate openly with one another.

Barbara now continues Tom's vision through the work of Skinner Leadership Institute. Barbara is someone I have come to love and admire as a servant leader and ambassador of reconciliation. We often speak to groups about our friendship, and people will say, "If you two can love one another, anyone can, because you could hardly find two more different people."

Barbara meets regularly for prayer with members of the Congressional Black Caucus and other leaders to offer support and encouragement. She helped get automotive training at Ballou High School in the inner city of D.C. and co-leads a mentoring program to teach students how to show respect, be responsible, and perform a job. This is making a big difference in these young people's lives, building character, and giving hope and a new vision for their futures. She works tirelessly to raise consciousness of the needs of the poor and bring people together across cultural, racial and political differences.

For years regular prayer has kept us together. Since January of 2007 we have prayed on a conference call that convenes every morning with another pastor, Leversie Johnson from San Francisco. I join every weekday and it is a privilege to see the way God has been faithful to answer our prayers. Often there will be four or five friends from across the country joining the conference prayer line. Leversie is a devout prayer warrior who has truly blessed my life. She and Barbara have taught me much about the power of prayer and passion for reconciliation.

Also through my friendship with Barbara, Grace Nelson and I were the first two white women to be asked to join twelve professional African-American women who call themselves the Generals. We meet twice a year, once for a retreat and then at the National Prayer Breakfast. We also pray over a conference call the first of each month, which keeps us in touch with each other and our prayer needs. Twice we have had our Generals' retreat at our family home, Gascony, on the Chesapeake Bay. We had a fabulous time of sharing Christ and encouraging each other—laughing and singing worship songs. We also sang a few of Aretha Franklin's songs such as "Chain, Chain, Chain" and danced the Electric Slide.

Beyond my covenant relationship with Barbara, who lives over three hours away from me in Maryland, I recognized the value of friendships with those who live near me. I have a wonderful African-American friend from our area named Carolyn Hines. Carolyn, who grew up in the civil rights movement, worked in voter registration drives, sit-ins, and demonstrations. We have shared stories together about our lives and how her family received threats from the Ku Klux Klan. Carolyn devotes her life to healing and reconciliation between people.

Fourteen years ago we decided to have a Christmas party in my home and invite our friends so they could get to know one another. Everyone arrived dressed for a good party, but was a little leery as to the purpose of our gathering. We immediately put them at ease as I announced, "This is a gathering of friends. Our only purpose is for Carolyn and me to *give our friends away to one another*. There is no project, no fundraiser, no commitment, only to come to know one another as friends, pray, and share our lives together." There was a huge sigh of relief.

We have gathered our "Lunch Bunch" twice a year for fourteen years. We enjoy lunch, then each person chooses what I call an angel card. It has a word and picture representing joy, love, peace, sisterhood, laughter, etc. Each person shares something of her life that is prompted by her card, then we pray for each other. Amazing friendships have developed and broader understanding of the differences that would too often divide us.

God is not Republican or Democrat, black or white, Baptist or Episcopalian, yet we seem to think in terms of categories. Over the years of my friendship with Barbara, Leversie, and Carolyn, it has become less important that we are Democrats or Republicans, but more important that we share a love for Christ and one another.

Barbara has said, "Every person we meet is our neighbor. It is easier to talk about reconciliation than to walk it, but if a difference there is going to be, let it begin with me." Building a true friendship across racial, cultural, or political diversity can be one of the most rewarding experiences of your life. The Devotional Guide at the end of this book has a copy of our "Ten Commandments of Our Friendship" written by Barbara and me. I hope this will be helpful to you in building relationships outside of your comfort zone.[2]

God works in amazing ways. He sent me into a place of fear—the inner city—to release me from that fear and to help heal me from my past brokenness. Initially after I was raped I had wondered if I would ever be normal again—if I could ever trust again. Barbara, Leversie, and Carolyn's friendship have helped me learn to love and trust again; and Tom, John, and Sam were wonderful mentors on my journey of healing.

Fear to Freedom

To Those I Love

When I die, give what's left of me to the children
and the old men that wait to die.
And if you want to cry,
cry for your brother walking in the street beside you.
And when you need me, put your arms around someone
wanting to be held and give them what you need to give to me.
Look for me, in the people I have loved.
And if you cannot give me away at least let me live less in
the anguish of your heart than in the sparkle of your eyes.
You can love me most by letting hands touch hands,
and letting go of what needs to be free.
Love does not die—people do.
So when all that's left of me is love, give me away.
I'll see you at home in heaven.
—*Anonymous*[1]

CHAPTER 12

Enlarged Territories

The prayer of Jabez says, "Oh, that you would bless me and enlarge my territory. Let your hand be with me, and keep me from harm so I will be free from pain" (1 Chron. 4:10). While I was experiencing the power of reconciliation in my own life, Paul and I were given the chance to have our territories enlarged to see the power of faith and reconciliation in action throughout the world. During Paul's time in Congress, God enlarged our worldview in such countries as China, Israel, Russia, and Ethiopia. Special people we met were true ambassadors for Christ. This broadened our compassion and respect for other countries, cultures, and people who have broken free from fear to live in freedom.

IN CHINA, THE FLAME OF FAITH KEEPS BURNING

In 1978 Paul and I joined a delegation of members of Congress for a visit to China. When we arrived, we felt we might have landed on another planet. Everyone wore gray or blue Mao coats. Thousands of people rode bicycles through the streets where big red billboards portrayed propaganda statements like "We have friends all over the world" and "Workers of the world unite."

Fear to Freedom

The first day we met in the Great Hall of the People with Deng Xiaoping, the Chinese leader and secretary general of the Communist Party. This was in the early days of China's outreach to the West. This leader of over a billion people spent ninety minutes visiting with our delegation of U.S. representatives who served on the House Armed Services Committee.

Before leaving for the trip, we asked friends from the National Prayer Breakfast if there were any contacts in China we could meet. We were given the name and phone number of Dr. K., a research physician who once attended the Breakfast from China. We asked someone to place the call and only identified ourselves as participants in the Prayer Breakfast from the United States. We were given in response this message: "Meet Dr. K. on Sunday in front of Beijing University at 10:00 a.m. sharp." On Sunday, we were a little anxious as the taxi dropped us at the entrance of Beijing University. Then we saw an elderly gentleman walking up to us with a big smile on his face. "You must love Jesus if you have come to bring greetings from the Prayer Breakfast. God bless you," Dr. K. exclaimed.

He gave us an embrace and we spent a most remarkable morning visiting the underground churches. I was awed at the courage of these people who were practicing their faith even though this was strictly prohibited by the government. These house churches were packed with people celebrating their love of Jesus with wonderful music and worship. It was amazing to see the strength of these men and women's devotion to prayer. Their lives could be in grave danger because of this, but their joy was overflowing. "This is where we get our strength for each day. We must keep the flame of faith burning," explained Dr. K. Then he told us his own story.

Dr. K. and his wife were both medical doctors before the Cultural Revolution. He was a cancer specialist, which was rare in China. During the revolution, intellectuals were considered a threat and were "sent down" in order to level all the classes. Dr. K. and his wife were separated from each other and sent to different parts of the country. For four years Dr. K. worked on a farm, picking tealeaves, apart from his family, friends, and profession. One day the son of one of the party leaders became ill with cancer. Someone in authority asked, "Where is that cancer specialist we sent down?"

The officials found Dr. K. and brought him back to care for this young man. The son returned to good health and Dr. K. was given a position at the

Enlarged Territories

Beijing University to further his research and cancer work. Unfortunately, his wife had died during their separation. Dr. K. said, "We all lived every day in fear but through all these trials, our faith sustained us." In America we take so much for granted. It's amazing how in places where you find the worst persecution, you often find the deepest faith. It was an unforgettable trip, and I will always be in awe of Dr. K.'s devotion to Jesus.

I never imagined I would be back in China a year later. In 1979 several friends joined me in founding Friendship Imports, a decorative arts and crafts wholesale business. It was a risk to start my own business, but I thought of Dr. K. and I realized it was time to step out in faith and put aside fear of any kind in my life. Paul encouraged Penny Taylor, Martha Field, and me to stop talking and go out and do it.

Three weeks later we had visas, an invitation to the Canton Trade Fair, and tickets in hand. We bought for several companies and later developed catalogs for clients such as Horchow and The Smithsonian. We loved the Chinese people and were about the only women traders at that Canton Trade Fair. Buying wholesale with multiple quantities was difficult. I remember the last day we bought the entire antique reproduction showroom—one of everything—to sell to our clients and gift shows across the country.

On our day off from business, our precious Chinese interpreter, Sian, took us sightseeing. On the way home on the bus after visiting a Buddhist Temple, Sian whispered, "What do you believe?" I had the opportunity to share Jesus with Sian. She hugged me and said, "A missionary when I was very young told me about Jesus. I thought some of the old people in America believed but not the young people." A courageous missionary had planted a seed of faith many years before. Now I had the opportunity to encourage Sian to open her heart to Jesus' love. Over these seven trips to China, little did I know, God was also planting his seeds in me. I would return many years later to be part of the building of churches in China as restrictions on practicing religion began to ease.

Putting aside my fear and building my confidence, it seemed God was inviting me to participate with him in new adventures. Even in China, so far from home, I was blessed to have this opportunity to share my love of Jesus with someone. I began to understand that going through my painful journey had actually made me a stronger and more compassionate person.

Fear to Freedom

The purpose for my life was developing to walk intimately with God, to love and forgive everyone, and to help others on their healing journey to live free from fear.

FAITH IN RUSSIA PERSEVERES

In 1984 Paul and I had another defining international experience in Russia as we witnessed how the power of faith survived even through persecution and fear. Paul and I joined a delegation of senators from the Foreign Relations Committee to travel to the Soviet Union. It was a productive trip and the last day, we visited the site of a church in Moscow that was destroyed by Stalin during his purge of religion. The old cathedral had occupied a prominent site in Moscow, so Stalin ordered his engineers to tear it down and build the tallest building in the world. He wanted to construct a building taller than the Empire State Building to display the expertise and power of the soviet state. Several times as the building took shape, it fell to the ground. Finally the idea of building a skyscraper was abandoned. Stalin then had his engineers build the largest swimming pool in the world on this site of the church. For decades, thereafter, the faithful in Russia would bring their children here to be baptized for they knew this was holy ground. Today the 19th-century Cathedral of Christ the Savior, destroyed by Stalin in 1931, has been rebuilt on this very site.

I will always treasure our last evening when we attended the Easter services at Zagorsk Monastery. During the period of Glasnost and Perestroika, Gorbachev began easing economic and political restrictions. There had been much persecution for any expression of faith and in the past on an Easter eve, the internal police would have been standing at the gates of the Zagorsk Monastery in order to deter the faithful from coming to worship.

On this evening we witnessed the celebration of the thousandth anniversary of Christianity coming to Russia. Tonight there were no police in sight. It was amazing how people who had experienced so much persecution for their faith, overcame their fear as a constant stream of Russians walked through the evening mist to worship. There were three churches celebrating mass within the monastery grounds. As we entered the sanctuary of one of the churches, Paul asked our guide, "Why are there no seats?" He replied, "Surely you would not sit in the presence of God."

Enlarged Territories

A standing-room-only crowd filled the ancient church that was dark except for the lighted candles on the altar. At midnight the priest turned to the congregation, raised his candle, and declared, "Christ is risen!" Then hundreds of Russian voices responded, "Christ is risen indeed." The priest passed the light to the people standing next to him, then, they in turn lighted the others' candles. In a moment, light shot through the darkness and exploded through the darkened sanctuary. This celebration of the new life in Christ became a rallying call. "He is risen, he is risen indeed," everyone chanted.

A priest then took up the cross and holding it high, marched up the aisle. The entire congregation fell in step behind the Cross of Christ. We walked out onto the grounds of the ancient monastery and were joined by the congregations of the other churches. As we walked behind the cross, the church bells rang out a thousand times to mark the millennium of Christianity coming to Russia. Our hearts were deeply stirred as we left the celebration service.

At 2:00 a.m. our plane lifted off to carry us home to America. As we landed we all broke into singing, "God Bless America." Our own freedom was now more precious than ever and we were proud to be Americans. I personally appreciated in a new way how many in the world may live in fear of freely practicing their faith, but they are courageous and strong because of their love of Jesus. Jesus had overcome my own fear, and I was humbled to experience these Russian believers who had overcome so much.

THE HOLY LAND THROUGH JEWISH EYES

On a personal trip to the Holy Land in 1983, Paul and I saw how God does beautiful things when we respond to his call to love one another across differences in faith and cultures. I had experienced this through the National Prayer Breakfast and also personally through the message of reconciliation that God had planted deep in my heart. Jesus can bring divergent people together through the power of love and forgiveness. I had been raped by a black man, and now some of my dearest friends were African-American pastors. This land had been torn apart by the deep division between three religions. Now we were visiting Israel with some wonderful Jewish friends united by our love for each other and respect for each other's faith. It was wonderful to see this special land through their eyes.

73

Fear to Freedom

Here we first met Nono, our guide who knew Israel inside and out. He taught the Bible on the seaside of the Mediterranean. He studied the Old and New Testaments because he guided both Jewish and Christian groups. Nono presented each site we visited with such dramatic realism that we felt we were there in earlier times.

Our deep friendship between the couples allowed us to honor each other's faith journey as we toured through this Holy Land. When we entered Jerusalem chills came over me as Nono gave us palm leaves. I imagined what it was like to be present when Jesus entered on Palm Sunday on a donkey. When we arrived at the garden of Gethsemane, I could not hold back the tears of love I had for Jesus; he who wept tears of blood for me in this place.

The warmth, love, and honesty were such beautiful things to witness between people of different faiths. In experiencing the Holy Land together, our hearts had become one. We talked together about how people of different nations and faiths get so far away from loving and accepting one another.

We climbed Masada and an amazing chapter in Jewish history unfolded before our eyes. In the year 73 AD on this mountaintop, 960 Jews who had courageously defended Masada chose to take their own lives rather than fall to the Romans. Standing in the midst of the historic remains of this ancient fortress, Paul and I were given a mother-of-pearl Bible from the Holy Land that each of our Jewish friends had signed. We prayed for the battles of the human spirit waged today, for peace in the world and peace in our hearts. We also visited the Holocaust Museum, which brought all of us to tears for the devastation of so many lives. Sharing these experiences deepened our friendship forever.

Several years later we returned on a personal trip to the Holy Land with our prayer group from Congress and several other friends. Of course, I asked Nono to be our guide. This time we started in Jerusalem and ended in Bethlehem. We shared with Nono along our travels about the purpose of the National Prayer Breakfast where people from all faiths could come together in the Spirit of this man Jesus from Nazareth. Nono knew much about Jesus through his study of the Bible. His father and grandfather were rabbis, so he had never really considered who Jesus might be in his heart.

When we finished our visit to the birthplace of Jesus in Bethlehem, we gathered together to pray. Nono had tears in his eyes. He wanted to know more about Jesus and was willing to come to the Prayer Breakfast to experience firsthand this reconciliation across different faiths where we could learn to love God and one another.

We left Nono and crossed the border into Jordan, where we met with King Hussein. We talked about Jesus and he was very warm and responsive as we all joined in prayer.

Nono did come to the Prayer Breakfast for the next ten years and often talked with Jews, Christians, and Muslims about Jesus of Nazareth, who was a man of love and reconciliation. He would challenge others to come together in friendship and understanding in the Spirit of Jesus to learn how to give up our divisions and look for unity. Nono is now deceased, but he will always be remembered as a gentle, compassionate man who truly was an ambassador of reconciliation, love, and peace.

IN ETHIOPIA, FAITH SURVIVES IN DROUGHT AND PERSECUTION

We experienced fear in a different way in Ethiopia in 1985 during a devastating drought and famine. People feared for their very lives from the hunger that had engulfed this nation. We visited the feeding camps, where I held children in my arms whose arms were no bigger than a fifty-cent piece. At the Sisters of Charity camp, I asked a doctor how he decided which children can come through the gate with so many pressing to find food and medical care. His answer was, "I never look into the eyes of the mothers."

We were amazed how only six nuns were responsible for feeding thousands of people. We asked Sister Berdelia, the nun in charge, how this was possible. She took us to see their prayer room and explained, "It is here every morning at 5:00 a.m. that we come for strength and guidance. We call this our generator room. As we take our communion and morning prayers, Jesus sustains us for the day. Surely in our weakness, he is strong." Jesus calls us to love the least of these. How wonderful to see the power of love and prayer in the midst of situations of great devastation and fear.

Another reason for traveling to Ethiopia concerned a different kind of fear. This involved the persecution of the Ethiopian Jews by the dictator Mengistu. America was aware of the covert airlift by Israeli operatives of many of these Ethiopian Jews to Israel in a project called "Operation Moses," which began in November of 1984. By 1985 some 8,000 Ethiopian Jews were resettled in Israel.[1] Now there was grave concern for the Jews that remained. The airlift angered Mengistu so much that he began severely punishing those who remained.

We drove in a four-wheel-drive vehicle through difficult terrain until we finally reached the villages. The Ethiopian Jews welcomed us warmly, and the scantily clothed children giggled with laughter at these strange-looking Americans who brought pencils, toys, and jars of bubbles to blow. These people had lived isolated from the world all their lives, and yet, their faith in God was what had sustained them.

One little girl and I quickly connected. She took my hand and led me to her small straw hut where her mother and sister were sitting around the fire cooking. Near them were the straw beds where they slept. We couldn't communicate by words, but the language of our hearts allowed us to speak. I said, "God bless you," and cupped my hands in prayer. The mother's face lit up and she sent the little girl to fetch her father. When he arrived the mother said something to him and he started digging under their straw sleeping mat. He produced an old book wrapped in rags, held it out, and gently placed it in my hands. I unwrapped the book and looked into his smiling face, realizing that this was something precious to him.

I could not understand what had just happened, so I asked our interpreter to help us communicate. The interpreter explained that the old book was the Torah, the first five books of the Bible. This Word of God was their life. These were the sons and daughters of Abraham; people of courage, people of faith, people of the Word. Even in the midst of fear, their faith had sustained them. The Torah had given them strength to endure.

I was sad to leave and say good-bye, knowing the great poverty and persecution that engulfed these lovely people. We had no idea of the danger they faced. The Ethiopian government was furious that we had traveled to the village of these Ethiopian Jews and wanted to make a statement. Two Ethiopians who worked for the U.S. Embassy in Addis Ababa had accompanied us to the Falasha village and that night they were savagely beaten.

Having struggled when being attacked myself, I identified with these Ethiopians and those in the village who were victims of much hatred. There is a fellowship of suffering that connected my heart to them and especially the innocent children. Jesus' heart was always to draw the little children to come to him and receive his love. Red and yellow, black, and white all are precious in his sight. God is building a diverse and wonderful family among the nations, and even though I could not imagine the devastation of hunger and fear that these people live with every day, their courageous spirit touched me.

Paul was upset at what had happened and when we arrived at a rural airport to fly back to the capital, there was more trouble. Soldiers carrying guns refused to let us board the airplane, accusing us of having contraband in our luggage. They pulled everything out of our suitcases and searched us again. I must confess I was terrified as I wondered how we would make it back home safely. Finally they let us go. We had experienced a small taste of what these people live with every day where fear is a way of life.

Holding a dying child from the feeding camp in my arms, knowing she might not make it through the night, I came to believe that every child is my child. This precious little Ethiopian girl who snuggled in my lap was also my daughter. Our lives were all intertwined. I prayed, "Protect this little girl whose eyes twinkled with love and keep her from fear. Let her faith keep burning and grow with the Torah alive in her heart. God bless those who in the midst of persecution, stand firm in their faith and find freedom in you." We are not separate from one another, but called to be God's worldwide family.

CHAPTER 13

Coming Home

Our congressional life was full of extraordinary experiences, but our family was the most important thing in our lives. Having such a demanding public career presented both of us with the challenge of balancing work with raising a family. Although I had come through a great deal of recovery from my past woundedness, at times always being in the public eye was still difficult. Giving up the travel to China and working in Washington, I thought, might also give me more time at home.

So in 1982 I left Friendship Imports and joined The Lascaris Design Group, a Washington, D.C.–based international interior design firm led by Carol and Climas Lascaris. Carol had accompanied me on an earlier buying trip into China with Friendship Imports where we had an amazing opportunity to buy wonderful items from the antiques warehouses. My first responsibility with Lascaris was working on a palace for King Hussein of Jordan. We did a turnkey job, which meant Lascaris did everything from the initial design and installation to flying in the grass sod for the official opening.

For three years I tried to balance caring for the children, working at Lascaris, and being a full partner with Paul in our many congressional activities. I thought I was doing pretty well until one day our babysitter surprised me by bringing my little son into the office at noon, just as I was giving Climas some bad news about a delayed marble shipment. When I saw Paul, I told Climas I needed to go have lunch with my son and everything else could wait.

Fear to Freedom

As we walked hand in hand along the river in Georgetown, I realized I was missing precious moments with Paul and Mary Katherine. Even though I really enjoyed my work at Lascaris, I thought about my priorities and knew my family was the most important thing in the world to me. I remembered how I had left my television show that I had loved, and how God had worked this for good in my life and opened new opportunities. Now was another moment of decision. I needed to trust my heart and keep my eyes on Jesus and his priorities, not on the circumstances that made leaving my present job difficult. We were building a new house and depended on my salary, but my children especially needed me at this time.

A peace came over me as I made the decision to leave Lascaris and become a full-time mom. I bent down, held Paul's hands in mine and told him, "Mommy is coming home." His hug and great excitement confirmed this was the right decision.

To the shock of the firm, I went back to the office and told Climas I was sorry, but I was resigning to put being a mother first. It became clear to me that everything else fell away in importance compared to my innermost emotional need to care for my children. I had learned from my past healing journey the importance of facing difficult challenges and making a decision that was the healthiest for my family and me. It took me a month to complete my work before I left, which was hard for our son, Paul, to understand.

The morning of my last day of work, my four-year old son took my face in his hands, looked into my eyes and said, "Mommy, when you come home to me it's going to be the happiest day of my life." With tears of joy I hugged him. That day I came home for good. It was the right decision and I never looked back.

MARY KATHERINE'S STORY

These had been wonderful years in Congress filled with a few tears, lots of laughter, some challenges raising two children in public life, and extraordinary experiences. I remember a funny story about our daughter when we were running for the Senate. Our children thought a normal weekend was riding in parades and going to fish fries. Finally one morning, in her then six-year-old words, Mary Katherine told me she was having something of an identity crisis because everyone called her Congressman Trible's daughter. I looked down lovingly at her and said, "Next time someone calls you Congressman Trible's daughter, you say, 'No ma'm, I'm Mary Katherine Trible,' and you be proud of it."

I was concerned about her as a mother wondering whether all the political involvement and pressure of our busy lives might be hurting her self-esteem. I recalled how my own self-worth had been so damaged after the rape, and how I had to fight back against the feelings that I was not enough even as a child in my relationship with my mom. I wanted her to grow up a self-confident young woman. I talked to Paul about her comment and my concern for how this was affecting her. We prayed for Mary Katherine and agreed we would be more aware of her feelings.

The next weekend we were lining up for the parade in Virginia, and the mayor's wife came up to Mary Katherine, who was walking in front of us. She leaned down lovingly to Mary Katherine, smiled at her and said, "Oh, you must be Congressman Trible's daughter." To which our daughter replied, "No ma'm, that's not what my mother says!" There was a moment of shock and then a roar of laughter from all those gathered. Somehow we still made it to the Senate.

A CHRISTENING I WILL NEVER FORGET

I also remember my most embarrassing moment of our congressional life. I was very honored to be chosen to be the sponsor for the nuclear attack submarine, the *USS Newport News*. March 15, 1996, was the date for the christening of the submarine that had been built at the Newport News shipyard. This was also the one hundredth year of the shipyard so 25,000 people had gathered for the celebration. Paul, as the U.S. senator, was the keynote speaker, and my job was to christen the submarine by cracking a bottle of champagne over the bow of the boat. It seemed like a very exciting task, but one that I was certainly up to. A camera was focused on the bow so that when the bottle broke, they knew to knock out the blocks and this huge submarine would shoot down the runway, splashing into the James River with the officers on deck saluting the crowd.

Paul finished his speech and it was my big moment. Mary Katherine, now ten years old, stood by my side as the honored junior sponsor. The band was ready to play as I spoke enthusiastically into the microphone, "I christen you the *USS Newport News*." With all my might I swung and struck the bow of the submarine with the bottle. To my surprise, there was only a thud! The bottle didn't break. Again I went through the motions: "I christen you . . ." and again another thud. My pulse was racing and my anxiety level heightened when a third time—and yes, a forth time—I crashed the bottle against the bow and nothing happened!

At this point I was praying like crazy. As a last resort I walked calmly over to the microphone and said to the crowd, "I need your help. Will you give me a one-two-three and together let's christen this beautiful submarine." The president of the shipyard looked worried. Thank goodness, the secretary of the navy noticed the red, white, and blue bunting was cushioning my blows and lifted it up. I reared back for the swing of my life and 25,000 joined me in shouting, "One, two, and three." I let go with all my might and the champagne bottle broke. The band played, confetti filled the air, the sub went crashing down the runway, and the officers in their crisp uniforms saluted.

I was so thrilled the submarine was finally christened that I held the bottle of champagne over my head as a sign of victory. Quickly, the president of the shipyard came up behind me, grabbed the bottle, and threw it overboard. I had completely forgotten that the bottle was attached to the boat that was streaking down the runway. The last thing I needed was to go overboard myself!

No one will ever forget that christening and each year at the party to celebrate the new crew and officers of the boat, they love to replay all five strikes in fast-forward motion. For years my christening adventure appeared on a television's funniest videos program. I just laughed along. I think humor is good for the soul, even when the laugh is on us!

I was thankful God had taught me lessons through the years about the importance of persevering and having courage in the face of trials. I had learned I could not run away from challenges, although I admit, after the fourth hit with that bottle, I was about to think running might be a good idea. Also I realized the importance of reaching out to others for support—we do not have to go it alone. Lastly, a good laugh never hurt anyone.

Coming Home

A DIFFICULT DECISION

The biggest challenge for us, however, was finding time for our family. During the week, meetings with constituents and legislative hearings filled the day and the debates on the floor of the Senate would often go late into the night. You could never definitely tell a child Dad could make that game or school play, and on weekends Paul was crisscrossing the state. We missed him a lot but understood he had important responsibilities. Two years later in 1988, Paul was coming to the end of twelve years of public service in Congress—six in the House of Representatives and six in the Senate. Paul expressed that he was frustrated over not seeing his own children grow up. At the end of his term, our daughter, Mary Katherine, would be twelve and our son, Paul, eight. Paul was feeling sad when he missed watching a Little League game or seeing Mary Katherine play soccer. Paul wanted to be there for that all-important birthday party, yet often he would need to be on Capitol Hill voting. In the Senate late-night sessions were a way of life.

Paul decided to leave the Senate and not run for re-election. He explained:

> In life it is not so often the bad, but the good that distracts us from the best. It's the good that is the enemy of the best. Our jobs, the committees on which we serve, the good causes for which we work distract us from what matters the most in life—our God and our family. We're just so busy that we don't have time for those things that matter the most.
>
> At the end of our days no one says, "I wish I had attended more meetings. My God, I wish I worked longer days. I wish I had closed more deals." Rather, we regret the opportunities lost to learn from a father, to hug a child, to say thanks to a dying and loving mother. Life is about choices and I felt the right choice was to give up my Senate seat.

Paul was a great father, and he made a rule to be back home on Sundays from his tours around the state. But if he served another six-year term, Mary Katherine would be in college and he would have hardly known her. Paul's decision not to run for reelection sent shock waves across Virginia. Few politicians then walked away from public service, especially for family.

Fear to Freedom

Paul felt convicted by his faith and his love of family. It was terribly difficult because people just did not understand why a forty-one-year-old successful senator was walking away. We were sorry and asked forgiveness of supporters who were upset. This, however, was the right decision for us. I admired Paul's courage and loved my husband more dearly for making it.

The press could not get over this decision. Ambitious young politicians are not supposed to walk away from power. The next day the press called Paul's office in Washington and said, "He's dying, isn't he?" Fortunately, that was not the case. About a week later, a political reporter for the *Richmond Times Dispatch* called Paul's mother, Katherine.

She was the most wonderful person in the world, but was absolutely the last person Paul ever wanted to talk to a political reporter. The reporter said, "Mrs. Trible, I understand your son has become very religious." To which Paul's mother responded, "Religious, he's not religious, he's an Episcopalian." The reporter was so amazed by her response he did not know what to write.

There were other reasons that affected Paul's decision, but the family was definitely the most important. Paul shared his concern about politicians staying too long in Congress:

> Our founding fathers believed we should have citizen legislatures. Their idea was that people should go to Washington and serve for a time and then have the good sense to come home. When our elected officials stay too long, they lose touch with reality and public service becomes a job. They begin weighing every vote on how it will affect their job security. We need more political leaders who have the courage to make politically unpopular decisions, notwithstanding the personal consequences of their actions.
>
> I also had become increasing frustrated by the glacial pace of the Congress. There was too much political posturing and rhetoric and the absence of real action. I missed my family very much. I realized my children were growing up, and I wanted to share more of our lives together. For me, the time to come home was now.

Coming Home

I realized what my husband had always said was true. "This world is not going to be shaped by great nation states or powerful parliaments or mighty armies, but by people who love God, love one another, and reach out and change the world for good one person at a time." Even though I never dreamed we would be leaving public service, I was excited for what God had in store for us. We made the decision, told only a few people, and recorded the televised announcement. We picked up our children from school and got on a plane to New York City.

That night as all of Virginia was hearing that Paul was retiring from the Senate, our family was watching the play *Les Miserables*. It is a powerful story of reconciliation and love and ends with the line, "To love another is to see the face of God." After the play, we returned to the hotel and tears ran down my face as Paul told the children about our new beginning. We had made this announcement about a year before the end of his term so others could make their plans to run for the seat. We did not know what was in store for our family once Paul was out of Congress, but we would be together, and we trusted in God's guidance just as we had trusted in God's guidance before in difficult times.

THE PRAYER ROOM—MY HIDING PLACE

In our last year in Congress, I had an extraordinary experience I will always treasure. During our twelve years one of the things that had meant the most to me were my times with the Lord in the Prayer Chapel off the Rotunda of the U.S. Capitol. This was my intimate place, my *hiding place* for prayer. I thought about the many leaders of our nation who had knelt here asking for God's provision for their families, personal challenges, and guidance for this country that they were privileged to lead.

One day Paul asked if I would take Jim, a political supporter, to lunch in the Senate Dining room. Paul explained he would be involved in votes and could meet him later. I had only met him once before at the Republican National Convention, but I knew he was a man strong in his faith.

We had a nice lunch and then I asked Jim if he would like to visit the Prayer Room. I described the beautiful stained-glass window of George Washington kneeling in prayer. Here are etched the words "This Nation under God," the Scripture "Preserve me Oh God for in thee do I put my trust" (Ps. 16:1 KJV), and the national seal with the American eagle.

Fear to Freedom

I told our friend I was always reminded here of God's promise, "If my people, who are called by my name, will humble themselves and pray, and seek my face and turn from their wicked ways, then I will hear from heaven and forgive their sins and will heal their land" (2 Chron. 7:14). We talked about the many challenges facing our nation. I recited one of Paul's favorite quotes from the National Prayer Breakfast. In Congressman Guy Vander Jagt's speech he attributed the following thoughts to the French journalist, Alexis de Tocqueville, who sought to answer the question "What makes America great?"

> I searched for America's greatness in her matchless con-stitution and it was not there. I searched for America's great-ness in her rich and fertile fields and her teeming industrial potential and it was not there. I searched for America's great-ness in her halls of Congress and it was not there. It was not, he said, until I went into the heartlands of America and into her churches that I discovered what it is that makes America great. America is great, he wrote, because America is good. And if America ever ceases to be good, America will cease to be great.[1]

Jim shared some thoughts about the Holy Spirit and read from John 15 in the historic Bible that lay open on a table in the Prayer Room. This is the Scripture where Jesus reassures his disciples that although he is leaving, he is sending the comforter, the Holy Spirit that would be with them always. Jim and I prayed together and then he left to meet Paul.

I remained deep in thought about how we were giving up the U.S. Senate and walking off to a new season. I got on my knees and surrendered to God my fear of our unknown future and all we were leaving behind. "I am completely yours, Lord. I trust you with my family and my life. I need your Holy Spirit to draw me close. I pray you will guide and direct our future and each moment of my life."

For the second time in my life, that blanket of warmth of the Spirit fell on me as it had that day of the robbery eleven years before. This was the most powerful experience of the closeness of Jesus through the Spirit I had ever known. God's presence was so real to me, and I was embraced fully in

Coming Home

unconditional love and tenderness. Tears fell as I recalled the faithfulness of God in all that had happened over the last years in Congress.

I recalled that when I was a young girl Willie would often sing a wonderful gospel song, "He Touched Me." This intimacy in the Spirit touched me in a way that made me whole as never before. I did not know what the road held for Paul and me on our journey, but I knew God was the one who was with us on the road. We were not alone on our journey.

WHAT'S NEXT?

As soon as we left the Senate, the pressure began building for Paul to enter another race—this time for governor. Some in the Republican Party reasoned with us that we would have more time for family living together in the Governor's Mansion. Serving as governor was also limited to the commitment of a four-year term. Here we were faced with another brush with politics just when I thought we were free. Paul was very uncertain about entering this campaign, but was strongly persuaded by others that this was his responsibility. Several delegates even walked him across the colonnade at Washington and Lee University, and talked about the willingness of George Washington, Robert E. Lee, and other Virginians to make sacrifices to serve the public.

After much prayer, Paul took two days away to make his decision. The last morning before returning home, he opened the Bible to a Scripture in Galatians: "And let us not grow weary while doing good, for in due season you will reap what you sow if your heart does not grow faint" (Gal. 6:9). Our hearts had definitely grown faint in politics. Paul felt a responsibility to run and said yes to the campaign for governor. It was a difficult race, and we lost by a few thousand votes in a tough primary, which was disappointing. Now, however, we were set free from a lifetime in politics. When God closes doors in our lives, windows often open.

We went to Boston for a wonderful sabbatical and Paul taught a course on Leadership and Politics at the Institute of Politics at Harvard's Kennedy School of Government. Our children enjoyed their new schools, and this was a refreshing time for all of us. We toured New England on the weekends, visited many historic areas, and enjoyed the vibrant color of the leaves in the fall.

Fear to Freedom

Occasionally our son and I would attend Paul's class at Harvard. Many of his students wanted to enter politics, and aspired to become senators or even president. One day the class was discussing the burdens of political leadership and public service, and a student turned to our nine-year-old son and asked, "What was it like having your dad in the Senate?" Our young son said, "You know, for nine years I never really saw my dad and then we moved to Boston, and it's just been wonderful." Paul and I both had tears in our eyes. We had lost too much time away from our children and now we wanted to take advantage of every moment we had together. Out of the mouth of a child had come real truth. We had made the right decision. It had been time to come home.

My brother Gene and Me

On our farm with Dad

America's Junior Miss 1967

Jr. Miss with Anita Bryant

Mom's kiss on the cheek

Our Wedding Day

Rosemary's Guestbook

Paul and President Jimmy Carter 1977

President Ronald Reagan

Prayer Breakfast with Billy Graham and
President Reagan

Campaigning with John Warner and Liz Taylor

Christening the USS Newport
News Submarine

Senate Swearing in with George Bush

Family at Christmas

President George Bush with Family

On the White House Lawn

Barbara Bush

Tipper Gore and Hillary Clinton at White House

Laura Bush

Time with Each Other

My "elephants" Grace Nelson & Linda Slattery

Prayer Group Friends 2009

My Forever Friend René   "The Generals"

"Soul Sister" Barbara Skinner

Hope Needed For Ethiopia

Mother Teresa At Nat'l Prayer Breakfast

Praying with Mother
Teresa in Calcutta

Dear
Paul and Rosemary

God bless you
Mc Teresa mc
13-5-94

Cambodian Orphans

Cuban Church
Dedicated to Mom

ICM team on Great Wall in China

Joyful Chinese Children ICM trip

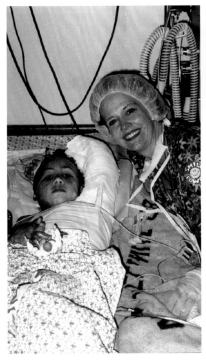

Burn victim, Operation
Smile in Gaza

Celebration CNU Seniors

Prayer Group with Amy Grant

Students with Ambassador Tony and Janet Hall, Rome

Groundbreaking at CNU

Andrea Bocelli Performs at CNU

CNU Graduation with Senator Bob Dole

Celebrating Friends

Son Paul III's Oxford graduation

Christmas with the family

38 years Together

Norman Rockwell published this mosaic that was reproduced by Venetian artists for the 40th anniversary of the United Nations in 1985. It was presented to the UN by Nancy Reagan

CHAPTER 14

Saturated By Love

After Boston we returned to Virginia and Paul practiced law, then led a public affairs company in Washington, D.C., Paul had been a young, free-enterprise Republican who talked a lot about risk, reward, and bottom line. But he didn't understand what those words really meant until he and his colleagues were rewarded on the basis of their productivity and performance.

It was a wonderful learning experience for Paul and an opportunity for him to further develop his leadership skills. These were also great family years, when Paul never missed our children's soccer or lacrosse games. This brought us all great joy. We built a home in Williamsburg where Mary Katherine finished her high school years and both children were active in the ministry of Young Life. We were enjoying this season in our lives out of the public eye. Mary Katherine headed off to the College of Charleston and Paul III had two and a half years left in high school.

Then another unexpected window opened. Paul was serving on the board of Christopher Newport University and had come to care about the future of this school. Newport News had been an important part of our congressional district, and CNU was a young, public university that was facing many challenges. As the former president was retiring, the university determined they needed a president who could provide energetic, visionary leadership. Paul became a candidate, and when he first came home to tell me the news, I must admit I was surprised. This would be another dramatic new career in our lives. For all of our years of marriage, Paul had stayed in the same job no more than six years. Again this was a time of uncertainty as to what the future might bring.

Later that day I drove to the CNU campus, and prayed, "Lord, could this be you guiding this decision?" Paul didn't have a PhD and wasn't a career academician. But as I looked into the faces of the students walking to class, I realized we had always loved college-age students since our days with National Student Leadership, and this might be a wonderful opportunity. Paul III might also enjoy being involved in college life as he finished high school.

I also knew that, although neither Paul nor I missed politics, we both missed the opportunity to serve and make a difference in people's lives. In December, Paul was elected president of Christopher Newport University and he took office on January 1, 1996. He explained to me, "It's as if God said, 'When you left the Senate you gave up public service you loved for a family you loved even more. Now that your children are older, I'm going to give you the opportunity to reengage in the life of Virginia.'"

A brand-new season began. I could never have imagined the incredible gift God had in store for our lives, and that this would become another important step on my journey from fear to faith to forgiveness to freedom. The whirlwind of our new responsibilities was both exciting and challenging. Both of us were adjusting to new roles, and I was inspired by the new friendships I was making with students.

On February 1, 1996, we drove to Washington to participate in the National Prayer Breakfast. We wanted to renew many friendships we had made around the world over those twenty years since we first attended in 1976 when Paul first came to Congress. That afternoon I went to the program of Praise and Worship that Pastors John Staggers and Sam Hines always led. A wonderful African-American pastor challenged us as he preached on Ezekiel, saying, "What would you have done if God told you to preach to a cemetery? I mean, you would have thought God had lost it! Right? But God called Ezekiel to preach over dead bones when the situation looked hopeless. How could a bunch of dead bones live again? Only through the Spirit of God!"

God asked Ezekiel to believe the impossible was possible as he took Ezekiel to the Valley of Dry Bones and asked:

> Son of man, can these bones live? I said, 'Oh Sovereign Lord, You alone know.' God said, I will cause breath to enter into you and you shall live . . . . Then He said to me, 'Prophesy to these bones . . . I will make breath come into you, and you will come to life. And as I was prophesying, there was a noise, a rattling sound, and the bones came together, bone to bone. . . . but there was no breath in them.
>
> Then He said to me, 'Prophesy to the breath . . . Come from the four winds, oh breath, and breathe on those slain that they may live . . . So Ezekiel prophesied as he commanded me, and breath entered them; and they came to life and stood up on their feet—a vast army (Ezek. 37:3–4, 6, 9–10).

I was greatly impacted by the way this pastor brought to life this amazing Scripture. Two thoughts came to mind. First, I recalled how Doug Coe's son, Jonathan, became ill with leukemia and fought hard for his life. Jonathan had led the vision for the Student Leadership Forum and dreamed of God gathering an army of young people who would love God, love each other, and go out and change this world for good—an army strong in the Spirit like Ezekiel's army.

Jonathan was married and his wife was pregnant with their first child when he told the doctor, "If I live, I will see my new baby born and continue to devote my life to student leadership. But if I die, I will be with the Lord." Jonathan's precious daughter was born a short time before Jonathan died in 1983.

Secondly, I thought of Matt Hall, Tony and Janet Hall's son who was now fighting leukemia. Janet was one of my prayer partners and close friends while Tony and Paul served in Congress. Matt's and our son's personalities were very much alike. They loved sports, adored surfing, were the same age, and had grown up in the demands of the congressional life. I was devoted to Matt and his healing. I had already dealt with the pain of other close friends, Peggy and John Bowditch, when their son, my godson, Leland, had died in a car accident. I wanted desperately not to have another person I love go through that terrible loss.

I wondered if there could be some connection between Matt's illness and what God was saying through this Scripture about the Valley of Dry Bones. Could this be a key in the Word showing us how to pray for Matt's bone cancer? One time, the cancer had gone into remission and Matt and his dad went on a wonderful trip to Egypt through the Make a Wish Foundation. The cancer, however, returned with further complications. We somehow needed to believe the impossible was still possible for Matt's healing.

I had joined the Hall family in New York for Matt's bone marrow transplant. The doctors said that Matt could die in twenty-four hours because they had to kill everything in his bones in order to inject a donor's new marrow. Matt's bones were "dead" like the bones in Ezekiel's valley. I sat outside the hospital room praying as I watched the doctors slowly put life back into Matt, giving him the new bone marrow from a matching donor in California. All went well for months—until Matt's cancerous bone marrow started growing back and destroying the donor's healthy marrow. I was devastated and could not imagine how much this hurt Janet, Tony, and Matt's sister, Jyl. Friends and family pressed in with prayer.

We had hoped for a miracle that Matt would be cancer free to live a full and wonderful life. He was such an incredible young man who had a great impact on hundreds of people through his bravery in fighting this cancer. Now timing was critical because in a week Matt would receive a life-threatening experimental treatment at the National Institute of Health in Washington, D.C., I prayed that the Spirit would bring life back into Matt's bones like that mighty army and his healing would bring glory to God as in the Scripture in Ezekiel.

I pondered these thoughts after I returned from Washington. For the last year I had been drawn to contemplative prayer and usually set my alarm to pray for thirty minutes to an hour to begin my day. When I awoke on Saturday morning, I felt there was a real sense of urgency. "Don't get a cup of coffee. Don't brush your teeth. It is critical you pray!" I sat up in bed and began to earnestly pray.

Saturated by Love

I was praying for Matt when a clear image of a pumpkin came before my mind. It was as if God's hand was reaching into the pumpkin and pulling out all the seeds and stuff inside one handful at a time. I thought how, at Halloween, you cut a pumpkin and take out the center to carve the face you want to create so the light shines through. God seemed to want to pull "stuff" out of my life like this pumpkin. The thought came, "I must carve out some of your seeds so my light will shine through you." Then the second image was of a pencil. I recalled how Mother Teresa had once said, "I am a little pencil in the hand of a writing God who is sending a love letter to the world."[1] What an incredible visual image that was for me. God's own hand had written Mother Teresa's life, which had brought happiness to so many. I thought how I would like for God to "write" my life. Then to my surprise in this image, God turned the pencil around and with the eraser began to erase a part of me.

"Yes, Lord," I prayed, "I am willing to be erased in whatever way you see fit—let there be less of me and more of you. I pray these images of the pencil and pumpkin will allow me to decrease, so God can increase in my life. Pull out whatever you desire, mold me into your image, erase whatever is thy will so that your light shines through my life."

I realized how during my earlier journey of healing, it was God's light that had seen me through the darkness of my pain and at times been used to help light others on their path to freedom. I knew there was more I needed to learn about surrendering fully to Jesus. What further needed to be erased?

I recalled how I had read about Mother Teresa praying that God would penetrate and possess her so completely that her whole life would be a radiance of the Lord. The light would be all from God—none of it would be hers. I was just a simple woman, but in my heart I truly wanted to radiate God's joy. I was open to his leading.

The last image was, of course, Ezekiel and the Valley of Dry Bones. Again it seemed this was the way to pray for Matt since it was his bone marrow that was dying from the cancer. When I opened my eyes two hours had flown by in prayer. I did not understand why these three images had come, but I felt it had to do with trusting and praying faithfully that Matt would live through this next terrible treatment a week from that Saturday.

Fear to Freedom

The following day was Sunday and Paul and I went to Grace Church in Yorktown. I was shocked that our pastor, Carleton Bakkum, also preached on Ezekiel's valley! Now, I am someone who loves visual examples, but even I thought this was a little crazy. What could these images of a pumpkin, pencil, and this valley of dry bones really mean? As we were leaving church I said in jest, "I guess I'm going to have to go to a morgue and get a bone to represent this Scripture. It's everywhere!"

God sometimes works in mysterious ways, and I believe he must have a sense of humor. When we arrived home from church I asked Paul to help me remove some cardboard boxes I had cut up and placed on our driveway so the women in my prayer group would not slip on the new-fallen snow. The snow was now melting and the pieces of cardboard were all wet and soggy across the walkway.

To my complete surprise as I moved one of them, there underneath was a thick white bone about ten inches long. Amazed, I realized how specific God is when we pray. I could hardly believe my eyes. I felt God was in every minute detail of my life. I prayed, "I'm listening God, what do you want me to do?" I felt I needed to go to D.C. and share with Tony, Janet, and Matt about Ezekiel!

I left for Washington the next morning and joined Barbara Skinner to hear Pastors John and Carol Arnott of Toronto Airport Christian Fellowship in Canada talk about the power of the Holy Spirit. There was a tremendous movement of the Spirit at this church, and Matt and his family had gone there for healing prayer for Matt earlier in the year.

I spent the night at the Halls' and the next morning I shared all that had happened that week. John Arnott came over and prayed with Matt, then asked if any of the family members and friends would like to say anything. I shared about the Valley of Dry Bones, and we asked God for Matt's bones to be healed that he might stand for Christ as part of the army of God.

I asked John how we as friends could support Matt, and I remember he responded, "Saturate Matt in prayer. Soak Matt in prayer." As I drove home that night, I stopped by my friend Linda Heath's house and shared with her all that had happened. I asked her to join me in trusting God for Matt's future.

On that Friday, February 9, 1996, I spoke to the President's Leadership Program at CNU on character and leadership. Afterward I was to join Peggy

Saturated by Love

Bowditch for a weekend retreat at her home with six college girls. Two of these young women had recently been raped at other universities. I had been talking to the girls by phone and trying to walk with them through the initial trauma.

This weekend we planned to create a special time together to encourage the healing process. This meant plunging back into sharing my old pain with all its emotional impact. One of these girls, however, had been suicidal the week before. I could understand her coming to the point of wondering if life was worth living. You are so broken that you just don't know how to respond to the emotional and physical symptoms of fear such as headaches, nausea, and lack of sleep. I was always grateful when God would bring me face-to-face—victim to victim—so my own experience of pain and practical tools that led to my healing might help others wounded by this devastating crime.

I left the university as a terrible winter snowstorm began to rage. En route I called Peggy to say I would be a little late, as I needed to pick up the food. We hoped that the girls would be safe on the road, but I felt confident driving as I had a four-wheel-drive Explorer. I set off for the retreat in Gloucester in wonderful spirits as I was looking forward to being with these girls.

I listened to a praise tape as I traveled down Interstate 64. The traffic around me was bumper to bumper since everyone was headed from work on a Friday night, wanting to get safely home in this terrible storm. I was trying to be cautious in my driving but suddenly my car skidded on the snow. I touched my brakes but then the car went completely out of control. The windshield was so covered with the torrents of snow that I could hardly see the road ahead. I panicked. It was all happening so fast I could not even think clearly.

The car then began to slide to the left and I was afraid I would plunge into the center median. Then when I tried to adjust the wheel to the right, my car began to spin as if it were on black ice. The Explorer was now headed toward the side railing and I thought I was going straight over the high metal railing to my death.

I cried out, "Oh, my God." I don't know how to describe it, but my spirit leapt. This tremendous peace came over me and calmed my fear. I felt I was not alone. Then suddenly there was a swishing sound. To this day I will never understand exactly what happened. The front of the car moved around very quickly, so only the back hit the railing, and the car stopped in the middle of the road facing the traffic.

I don't remember if I hit my head hard or not, but I rejoiced that I was safe! I was OK! My car had spun around until I now looked straight into the line of stopped traffic that had been behind me on Interstate 64. Snow was blowing everywhere. My heart was pounding and I began praising God, "Thank you for saving my life!" Then I thought, I must get out and see what happened to the car. I stepped out and looked at the back of the car fender. I couldn't believe that there was not more damage.

A man who was stopped behind me began walking toward me. I immediately reached out to him as if he were an angel sent to rescue me. His name was Ron, and he said, "That accident was amazing, are you all right? Is the car terribly damaged? I can call for help." I was thankful for his kindness, but replied, "I don't see any reason why I can't just drive away. I'm all right. Will you help me with the traffic so I can turn the car around and get going the right way?" With Ron's assistance, I made a U-turn. He then followed me as I drove down the road very slowly until I got to the first exit and waved good-bye.

My emergency lights were on. My praise tape was blaring. I thought I might share with these girls at Peggy's house the way God's amazing grace had just saved my life. I was aware of feeling a little confused. I had to concentrate to negotiate the exit turn. Perhaps I was more shaken than I thought since I turned right instead of left.

When I realized I had gone the wrong way, I pulled into a Texaco gas station. My eyes felt heavy. Something was different. I felt I was seeing through a tunnel as if something was affecting my vision. I asked the man at the station how to get to Yorktown and he confirmed my directions. I felt a little overwhelmed and decided I needed to stop and pray.

A wonderful gentle spirit and peace filled me. I realized I was more affected than I thought by the accident. There was a phone booth nearby, but I could not seem to move to make a call. I just closed my eyes and began to thank God again for saving my life. I prayed for specific people and circumstances. On top of my list was Matt Hall because I knew the next day, February 10, was the day his terrible treatment was scheduled at the National Institute of Health.

Saturated by Love

I was continually embraced by this wonderful light that flowed all around me. I remember asking, "Lord, how can I saturate Matt in prayer? Do you want me to take Matt's fear upon me? I'm willing, if this will help." I kept going deeper in prayer and was comforted that God's Spirit or presence felt right beside me. I felt like Joy, my name for the Spirit, was my intimate friend—loving, endearing, and gentle—always bringing me back to a deep sense of peace. This seemed strange, I thought. I should be anxious, but I am not. I should be fearful, but I am not. In fact this presence, Joy, has brought more contentment than I ever felt possible in what was a very unusual situation.

I lost all concept of time, but I must have been there several hours. At some point, I turned off the car ignition and lights, and locked the doors. I thought of the unusual images from my prayer time the week before, and I laughed that someone might just think this was all crazy. I also asked the Lord to comfort Peggy and assure her that I was all right. I knew the nightmare of fear she had experienced when the police had arrived at her home and told her about Leland's accident. I did not want her to be afraid for me.

Again I asked, "How can I soak Matt in prayer? Please help him through tomorrow's treatment." I prayed, "Teach me how to love you more and live in your presence. Bless these girls, especially those in such pain. Thank you for saving my life. Please use it for your glory." My hands were at my sides and my feet crossed. I began to shiver with the cold on the outside, but inside I felt the warmth of God's love like a blanket. I was not afraid, but always embraced by Joy.

Logically I could not explain what was happening to me, but I was in a place of complete contentment. Then I heard the sirens coming. I asked Joy, "Is that for me?" and I felt I heard the answer, "Yes." "Am I supposed to go with them?" Again the word "Yes." An ambulance pulled up and the crew started knocking very hard on the window. One guy said, "We're going to have to crowbar the door. It's locked and the woman looks like she's unconscious."

I laughed inside. After God saved this car from being totaled, Paul would be so upset with me if I let them crowbar the door open. I asked, "If I go, Lord, can Joy stay with me?" I then realized I was shaking from the cold but I couldn't seem to move. I asked Joy, "How are we going to open the door?"

Fear to Freedom

Somehow God gave me just enough strength to move my left-hand baby finger up so I could barely touch the unlock button. The rescue squad immediately rushed in and lifted me out of the car. My arms and head fell limp as they put an oxygen mask on me. I was shaking uncontrollably as they put blankets around me.

I felt like I was looking down on my body lying on the stretcher in the ambulance. I was observing myself as if I were a witness to what was happening. I felt calm. I felt safe. I felt completely unafraid. A policeman had come and tried to determine who I was from my driver's license. He said he thought my husband had been in politics and he would try to contact him at our home address on my license. I was relieved Paul would soon know what was happening.

Meanwhile the rescue workers tried five times to get an IV into my veins that kept going flat. They said I was unconscious and my eyes were completely dilated. I could hear every detail and felt I'd never been so conscious! I was aware of the strong light beam when they shone an eye instrument directly into my pupils. It was as if my eyes were covered with little robin eggshells and I could see nothing. My veins kept blowing until finally one man said, "I think we've got to put this one in the wrist but this may be painful." I prayed Joy would help them insert the IV. Finally it went in smoothly.

As they drove to the hospital with sirens blazing and lights flashing, it felt unreal, like a comedy. I felt lighthearted inside, continually embraced by this beautiful light and warmth and always in the company of the Spirit. The rescue workers talked about what they had for lunch, and one described his great date the night before. There was nothing I could do but be totally surrendered to the Lord, who gave me this amazing peace in the midst of all that was going on around me.

When we arrived at the first hospital, the rescue squad told the doctors I appeared to be in a coma. They could not get any response or movement although my vital signs seemed normal. They said, "Perhaps she is a diabetic or on some drug. We did find this strange white bone in her purse. The police took her ID from her wallet and are going to notify her husband."

I could clearly hear everything going on and laughed inside about the bone in my purse. I guess it did seem a little strange, but I was planning to share the Scripture of Ezekiel with the girls at the retreat. I felt I was in a different place looking onto this scene yet totally secure, embraced in Jesus' love.

The most difficult time was what took place next in the emergency room. There was shouting all around because the hospital was packed with many people who had been in accidents in the snowstorm. I remained peaceful inside until one male nurse, using an instrument to test reflexes, hit my knees several times. I showed no response, so he dug the pointed end into my foot and that pain was severe.

This instrument actually pierced a hole in the bottom of my foot so it was bleeding. I wanted to cry out inside, but I could not move or speak. The medic saw no reflex response and was puzzled by my condition. I felt Jesus gently comforting me, restoring my peace: "That's so you might know just a little how it felt when the nails pierced through my feet."

In the ambulance, they had tried ammonia several times to awaken me. Now the emergency room nurse held the smelling salts up to my nose for a long time, convinced I would revive. The ammonia was burning through my head and body. I was concerned it was going to cause a migraine, like I had suffered for many years. She didn't stop until a doctor came in and said, "That's enough!" I don't think God meant for me to have any pain, but even then, Joy comforted me inside. "Forgive her. She is just trying to save your life." I was at peace again. The police had gotten in touch with Paul and they put the phone up to my ear. I desperately wanted to talk to Paul and assure him I was OK, but I was unable to talk. There was nothing I could do.

The doctor explained to Paul that it appeared I was in a coma-like state. Although I was not responding in any way, I seemed not to have been badly harmed physically and my vital signs were good. When I heard Paul's voice, I managed a slight quiver of my lips that looked a like a crooked little sideways smile. Everyone got excited and encouraged as this was the first movement they had seen.

Paul and our friend John Bowditch arrived from our home in Williamsburg. I was then transferred by ambulance to a second hospital because it was where my family doctors practiced. There I was examined by Dr. Harris, my neurologist, who had treated me for my migraines, and Dr. Chessen, a friend and psychiatrist. I regularly took medicine every night for the migraines that I had experienced for fifteen years. Because I could not swallow any pills, I heard Dr. Harris say I could take my medicine the next morning. I knew I needed my medication as the ammonia had caused my head to throb, but I could not communicate this to Dr. Harris.

I was comforted that several friends, including René, had gathered to pray. My friend Linda Heath asked to pray with me alone for a few minutes. As she prayed, my spirit began to soar. I knew she was concerned and wanted me to return, but my heart took flight instead. I had this incredible experience of soaring as if I were an eagle in flight over majestic mountains. I flew over beautiful rivers and lakes. The wind felt cool on my face and my heart was full. I had never experienced anything like this new sense of freedom.

Then very abruptly the doctor returned and asked Linda to stop praying and leave. I felt my heart crash. I longed to remain soaring on the wings of this amazing love. Later, I wrote this poem to try to express my experience.

I Soar

The world would draw me back
But no, no!

Be free from the bonds of fear.
My lover calls
Come, Come, my *Beloved*
Come fly with me.

My heart takes flight to soar.
As an eagle rides the wind
Up mountain slopes
To descend at great speed,

Only to soar again.

CHAPTER 15

My Near-Life Experience

What I am going to describe in this chapter is very personal and may seem surrealistic to you. It does to me sometimes. However, the first night in the hospital was the most wonderful experience of my life. It took me to a new level with the Lord, and my memory of it has a vivid quality. I truly believe I experienced passing for this brief time through the curtain between the visible and invisible world on that first night. I understand that this may seem more than a little unusual. All I can do is tell you honestly what happened to me that night and hope that this blesses you as it did me.

The doctors and everyone finally left. Paul fell asleep in the chair beside me, and it quieted down for the night. I had an unusual feeling I was in this world, but not of it. I remained surrounded by a warm blanket of love. This beautiful, diffused white light had never left me since I was in the car praying. The light pierced the darkness within me, constantly comforting me and taking away all fear and anxiety.

Fear to Freedom

The light had movement and life, and its warmth continued to be a blessing. In the middle of the night, I awoke in my spirit and became aware that the light seemed now to be guiding me forward. It was as if I was entering a new place and being transported into another dimension. The white light around me opened up to a beautiful blue as I saw a field with what looked like wheat blowing in the wind.

At first it looked like individual lights coming toward me. Then I was so surprised and overjoyed when I recognized these figures approaching me were dear friends who had come to greet me. It was like a welcoming committee! The first person I saw was Leland Bowditch, my godchild, who had died in an automobile accident almost four years before. He apparently fell asleep, hit a tree head-on, and was killed instantly only minutes from his parents' home. When my car had gone out of control, I thought this was how I would also die.

Leland was so handsome and looked exactly as I remembered him. I have always kept a picture of him in his tuxedo by my bed. We greeted each other lovingly. Seeing him brought me such great joy. Then Leland asked me to share several things with his family.

"First, hug my mom. Hold her for me and tell her how very much I love her. I'm worried about the pain in her legs, so help mom find the doctor she needs. (Peggy has had difficulty with post-polio syndrome and she had recently fallen and broken her foot and ankle.) Tell Dad that he was the greatest dad ever and not to feel guilty because there was nothing anyone could have done. Tell Mom, Dad, and Sherwood (Leland's brother) that when I died I didn't feel any pain. (I discovered later this was one of his family's main questions.) Tell them I am with Jesus, and that God has a lot for them still to do to love others."

I told Leland, "This very weekend, Peggy has a group of college girls at your house on a retreat where she is loving and caring for these students. I was supposed to be there too, but how amazing that, instead, I am with you!"

Next to Leland was Tom Skinner. Tom had been diagnosed with leukemia about the same time as Matt Hall. I told him how touched I had been by his home-going celebration. It was so wonderful to see him again. I could not remember all the details of our conversation, but Tom spoke of the Kingdom of God that he was experiencing firsthand. Then he said, "Rosemary, take care of Barbara for me."

Next to Tom stood John Staggers and Sam Hines. Here were my dear African-American friends who both had died during the last two years. We talked about our mornings together at Shiloh Baptist Church and work in the city during our years in Washington. I thanked them for being great mentors and incredible brothers in Christ.

What a joy to see them again looking so vibrant as they were still dreaming of people coming together as one; black and white, rich and poor, powerful and powerless, learning to love one another as Jesus had taught. They said they continued to pray for Washington, D.C., to become a City Set on the Hill for God.

Beside them I was thrilled to see again Jonathan Coe, whom I loved like a son. We reminisced how he had visited Paul in the Senate to share the vision of Student Leadership. I shared how much everyone missed him. I told him how the Forum was still powerfully making a difference in young people's lives, encouraging them to be leaders led by God.

He spoke lovingly of his wife and daughter. Then he asked me to hold his mother and tell her how much he loved her. (Interesting how both boys wanted me to physically embrace their mothers as if their arms were holding them and express how much they loved them.) He then said specifically, "Tell my dad that everywhere he goes in the world, I go with him."

I was amazed as I began to realize that this next life is not some far-off place. These loved ones seemed separated from us by only a thin veil. It had been exciting to see these friends, and I was in awe of what was happening around me. Each one of these individuals had deeply impacted my life in a wonderful way. They appeared to be the same age when I had last seen them, yet now their faces radiated such peace and happiness.

Then I noticed a large figure standing behind Leland. I did not know who he was as he was deep in the shadows. Then this man stepped forward out of the darkness and into the light. For a moment I became anxious as I asked, "Who are you?" He replied, "I am the man who raped you. I would not be here except you forgave me and prayed that someone would tell me about Jesus and I would be set free." Could this really be true? It was twenty-one years since I had been raped. Could God have answered my prayer of so long ago? Could this man somehow have been transformed from a life of violence to receive hope and forgiveness? Maybe he could have been in prison, or did a friend reach out to him and share this love of Jesus? I will never know this side of heaven.

All I know was this moment was a great gift to my life: To be face-to-face with the man who had stolen my joy, and see him now at peace with God and forgiven of his sinful past. What a merciful God to answer my prayer. The power of forgiveness came to have new meaning in my life that night. This man was like the prodigal son who had returned home, accepted the love of the Father, and had been forgiven for his vicious crime against me and perhaps other women.

I thought about how when we forgive, it can open up an opportunity for those who have deeply hurt us to be released to become all God would have them to be. Unforgiveness can only lead to bitterness and bitterness to a hardened heart. I remembered the two girls on the retreat at Peggy's who had recently been raped. I wished somehow they could hear this story, and I could share how this miracle had touched me.

I knew I would forever treasure the gift of this night, yet with all the excitement I was exhausted. I seemed to fall into a peaceful sleep for some time. Then I was jolted awake inside my mind by the thought of Matt and his leukemia. I felt it was urgent to saturate Matt in prayer. I seemed to sense Matt was getting fearful about the next day's treatment. I asked the Lord as I had in the car earlier, "Would it help if you let me take Matt's fear upon me?"

Tears began coming down my cheeks as I saw a vision open up in my mind of a battle raging around me. A terrible darkness and continuous roaring sound surrounded me. Something fierce seemed to be swirling around in the blackness, but I could not look at it and had to turn my eyes away.

Then on the other side, I saw a man on a white horse with his sword drawn high. I thought it must be Jesus who was in the midst of some spiritual battle concerning Matt. The evil was so black. Fear gripped my heart and I continued to cry out and pray for Matt's life. As my eyes focused away from the darkness toward the light, I felt such an abundance of love. The vision departed, and I was calmed once again by the light. My fear was gone, as I felt embraced as God's beloved child.

My Near-Life Experience

Later, my husband Paul described to me his experience:

> We finally settled down for the night about 1:00 a.m. and we all were exhausted. I slept by you on the reclining chair but kept awaking to check on you. Nurses were coming in throughout the night, but from 1:30 a.m. to 3:00 a.m. you seemed to have this contented look on your face. You clearly were very active during this time, slightly nodding your head yes and then nodding no. You seemed to be engaged elsewhere, but there was no interaction with any of us. About 3:00 a.m. you began to cry, and I was so concerned because I could not comfort you. The sobbing finally stopped, and then you were calm and quiet for the rest of the night.
>
> At this point early in the morning around 6:00 a.m., I was overwhelmed and exhausted by the spectacle of the night. I've never had such an overwhelming sense of loneliness. I thought how my mother was walking off into the sunset and my father was not feeling well. Here I am and I may have lost my wife. I was overtaken by emotion.
>
> I remember coming close beside you and whispering, "My Rosemary, I love you so much. God, I pray you'll let her return to me." I had been gently rubbing your forehead just like your father used to do when you were a little girl. That had seemed to give you some pleasure. I had tried kissing you the night before, but it felt like a first kiss in grade school. There was no movement on your side at all. This time however when I kissed you, your lips gave the slightest response. This was the first sign of hope.

I was so overwhelmed by Paul's love as he awakened me with such tenderness. We had been married for twenty-five years, yet I felt now more than ever, how deeply Paul loved me. My heart rejoiced. I had not been able to speak at all since my time in the car, but I wanted so much to respond to Paul's affection. I strained out the words and whispered, "P-a-u-l, I love you." After the deep coma-like state of the night before, I now for the first time could communicate with great difficulty even though I still couldn't move or open my eyes.

CHAPTER 16

Fighting For Life

My love and concern turned to my children and then back to Matt. I struggled to verbalize the question "Where's . . . Paul?" Paul reminded me that our son, Paul III, was visiting overnight with a friend. He said, "I will contact him a little bit later in the day when you are feeling stronger." Paul at least was encouraged that after the long night, there had been some response and evidence of life and engagement with my surroundings.

He also assured me that he had talked with our daughter, Mary Katherine, who had graduated from the College of Charleston and was now working for the Medical University of South Carolina (MUSC). He told me she had wanted to come, but he thought it was better for her to wait. She had said, "I feel terrible I am so far away and can't help, but tell Mom I am praying for her."

Now my attention turned to Matt, for I knew this was the day of the NIH treatment. I struggled out the words, "How's Ma-a-a-at?" Every word I had to really force. It was all I could do to get the syllables out of the crooked side of my mouth. Paul went out of the room to call Matt's home number and got a recording. I then forced out, "N-I-H." He looked for an NIH number, and

107

Janet's sister answered the phone in Matt's room. Ruth said, "Matt's doing pretty well. He is getting prepared for the tough treatment today. Janet is down the hall with the doctors."

Ruth explained that Tony, Matt's dad, was experiencing some serious problems of his own. He had flown to his congressional district in Ohio and had been scheduled to fly back that evening to be at the hospital with Matt. But because of a bad snowstorm, (the same one I had been in) the plane could not land in Washington, Baltimore, or Richmond. Finally the plane landed in Newport News! Paul was absolutely amazed when Ruth reported Tony, Paul's friend from Congress, was in the Hampton Inn just minutes from where I lay in the hospital.

Paul called the Hampton Inn and rang Tony's room, but he was on the phone. It seemed busy forever and Paul finally asked the operator, "It's really important I get in touch with Congressman Hall. Could you send someone up and ask him to get off the phone and call me?" When Tony called, Paul gave him the shorthand summary of what had happened. Tony said he would come immediately to the hospital. He told Paul how upset he'd been the plane was routed to Newport News when Matt was so seriously ill at NIH in Washington.

How amazing that Tony's plane was re-routed to Newport News to bring Tony to be here with us at the hospital. When he walked into my hospital room with Paul, all of us were so encouraged, especially Paul, because he could see God involved in a miraculous way. Tears rolled down my cheeks when Tony gave me a hug. Although my eyes where still closed and dilated and I could not move anything at all, I felt an exciting reaffirmation inside that God was in charge of both Matt and me. I surrendered to God's total control of everything.

I wanted to tell Tony how I had seen our friends John and Sam. They had worked so closely with Tony praying for the inner city and the poor in D.C. and around the world. Again, I tried to force out the words that had been our vision, "A City . . . Set on the Hill for God." Tony squeezed my hand sweetly and said, "Rosemary, I know you are concerned for Matt. He's doing OK, and we all really want you to come back." Then Tony left the room as the doctors began more testing. Tony stayed with us throughout the day and was a great encouragement keeping us abreast of Matt's progress through his treatment.

Fighting For Life

We had been assigned to a room at the end of the oncology floor because the hospital was so crowded. A large waiting room was nearby where many friends gathered. Some remained through the night to pray for me. We were assigned two precious nurses, both of whom had a strong faith. They could not have been more attentive and loving in their care.

Dr. Chessen and Dr. Harris both returned in the morning, and Paul tried to give them some background on what had happened over the last week. He explained to the doctors my deep concern for Matt and the impact of the Scriptures about the bone and other images. The missing element of this whole thing was that they didn't know I had been in a car accident. Thus they were operating at a disadvantage.

Someone had called the ambulance and learned they had found me at the side of a Texaco station in the snow. Looking back on it now, they surely must have thought this whole situation was very unusual. After examining me again, Dr. Harris reviewed the CT scan of my head done at the first hospital and ordered an electroencephalogram (EEG) and an MRI. He said he would return after he got the test results.

Dr. Harris had taken care of my migraines for years and now I had a whopper from the overdose of ammonia the night before. I tried to communicate how badly my head was hurting by raising my eyebrows and using my crooked smile. I really think if I had been awake, I would have passed out because of the pain. The sweet nurse, Sandra, and friend René kept asking, "What's wrong?" It was like we were playing 21 Questions. They asked, "You need to blow your nose? You're too hot? Finally it was Sandra that asked, "Are you in pain? Do you have a headache?" I sighed with relief.

The doctor ordered a shot like I had taken in the past for my three-day migraines. I was relieved I would get some medication, but I hoped it would not knock me out. I did not want to miss anything the Lord wanted to show me. They would give me the shot just after the MRI, so I needed to hold on a little longer.

René then told me about her accident on black ice on Interstate 64 that morning on the way to the hospital. I got excited that this might be a way I could let them know about my accident. I tried to move my eyebrows again and forced out the words, "Me t-o-o! Sixty-four!" René got it. "You were in an accident too?" Everyone seemed encouraged to finally know there may have been an accident that might have been a trigger for my coma-like condition that first night.

Because of my terrible migraine, I was afraid the loud sound of the MRI machine would only make it worse—and it did. My friends from the night before came back to comfort me. Tom Skinner especially wanted to help, and he began to retell one of my favorite humorous monologues from his sermons. Then all five friends who had gone before joined hands and began to sing "Jesus Loves Me." I joined in the singing in my mind with Tom, John, Sam, Leland, and Jonathan. I felt so very blessed God had allowed them to be here to comfort me.

Dr. Harris came back late in the morning after the test results and encouraged Paul, reporting, "Although there's no absolute certainty in this business, I think the chances are very good that Rosemary is going to be just fine." He said my condition might be a dissociative reaction in response to the trauma of the accident and freezing cold. He thought I was going to come back strong but had no idea how long it would take. The fact I had begun to come out of the deeper state of the first night was a good sign, and I could strain out a few syllables. Sandra gave me the shot that I needed to ease my headache. I quieted down and slept deeply for several hours.

For me, the invisible became so much more real than the visible. It was like I was super-conscious in this other world around me. To this day, the quality of those memories are much more vivid than what happened just yesterday. There was a lifting of the veil. Yet when I try to describe it, words are inadequate to express my experience of the Divine. My heart was set free to experience whatever came in a new, fresh, and wonderful way. Jesus gave me new eyes to see; a new heart to wonder; a new mind to explore what might be in store for all who love God and seek his heart. Those few days I will treasure the rest of my life until we meet again.

Again I awoke to a raging battle in my mind. Like the night before, it was like I was experiencing a spiritual war over Matt's life. I was overwhelmed by the terror of the darkness and the sounds of the battle. Paul said later that I seemed to become agitated on the inside from what had seemed like a peaceful sleep. Tears kept falling from my eyes, making puddles on my cheeks as Paul gently wiped them off. I was intensely praying for Matt with all my heart. I believe this might have been during Matt's life-threatening treatment at NIH.

Paul went to pick up our son around 2:00 p.m. and told him about my being in the hospital. He held him close as they said a prayer together. When my son walked into my hospital room, my heart leapt for joy. I did not want him to be afraid for me. I was being held in the warmth of this beautiful light, and Joy was my constant companion. I could not speak these thoughts, but I desperately wanted to show Paul how much I adored him and reassure him that I was going to be fine.

Somehow I was able to make my first real movement since my time in the car. I moved my shoulder up a little to touch our son's hand that he held close to my cheek. Tears rolled down my face as Paul snuggled near and told me how much he loved me. I believe there were three critical steps that began my recovery from the first night's coma-like state: my husband's morning kiss; Tony's miraculously appearing in Newport News to be with me; and my son, Paul, holding me close.

Tony was about to say good-bye and leave to catch a 5:00 p.m. flight from Newport News to D.C. when he got a phone call giving him a good report from Janet at NIH. Matt had done amazingly well with the treatment. In fact he might be able to return home the following day. Janet said, "We all are hoping you will get better and open your eyes very soon."

Tony leaned over and gave me a hug. He said a prayer and thanked God for Matt, then asked God for my own quick recovery. Tony's being there in Newport News was the best comfort my husband could have had. It was the sign that gave him the encouragement that this was spiritually connected to what God was doing. We had to keep the faith. For me it was a wonderful gift of assurance of God's love.

All was quiet again and I felt no anxiety or fear. I had no concern whatsoever for the fact I still couldn't move except for my shoulder and little crooked smile or speak clearly except by forcing out a few words. God's presence was everything to me. His love enveloped me like a warm blanket while this amazing light surrounded me, calming and nurturing my soul. My eyes were shut tight as I was still in a coma-like state. However it was as if I could see in the spirit, and my hearing was multiplied tenfold.

In fact, throughout the day when people came into the room, I could sense their essence—a kind of glow when they knew Jesus. Sandra, the young nurse who had been so kind, had this glow about her. I learned later she had a strong faith and her dad was a pastor. When Carleton, my pastor, walked in my room the light around him was incredibly strong. I don't know how to explain it, but it was as if I recognized this essence. I encountered so many different people, and it was as if I was seeing them through Jesus' eyes.

On one occasion, a person walked in who said he was a chaplain. I did not know him and yet my spirit totally pulled back. He asked if I were deeply troubled or dealing with problems in my life. To the contrary, I felt totally enveloped by the Holy Spirit's love, and this was a time of extraordinary peace, not anxiety or fear. I was reminded of how Job's friends were judgmental about his sickness, and I felt compassion for this pastor.

After he left I pondered how my only moments of anxiety had been when I experienced the spiritual battle raging around Matt and when I first recognized the man who raped me. Now my attacker's image held no fear for me. This was truly one of the greatest blessings God has ever given me. I never saw him again after that night. Throughout the day, my other five friends kept returning and sharing with me. I never felt alone.

I wish that I could adequately describe the light that surrounded me at all times and that calmed and nurtured my soul. It appeared to me that people with this essence were surrounded by this diffused white light. My five friends that had visited me had this light, and I thought perhaps this could be like an armor of God that protects us. The radiance was not dazzling, but a soft, full whiteness that enveloped me with inner peace. It delighted me with a happiness and contentment that was beyond words and brought me closer to others who shared this light.

I rejoiced over the news that Matt was doing well. I thanked God and prayed he would keep Matt close and help him not be afraid. I entered into a deeper sleep and again, this intimate awareness of God's presence blessed me. I asked the Lord, "Am I to stay or go back? I am willing to stay with you if this is your will."

This is the only time I saw the image of Christ on the cross. My heart broke as I saw the blood coming from Jesus' side that had been stabbed and from his face where the crown of thorns pierced his head. Then in one transforming moment, Jesus looked directly into my eyes. Peace and love flooded my heart. That one gaze from Jesus changed my life forever. I fell deeply in love—that kind of head-over-heels love that completely overwhelms you with joy.

I felt beloved. It was as if Jesus were saying, "Be loved by me." This affirmation was a defining point in my life as I realized Jesus knew everything about me—all my joys, shame, and sorrows. He loved and accepted me just for being me—just as his child, Rosemary. I came to know that this was not my time to die. I was to return home.

Jesus then looked down at the foot of the cross where in Scripture stands Mary, his mother, and John, his devoted disciple. Jesus said to them, "Mary, behold your son, John. John, behold your mother, Mary." But to my surprise it was Matt and Janet who now stood there at the foot of the cross. Then with great compassion Jesus looked down at them and said, "Janet, behold your son, Matt. Matt, behold your mother, Janet." Christ had given them to each other in an incredible act of love. I didn't know if Matt would be healed in this world or the next. I had seen such happiness in Leland and Jonathan. There was no assurance for the future. What I did know was Matt's life was in God's hands, and I was to come home.

It was Saturday evening and I had experienced an incredible day. I still could not see or move except my shoulder, but I was finally able to speak more clearly. Paul and our son sat close beside my bed and I told them, "I want you both to go home. Get some rest. I don't know when, but I am going to be fine and I know now I am coming back. René said she would stay tonight."

I explained that before they left, I wanted to share with them the events of the first night. I did not know if I would remember any of this when I awoke. I asked Paul to please write down my story so I would have this memory forever.

I shared how I had been saturated by God's extraordinary love and shown the power of forgiveness and prayer in an amazing way. I told how I had been greeted by my five friends; Leland, Tom, John, Sam, and Jonathan who had gone before. Then I talked about seeing the man who raped me. I rejoiced that in some miraculous way, he had been forgiven and was in eternity as I had prayed for so many years.

Paul took notes and promised to write it all down when they got home. René came to be with me, and we prayed briefly together. I began to reflect on the way God had touched my life with the joy of his presence. Our time on earth is so short in the eternal sense. Whether we live to be 14, 45, or 70 years old, it is but a moment in our eternal lifetime. It came to me that our journey on this earth is like a service project to learn to love God, to love each other and learn to forgive. It is like a coat we put on and then lay down when our earthly life is finished. Death now held no fear for me.

My experience the first night in the hospital had some similarities to spiritual experiences that happen when other people have a near-death experience. This was triggered by the car accident. I don't have to fully understand why this happened. All I know is I will be eternally grateful for the blessing of this near-life experience. Because I had gotten a taste of the life hereafter, my life on earth will never be the same.

It was not as if heaven were up there. The intimacy was so very real with the friends that had gone before that it seems possible we can be one with the Divine right here. The Spirit longs to be part of our daily lives in the here and now. It seems to me that the dividing line between the visible and invisible worlds is very thin. I believe when we die, we enter into the presence of God to have fellowship with Jesus and those who have gone before.

Joe Girzone, who wrote the book *Joshua,* described at a retreat what death is like: "It's like seeing two trees in the forest. You walk gently through those trees and you're in the next life." I, too, had come to believe that heaven is not another world—God exists now and forever. The thing that concerned me the most was that I did not want to lose the intimacy I had felt of knowing Jesus in the here and now. I personally had somehow experienced that "crossing through" in a most gentle manner that seemed absolutely the natural thing to do. Time meant nothing and I was comforted that I did not have to fully comprehend what was happening, but trust God in it.

During those days, Jesus and the Spirit were such a part of me that I no longer mattered at all. The old Rosemary was gone. It was as if God had erased me like the first image of the pumpkin and the pencil. God had taken away all my fear and my need to be in control.

God's presence was all I needed, and the love of Jesus enveloped me like a soft comforter. The light surrounded me and nurtured my soul. The inner peace delighted me with a happiness and contentment that was beyond words. I had been caught up in the river of God's love, and it flowed over me in waves. How could I now keep from being caught up in the world's demands and pressures? How could I remain in this free-flowing river of God's love?

I slept very deeply until about 3:00 a.m. Then out of that place of deep intimacy, I awoke. I felt a warm mass like a ball of fire in my stomach. It shot up suddenly through my body and flew out when I opened my mouth. I was fully back. I opened my eyes for the first time in three days and I could see René sleeping beside me. I could move my arms and legs, and I realized I was really starving. My first thought in being back however was not excitement, but a sense of loss, as part of me wanted to be back there.

I felt I had left this cocoon of total love. Then I became concerned and said to myself, "Oh no, my husband and son aren't here." The very last words that Joy said so clearly to me were, "Rosemary, don't start being Rosemary so fast." How amazing that I had just had this incredible experience where I was completely free from all fear and anxiety. Then the very moment I am back, I start trying to control the situation!

I asked the Lord to forgive me, and I spent the next several hours fading in and out of the intimacy. I was praying, "How do I now live and process all I have been given? Who would understand and believe this unusual experience?" During this experience, I had lived with a fearless heart. Now I knew I needed to discover how to keep that fearless heart while living here on earth.

About 5:00 a.m., I knew it was time to awaken René. I swung my legs over the side of the bed and gently nudged her, saying, "I'm back." She shot awake, embraced me, and we rejoiced together. It was then to my amazement, I saw this light that shone clearly around René's body. There was this beautiful essence of light that just coated her about two inches thick, which I thought was a constant protective covering over those seeking God. I could only see the light for about twenty minutes, then my eyes were unable to focus on the essence that was of the Spirit.

I felt God had revealed to me that the things of the world that pull us down aren't important. What is important is that Jesus is with us. The "Christ in me, the hope of glory" is the holiness that resides in each of us and is the fullness of who we are. Jesus through this experience had truly set me free and given me a burning desire for God's love. I will not be fully satisfied until I return someday to be with Jesus.

Fear to Freedom

There was a deep sense of sadness at leaving this incredible place of eternal love and security. I wanted to gaze on Jesus and not fall back into the confusion of this world. I had experienced who I was as a spiritual being and not just a human being. How was I to bring this rich experience of the Divine into my everyday world and not completely embrace life as usual? It was a paradox of experiencing this afterglow of being with Jesus, and yet knowing how much I adored my family and friends and realizing it was not my time.

I was comforted knowing Jesus would someday come back for me, and I would return and never leave his loving arms. He is what is real in our life today. I had been liberated in a wonderful way to see life differently. I realized it was not all about me, but it is all about God. It is God's ability that mattered. I just needed to learn how to show up and be available to Jesus' guidance for the rest of my life here on earth. I asked René to help me write down some of my thoughts and feelings because I did not want to forget.

About 7:00 a.m. I called Paul and my son at our home and told them I was back and feeling just fine. I missed them both so much. I could not wait to see them and hug them. Also, I asked if Paul would get in touch with Peggy and see if she and John could come down to the hospital with all the girls. I had something of my experience I very much wanted to share with the girls before they returned to their colleges late that afternoon. I also wanted several other friends to come. I hoped he could make all this happen in a few hours.

I am sure when Paul got off the phone he wondered, "What am I to do now?" Paul and our son dressed and came quickly to the hospital. Dr. Chessen, however, arrived before them. When he heard of my desire to see all these friends, he said, "Rosemary you have had quite an experience. I do not want you seeing anyone but your immediate family for a brief time. You must rest today."

I turned straight toward him and looked Dr. Chessen in the eyes. I explained in just a few words a part of my vision from the first night that I felt these two girls who had been recently raped especially needed to hear. I asked, "Are you really not going to let me have this opportunity to share this part of the story? I believe God could use this to encourage these young women in their own personal struggles." He looked at me for a moment

116

then smiled and said, "I guess you're right. I'll let them come, but promise me then you will rest."

I reached over and thanked him. Life seemed all fresh and new. I was thrilled when my husband and son came in and ran to embrace me. We called Mary Katherine in Charleston, and I was able to reassure her I was just fine. She had been so worried and felt so far away.

Peggy, John, and the girls from the retreat came, and we had the most precious hour together. I held hands with each of these two hurting girls as I told the story of the power of forgiveness and my journey to freedom. We shed tears of joy and hugs as they left. I also had a sweet time with John and Peggy as I relayed all Leland had wanted me to personally share with them. I told them how Leland was so handsome and full of life.

I knew that day, and will always believe, that nothing will separate me from Christ's love. "Who shall separate us from the love of Christ? Shall trouble or hardship or persecution or famine or nakedness or danger or sword? . . . No, in all these things we are more than conquerors through him who loved us. For I am convinced that neither death nor life, neither angels nor demons, neither the present nor the future, nor any powers, neither height nor depth, nor anything else in all creation, will be able to separate us from the love of God that is in Christ Jesus our Lord" (Rom. 8:35–39).

CHAPTER 17

Death Is Not The Final Dance

The gift of my near-life experience taught me many things. I learned that death is not the final dance, but only the beginning of a new and full life in the presence of love. Spiritually God allowed me to move into another realm on that first incredible night, and I came to understand that we do not have to fear death.

While writing my book, I had an opportunity to meet Paul Young, the author of *The Shack*. This is a wonderful book in which Mack, the main character, spends three days with God (Papa), Jesus, and the Spirit (Sarayu) to discover healing from the devastating murder of his daughter Missy. The story wrestles with the question of where God is during times of great pain and brokenness. There is such delightful intimacy that grows between Mack and these three (the Trinity), who guide him through a powerful lesson in healing and forgiveness.[1]

I felt my three days in the hospital were also such a time of healing with these three—God; Jesus; and his Spirit, Joy—who guided me through each step. It was like God erased me physically so he could get my attention spiritually to let me know just how loved I am. I experienced the freedom of being in the presence of Divine love. God took my stolen joy and redeemed it through this taste of heaven. This gift of grace was a healing balm to my soul, and being saturated by love over three amazing days was an experience of deep holiness.

Max Lucado said, "Let me encourage you . . . God never said that the journey would be easy, but he did say that the arrival would be worthwhile."[2] We came from God and will return to God. God who gave us life awaits and at some point we return to the Father. The loss, however, is so difficult for family, friends, and loved ones left behind.

On July 12, 1996, five months after my accident, Matt Hall died. Two weeks before he went to be with God, I had another image about Jesus as the Good Shepherd that came to me during my early morning prayers. I was a little lost sheep crying out for the shepherd. He came for me and I felt him lift me up and gently place me on his shoulders where I felt safe and at peace. But as Jesus walked off, I realized it was not me, but Matt, who was on Jesus' shoulders.

I know Matt will be held throughout eternity in God's loving embrace. He will experience no more of the pain and suffering that filled his last years. "I have fought the good fight, I have finished the race, I have kept the faith. Now there is in store for me the crown of righteousness which the Lord, the righteous judge, will give me on that day" (2 Tim. 4:7, 8). Matt fought the good fight. Matt finished the race. Matt kept the faith. Matt won the race of life and crossed that finish line into peace and joy forever as God's beloved son. The glimpse I received of God's amazing love gave me a new perspective, and comforted me in the difficult time of Matt's passing.

Through my experience, I also learned new lessons about surrender, trust, reconciliation, and forgiveness. I began to understand how we grow from pain and that even the most difficult experiences can be used for good. My story became for me a pearl of great treasure. Pearls become a precious jewel through pain and suffering. I have heard the expression that we are human beings having a spiritual experience. Now I have embraced the mystery that I am a spiritual being having a human experience. Those three wonderful days brought me closer to Jesus than any time in my life as my heart was pierced with God's love and overwhelming tenderness.

I came to realize that we focus on the visible, but it is the invisible that is real. We get so caught up in this world and its distracting noises that it is hard to step back and hear the Spirit. Jesus drew me to a special dwelling place of love as an experience of oneness, acceptance and, also, Joy.

I came to believe that next to love, forgiveness is the most powerful force on earth. My healing deepened when I realized the impact of the prayer of forgiveness I had offered my attacker nineteen years before. When I forgave this man, it not only released me, but also released him to be redeemed by God. When we don't forgive, we can allow lies and bitterness to grow that will destroy us. I released my rapist from my judgment that night and put my trust in God's mercy. Somehow, some way, God's love must have burned great evil from my rapist's life and opened a way for his redemption through the power of Jesus' love.

I learned the importance of surrender and found peace like I had never known. It was time to totally let go of Rosemary. I needed only to trust wherever God desired to lead me and to understand that my job was to follow. When I first returned from my coma, this world seemed so clanging and noisy. I missed the calm that had surrounded me. During the days in the hospital, I was in constant communion with the Spirit in a relationship I can best describe in terms of friendship. I experienced this third person of the Trinity, Joy, as an intimate friend. This gave me such peace as I shared my deepest thoughts, fears, and joys. God granted this revelation of love and engraved it deeply upon my mind and heart.

I needed not be anxious about the past or the future but to live in the present. The last thing the Spirit said to me as I awoke was, "Rosemary, don't start being Rosemary so fast." My heart's desire is not to return to the old Rosemary, but truly to die to myself and live for God in the here and now. It is easy for our egos to start controlling our minds and let worry and anxiety take over. Yet, I began to see how we are capable of oneness with each other and the Divine now—today—not just in eternity, so we need not experience such unease or fear in our lives.

One of the most powerful lessons was that I learned to accept myself as I am. When the evil of my rape happened to me, it was as if this man infected me with a disease that caused fear, lack of self-worth, and shame. I had not been able to control what had been done to me, and then, it seemed I could not control life itself. I could not make it right in my mind and heart, and that was painful and frustrating. I must have asked myself a thousand times,

"What's wrong with me? Why can't I just get over this?" But I learned I do not have to have it all together—Jesus loves me in the midst of my brokenness. What a relief! It is OK to fail and have challenges. It does not mean I am bad or inadequate, but I'm just having a difficult day.

It was important that I not let pain and fear destroy me. A man who rapes you does not just want to destroy you for a night—he wants to destroy you for a lifetime. Just before he left through the window that night, he injected me with an extra dose of fear as he whispered in my ear, the gun at my temple, "I will kill you if you tell. I know where you live."

Along with rejecting this fear, I needed to reject the lies I was believing about myself. My heart breaks for the many women who are walking around with a devastating secret and saying to themselves, "I'll die if anyone knows about this—no one will ever look at me in the same way—how could someone still love me, or ever love me, if I can't even love myself?" This lie can be implanted not only through being raped, but also by other kinds of painful circumstances—circumstances that can steal your peace and destroy your self-image.

Sometimes because of a trauma in our past, we don't know what "normal" is. We get stuck in our heads instead of living out of our hearts. We may think, "If anyone really knew this about me, I couldn't live with the shame or brokenness. I am unloved, never enough, abandoned." So we bury our painful secret in our souls where it eats away at our happiness. We become one person on the inside and another on the outside. I have good news! You do not have to live with these tormenting secrets! The Spirit already knows everything about you and does not judge you, but weeps as you weep. God wants only to draw near to comfort you.

Instead of trying to mold Jesus into our culture, we can come to know Jesus as Lord of our life—decide to follow him and trust him with our pain. If you ever really know in your heart you are loved by God, everything changes.

When Jesus looked at me from his cross, I felt so loved. Here was the tenderness of a father loving his little daughter and picking her up in his strong arms and saying, "Don't worry. I am strong and wise and forgiving and all knowing. You can trust me and I will take care of you. Come into my loving arms and find rest for your soul. Receive my healing—and know my love. I know how much you've been hurt. I am the one who understands. I am the one who heals. I am the one who forgives. I am the one who is full of ultimate love. All is well, for I am who I am."

Through this experience with death, I truly came to live and I am willing to stake everything on the fact Jesus is real today and he is love. There was great freedom in turning my life over and resting in the intimacy of this loving relationship with a living God. I could be the Rosemary I am, not strive for what I am not. I realized how foolish it was to keep trying to be in control of my life, other circumstances, and certainly other people. I could stop with all the striving; to please others, to be perfect, to handle everything that life brought my way. I could let go of a life of performance and the obsession of wanting to fix others and myself. Now when the going gets tough, I whisper, "Come, Joy, I need you."

Neither do I have to be perfect to please God, but rest in his love. In *The Shack*, Sarayu, who represents the Spirit, encourages Mack, "Trust is the fruit of a relationship in which you know you are loved. For now I just want you to be with me and discover our relationship is not about performance or your having to please me. I am good and I desire only what is best for you. You cannot find that through guilt or condemnation or coercion, only through a relationship of love. And I do love you."[3]

This is the kind of freedom and hope that God promises through his Son. "He has sent me to bind up the brokenhearted . . . to comfort all who mourn . . . To bestow on them a crown of beauty instead of ashes, the oil of gladness instead of mourning, and a garment of praise instead of a spirit of despair (Isa. 61:1-3)."

In the movie *The Bucket List*, Carter asks his friend, Edward, two questions: whether he has found joy in his life and whether his life has brought joy to someone else. Far too many people have had joy stolen by circumstances and therefore have none to give to others in need. Caught in a cycle of fear, they are left living with "ashes of yesterday." I have learned our ashes of yesterday do not have to define us today.

My question for you is, "What or who has stolen your joy?" Maybe it is something from your past you have hidden. Maybe it is a present circumstance or person you are struggling with. Maybe it is a situation that needs

Fear to Freedom

forgiveness or someone you may feel you want to forgive. You can find joy. You can take back power. You can trust again. You can exchange:

Beauty for ashes
Gladness for mourning
Praise for despair!

Jesus wants to remove our ashes of yesterday, but we need to give them to him and not hold back. We can hide our challenges from others, but we cannot hide them from God. Somehow even our ashes can become precious to us. They become our identity: "This is my pain, my cross to bear. Who would I be without my pain?" God cannot give the freedom we will not take.

Sometimes there is not a way out of suffering, but God provides a way through it. It is when we are most fractured and overwhelmed that we hear the Master gently calling. We are reassured that there is nothing we can do to make God love us any more and nothing we can do to make God love us any less. In the middle of fear, in the midst of painful circumstances, in the moments when you want to give up, remember you are loved and you can begin to love yourself. I came to believe:

When I was raped this love wept with me.
When I was afraid this love never left me alone.
When I was overwhelmed with fear, this love was holding my heart.
When I wanted to give up, this love lifted my spirits.
When I thought I would never dance again,
this love embraced me as his beloved.

Like the rainbow after the rain, God can make something beautiful follow the raging storms in our life. Pain can destroy us or make us stronger, wiser, and more compassionate toward others. You can let circumstances devastate your future or be willing to become healthier and freer than ever before. As I surrendered the ashes of my pain, God called me to a closer walk in his presence, and gave me a new passion for living as a reconciler with a purpose to help others who were wounded. I wanted to learn how to make this kind of radical love, forgiveness, and reconciliation an important part of my life.

Death Is Not the Final Dance

Over these last fourteen years, there has been a newness to life—a fresh sense of joy as I walk through each day more alive than ever before. God has been drawing me close to his presence, igniting my passions and helping to define my purpose:

To live in God's presence.

To love and forgive everyone.

To inspire and empower others to live free from fear!

These themes found throughout this book have directed my life, and I hope they will encourage you to walk closely with God, do what's right, and delight in God's purpose .

Be comforted! God is near and you are his beloved.

Be encouraged! The cycle of fear can be broken.

Be strengthened! God wants to use your passion for his purposes.

Be joyful! God's power will release you to live in freedom.

CHAPTER 18

Abiding In God's Presence

"Y ou will seek me and find me when you seek me with all your heart" (Jer. 29:13). These words invited me to draw near to God in my everyday life. I had felt such an incredible closeness to the Lord during my near-life experience and now my passion for living in God's presence is greater than ever.

Jesus certainly knew the importance of dwelling in God's presence. For him, prayer was a priority. Jesus taught, healed, preached, and then went away to spend time with his Father. Here he received the guidance, strength, and comfort he needed for each day. Likewise prayer strengthens our faith, helps us appreciate the joys of life, and brings us into the delightful presence of God.

St. Augustine said, "For you have made us for yourself, and our heart is restless until it rests in you."[1] What a difference prayer can make in our lives! Only here can our hearts find the true rest we long for.

I want to know God's purpose for me and my family. To do this, I need to spend time with Jesus in the Word and in prayer. After all, the most strategic person I need to reach with the love of God is me. I have called my time of prayer an Appointment with the King since I heard Becky Tiarabassi use that expression at a woman's retreat years ago. The pace of life today is full speed ahead, and the noise of life is so loud it can distract us from God, who is wooing us—inviting us to slow down, to sit and be still. What if we made an Appointment with the King for twenty minutes each day? We would still have twenty-three hours and forty minutes of our day left! We are so busy running and doing that we have lost what it means to just be still—to know that God is holy, faithful, and unfailing.

Elijah on the mountaintop did not find God in the storm or the wind or the fire but in a small whisper. God often whispers his love to us: "Come to me. Enter into my presence, and find rest for your soul. Come with no agenda but to be with me for you are my heart's delight."

I have come to believe that Jesus plus nothing equals everything. God is not concerned about our past except for the grace he gives to cover it. Today we can have a relationship through his son, Jesus, and the Holy Spirit. Jesus said, "I *am* the bread of life. I *am* the way, the truth and the life, I *am* the good shepherd." This is true for us today, not in the past tense. I want to know Jesus now—I want to learn to walk like him, and forgive like him, and love like him.

Jesus is alive today. He is healing, forgiving, restoring, and loving today. I believe he wants us to be part of his transforming work, but this flows out of our time with him. Instead of being with Jesus to develop this intimacy, and seek his vision, we seem often to focus on the *doing* instead of *being*. If what we do is who we are, then who are we when we stop doing it?

I am comforted that Jesus did not run through Jerusalem! If we are always running throughout every day, checking off our to-do lists and responding to our e-mail and text messages, we become exhausted. We must find balance by spending time alone with the Lord. On my calendar there are many entries for every day, but my prayer time, my Appointment with the King, is my highest priority.

Find a time of prayer that works for you. After I went back to work, it was difficult to continue my regular morning time of prayer. God let me know, "That's no problem. We'll just meet in the middle of the night when we can be quiet together." For the past eight years I am awakened sometime between three and four o'clock and have found this time to be the most precious part of the day. I enter into God's presence when my mind is not already focusing on the days' activities. If your heart's desire is to be with God, you can find a time that is best for you.

Abiding In God's Presence

A revelation from my near-life experience is the importance of living in his presence now. Jesus' Spirit lives in us and therefore we are never alone. Moment by moment, step by step, day by day, we can be one in Jesus as we open our lives to this transforming relationship. We are the ones who must open our hearts to the fullness of this love.

Billy Graham once said, "Heaven is full of answers to prayers for which no one ever bothered to ask."[2] Sometimes we do not know how to ask, what to seek, and how to begin to knock. "Ask and it will be given to you; seek and you will find; knock and the door will be open to you. For everyone who asks receives; he who seeks finds; and to him who knocks, the door will be opened" (Matt. 7:7–8). So keep knocking!

MOMENTS WITH MOTHER TERESA

Mother Teresa is a great example of this kind of radical devotion to love and prayer. Her life epitomized love, for she reached out to everyone who crossed her path—the rich and the poor, the powerful and those who were dying in poverty and filth. When people asked her how they could make a difference, she would often suggest to them, "Simply respond to what is right before you—love the person in front of you. You are called not to be successful but to be faithful."

I first had an opportunity to meet Mother Teresa in February of 1994 when she was the speaker at the National Prayer Breakfast. Because I was helping with logistics that year, I visited with Susan Mendies, who traveled with Mother Teresa and helped make her arrangements. She indicated Mother Teresa would rather not sit at the head table, but have a simple chair placed for her behind the dignitaries.

While others were eating their breakfast, President Bill Clinton, First Lady Hillary Clinton, Vice President Al Gore, and his wife, Tipper, came behind the curtain to spend time with Mother Teresa. I watched from the wings of the stage as Mother Teresa reached her arms around these two couples while she prayed for them. The program was about to begin, but the most important event seemed to be the scene I was witnessing. Five people sitting in folding chairs as this humble woman prayed for them—the leaders of our nation and the world.

Fear to Freedom

Mother Teresa was so small that we placed a box behind the podium so she could be seen when it was time for her keynote address. When she spoke, however, the authority of God seemed to come through her, and you could hear a pin drop in this crowd of five thousand who listened intently. She challenged the audience that represented some 146 nations to "Love until it hurts." She said:

> And so it is very important for us to realize that love, to be true, has to hurt. I must be willing to give whatever it takes not to harm other people and, in fact, to do good to them. This requires that I be willing to give until it hurts. Otherwise, there is no true love in me and I bring injustice, not peace, to those around me.
>
> You too must bring that presence of God into your family, for the family that prays together, stays together. There is so much hatred, so much misery, and we with our prayer, with our sacrifice, are beginning at home. Love begins at home, and it is not how much we do, but how much love we put into what we do.
>
> We can keep the joy of loving Jesus in our hearts, and share that joy with all we come in contact with. If we remember that God loves us, and that we can love others as He loves us, then America can become a sign of peace for the world.
>
> If you become a burning light of justice and peace in the world, then really you will be true to what the founders of this country stood for. God bless you![3]

I had another wonderful opportunity to be with Mother Teresa in the spring before her death September 5, 1997, when I traveled to Calcutta to work in the House of the Dying and the Orphanage of the Missionaries of Charity along with Susan Mendies. There I experienced Jesus as never before among the poorest of the poor.

Morning worship was in the Mother House at 6:00 a.m. Mother Teresa was in her wheelchair, and beside her was Sister Agnes in her wheelchair in the back of the crowded room. Sister Agnes was the first nun to join Mother

Abiding In God's Presence

Teresa in Calcutta. She was the contemplative nun who prayed while Mother Teresa was out serving. They were devoted friends who were paired in their lives in Christ. As Mother Teresa worked in the streets, her friend for forty-two years, Sister Agnes, kept a prayer vigil. Every morning the sisters repeated this prayer called "Radiating Jesus":

Dear Jesus, help us to spread
Your fragrance everywhere we go.
Flood our souls with your spirit and life.
Penetrate and possess our whole being, so utterly,
That our lives may only be a radiance of Yours.
Shine through us, and be so in us,
That every soul we come in contact with
May feel Your presence in our soul. . . .[4]

After morning prayer, I knelt by Mother Teresa's wheelchair and felt I was beholding Jesus face-to-face. Her dancing eyes twinkled with joy as her warm wrinkled hands, leathered from years of serving and loving, held mine. It was if I were looking into the eyes of unconditional love. Her challenge has stayed with me ever since: "Rosemary, be a woman of prayer."

I love what she said about prayer: "Perfect prayer does not consist in many words, but the fervor of the desire which raises the heart to Jesus. Love to pray. Feel the need to pray often during the day. Prayer enlarges the heart until it is capable of containing God's gift of Himself. Ask and seek and your heart will grow big enough to receive Him and keep Him as your own." Another of her favorite sayings I have engraved on a rock by my bed: "Do no great things, only small things with great love."[5]

I thought often of Mother Teresa's words as I worked in the House of the Dying. I saw all around me great love and felt blessed, in a small way, to care for those on the threshold of death. The hurt and pain was evident, but God's peace and love was even more present.

On this weekend nuns from across the world had gathered to determine who would follow Mother Teresa as head of the Missionaries of Charity. To help with the daily jobs, teenage novices had come from another province to work that weekend. That made me the oldest person serving in the House of the Dying. The doctor asked if I would give out the medications to each woman. He paired me with one of the novices, who checked the name on the individual cups of pills and bottles of liquid to determine the medicine was going to the right woman.

My mother had recently died, so my heart was particularly tender when I was with these women in their last days. I held each woman in my arms and spoke softly about my own mother's dying and how she had said, "Jesus is coming. He is coming for me." I will never know if any of these dying women could understand what I was saying, but I felt a deep peace in the midst of the dying. As I told them about my own experience in the vision of heaven, I looked into their eyes and felt somehow they at least knew they were loved and cared for.

I asked one of the nuns later, "How is this unusual peace possible?" She replied, "The peace comes from love. These women, many who have been picked up out of the gutters, now know they are loved. God loves them. They have been forgiven and may soon be free from their pain. She told me how one person had said, "I lived my life in filth, but I will die as an angel."

The next day I was not expecting to see Mother Teresa. Then I heard tiny footsteps coming from behind me and there she was. Her eyes sparkled as she asked, "Do you have one of my business cards?" "No, I'd love to have one!" I replied in total surprise. I told her about my time at the House of the Dying and how the next day I was going to spend time in the orphanage. She asked, "Do you love children?" I replied, "Oh yes, I have two children who I adore." "I'll give you one!" Mother Teresa exclaimed!

My jaw must have dropped open. But before I could speak, the nuns had come for Mother Teresa and whisked her away. Her business card read:

The fruit of Silence is prayer.
The fruit of Prayer is faith,
The fruit of Faith is love,
The fruit of Love is service,
And the fruit of Service is peace.

Mother Teresa changed the world through her life of loving everyone. Whether a leper everyone despised, an abandoned baby, the pope, or the president, each person was special to her and to God. She is buried, as was her request, in a simple pine box. This tireless and compassionate woman was loved by the poor and powerful alike. She lies in the Mother House where her last simple message reads, "From Mother—Love one another as I have loved you."

MY HEART OPENS TO CONTEMPLATIVE PRAYER

Mother Teresa's challenge to me ignited a deep longing to be a woman of prayer. Also the time I spent with Sister Agnes, hearing about her life of contemplative prayer (which she called "the Prayer of the Heart"), started my journey to learn how to come into God's presence in prayer. This led me thirteen years ago to begin monthly sessions with my pastor and spiritual director, Carleton Bakkum. We focused on the tradition and practice of contemplative prayer, and then we simply spent time praying. I love people. Yet everyday I am drawn more and more to abiding with God in silence. Silence blossoms inside you like a flower opening its petals to receive the sun. So too we can open our hearts to receive the Son.

Over the last ten years I have set aside times to retreat at Mepkin Abbey near Charleston, South Carolina, or the Monastery of the Holy Spirit in Conyers, Georgia, outside Atlanta. In one of my visits to Georgia, I developed a wonderful friendship with a monk, Father Thomas Francis, who has been a true blessing to my life as a spiritual director and mentor, and Brother Ed at Mepkin has been an encourager to me in writing this book. I have come to know and love the spiritual experience of spending time in a monastery.

I also completed a two-year program offered by the Shalem Institute for Spiritual Direction (www.shalem.org), which for thirty years has provided teachings on living a more contemplative life and being present with God in each moment. What I have been discovering is a rich Christian tradition of prayer and closeness to God that is often either unknown or unexplored in our modern world. Prayer practices such as praise, intercession, confession, or thanksgiving are well known. Praying the Scriptures (sometimes called *lectio divina*), drawing near to God through the beauty of icons and contemplative prayer are often less familiar.

Contemplative prayer has deep roots in Christian tradition. Through time, this way of praying has been called by different names, but in our day it is often called centering prayer or abiding prayer. This has been a way of being with God since the beginning of Christianity that came out of the prayer practice of the desert fathers and mothers.

Fear to Freedom

In Jesus' final teaching to his disciples at the Last Supper, he used the image of himself as the vine with his followers as the branches. It is a remarkable picture Jesus paints for us that our work is to *abide*. It is doubtful that in his all-night-long prayers that Jesus was preparing sermons or endlessly interceding for others. Many believe that these were times for abiding in wordless intimacy with his Father. "Silence is God's first language," said the sixteenth-century mystic, St. John of the Cross.[6] Should we not then explore the closeness of such drawing near?

Of course words are powerful tools to cultivate our relationships, but can we dare to be silent and just be? Surely, you've been with someone you love, sitting together in a special moment where if either of you spoke, it would only spoil the moment. How many times have we come to prayer with our list of needs and our suggestions as to how God might get busy providing for them? Can we dare to simply love God and let God love us?

I've been influenced by Teresa of Avila, a sixteenth-century Spanish mystic who was consumed by her love of God. In the book *Interior Castle* she describes a series of "rooms"—each representing a special level of closeness with God. She writes, "This Lord of ours is so anxious that we should desire Him and strive after His companionship that He calls us ceaselessly, time after time, to approach Him."[7] It was not mystical experiences she sought but deep intimacy with God. In other words, God wants to be with us—just to be with us!

Teresa combined times in prayer with action in the world. She was a great organizer, builder, and reformer. She provided leadership in her spiritual community and impacted her country and its leaders. The contemplative experience doesn't mean we should remain in solitude. Instead it cultivates a love for God that flows out into love for others. As Mother Teresa's prayer suggests, deep contemplation bears fruit in service and action. As we fall more passionately in love with Jesus, he flows his love through us to become his love to others.

Cynthia Bourgeault, in her book *Centering Prayer and Inner Awakening*, says of intentional silence, "The first step is simply to pull the plug on that constant self-reflective mind. . . . It's like putting a stick in the spoke of thinking. . . .so the more subtle awareness at the depths of your being can begin to make its presence known."[8] At one of her retreats, Cynthia described it this way: "Inside there is a flute playing but the boom box on the outside drowns out the sound of the flute. Centering Prayer helps pull the plug on our interior chatter to rest our monkey mind that jumps from one thought to another."

Cynthia led us into prayer by beginning with the phrase, "Be still, and know that I am God . . ." (Ps. 46:10). We repeated this Scripture and each time, dropped a word. "Be still and know that I am. Be still and know. Be still. Be." Repeating this process twice helps us center, letting go of scattered thoughts to begin Centering Prayer.

Some people get anxious just thinking about silence. Even when there is a pause in conversation, we feel we need to fill the moment with words. I have found it is wonderful to think about prayer as a loving relationship and contemplative prayer as simply being together with God. This is a place to encounter the Divine and be in communion—to bask in God's presence and rest in his promises.

Contemplative Outreach, cofounded by Father Thomas Keating, introduces lay people to Christian Contemplative practices. This organization provides Centering Prayer guidelines that are helpful, and it is a good resource for information on lectures and retreats (www.comtemplativeoutreach.com).

For me, Centering Prayer opens my heart to be still and listen. Like when we plug into an electrical socket to receive power, when we plug into the Spirit, we can access more peace and a sense of well-being. As we regularly stay connected to the Divine we can experience the ongoing joy such intimacy can bring. Many people have been encouraged in their faith by Rick Warren's book, *The Purpose Driven Life*. Mine might be called "The Joy Driven Life." As I spend intimate time in the Spirit, I feel Joy directing and guiding my life, and sharing moments of both challenge and happiness.

I have developed my own expression of these guidelines for Centering Prayer as a time when I **seek**, **surrender**, and **soak**. (An outline is found in the Devotional Guide.)

First **seek**. Set aside time to be with God in prayer and seek his presence. Choose a simple word that has meaning for you. It might be *Jesus*, *peace*, *love*, *Abba*, or *beloved*. My word is *Joy*. Before beginning, repeat a short phrase or portion of Scripture such as "Be still and know that I am

God." I use the ancient "Jesus Prayer," breathing in, "Lord Jesus Christ" and breathing out, "Have mercy on me." Repeating this several times settles my mind like a puppy turning around in circles before snuggling down to rest.

Next **surrender** thoughts. The purpose is not to sit in silence with no thoughts, but to practice gently surrendering thoughts that come up and releasing them. Cynthia calls it "the aerobics of letting go." Our minds jump from one thought to another, especially when we try to be still. When a thought comes, gently whisper your word in your mind a few times. The word is just a reminder, like a red string on your finger, to let the thought go and be with the silence.

Keating has used the metaphor of boats on a river to describe our running stream of conscious thoughts. Imagine yourself as a scuba diver who looks up from his peaceful water world to see the boats going by. "The temptation is to get interested in a particular boat, swim up to the surface of the river and climb on board. In other words, get caught up in a particular thought. Conscious thoughts and feelings may occur over and over again, but when we notice them, we say our word silently a few times and let them go."[9] Eventually our mind, body, and spirit come to desire this natural state of open awareness and peacefulness.

Then **soak**. Simply dwell in God's presence. Some call this a dwelling place, abiding place, interior garden, or hiding place. It is here that we can be restored by God's healing touch, transforming love, and holy rest. This is a time to know and be known by God. End by saying the Lord's Prayer and open your eyes when ready.

Words, cell phones, television, and noise fill our lives. The world says, "Do it fast, make your lists, always be busy." Try centering prayer for five minutes a day and see the peace that comes. Later you may want to increase your time. For me, and for those that teach Contemplative Prayer, twenty minutes truly refreshes the spirit. Prayer is about a relationship with God through spending time together. There is no "right way." Just trust your heart and be open as the Spirit leads you.

THE HEALING WELCOMING PRAYER

Another special prayer practice called the Welcoming Prayer has been especially helpful to me dealing with difficult emotions and facing my fear.

Abiding In God's Presence

Cynthia Bourgeault has a wonderful teaching on this kind of prayer. Instead of reacting immediately with full-blown emotions to a situation, turn toward the pain or fear and identify how you are reacting. What physical response are you experiencing, such as knots in your stomach or difficulty sleeping? "Don't try to change anything, just stay present," Cynthia explains. Gently welcome the emotion you are feeling "Welcome fear, welcome frustration." Next, surrender: "I give my anger, fear, pain or grief to you, God." The three-step process is as follows: 1. Focus and sink in; 2. Welcome; 3. Let go.

Cynthia shared with us at a Centering Prayer retreat about a friend who had recently lost her husband. In her grief she determined never to be home at five o'clock as this was her special time with her husband. They enjoyed a glass of wine and focused on their day and their love for one another. She set a schedule to play racquetball, go shopping, visit a friend, anything but be home at that time when her grief seemed to overwhelm her. I recall as she told the story:

> One day a storm canceled the racquetball, and she found herself at home at the dreaded hour of five o'clock. Having learned about the Welcoming Prayer, Mary decided to pour two glasses of wine, sit in their favorite place, and try this prayer practice of surrendering her emotions of loss. She fully experienced the sadness and loneliness, welcomed them, and let the grief go. She said, "It was like day and night. One moment I couldn't stand it anymore; the next moment I could."
>
> Sinking down into her grief, welcoming it, and then letting it go, she surrendered her deep emotions of loss and sadness to God. A wonderful peace came over her. From then on her favorite time of day was at five o'clock as she felt her husband's presence near to her as well as the presence of God. Cynthia explains, "Embracing the emotion takes away its power over you to rule your life."[10]

I have found this *Welcoming Prayer* to be a useful practice that can begin to release our dependence on our emotions that often trigger our reactions. We can begin to let go and let God enter into our daily lives and reduce the anxiety, pressure, and fear that powerful emotions can bring.

Fear to Freedom

How then, can I become more like Mary in this world that often calls me to become more like Martha? When Martha complained that Mary wasn't helping her, the Lord answered, "Martha, Martha you are worried and upset about many things, but only one thing is needed. Mary has chosen what is better, and it will not be taken away from her" (Luke 10:41–42).

The better part is being present to the greatest leader that ever lived. The better part is sitting at the feet of Jesus, the greatest lover of all times. I was inspired by the prayer life and love of Mother Teresa, Sister Agnes, Teresa of Avila, and Cynthia to lead a deeper life in prayer, so that I might hear the voice of love calling.

Desire

Desire, desire, desire
My heart cries out
For foolish desires,
For comfort and success,
Weak and worldly.

But you, Oh God
Fill my existence with a desire
For your arms to hold me
Your kiss to touch me
Your love to embrace me.

I long to dance in
The fire of your desire
To surrender my tiny heart
To be consumed by the
Heart of all hearts,

The heart of love.

CHAPTER 19

Forgiveness Sets Us Free

M y friend René's license plate reads 4GivEvr1. But, what if they don't deserve it? What if I don't feel like forgiving? What if they were to blame and it was their fault? Forgive anyway. Why? Because forgiveness sets us free. There have been times when I have asked for forgiveness in my life, and experienced the fresh balm of healing in receiving this gift. Also, when I offered forgiveness to the man that raped me, I felt new freedom in my life. I learned the power of forgiveness to change others. Forgiveness heals the heart.

I believe alienation is the biggest problem in our world. God's answer to alienation is reconciliation. When there is brokenness, there is a need for healing. If I had to describe Jesus' purpose in two words, it might be *reconciling humanity.* Jesus' call is to love one another as he loved us. And he loved and forgave some very diverse and difficult people—even his enemies.

I see reconciliation and forgiveness as two sides of the same coin. On the cross Jesus said, "Father, forgive them, for they do not know what they are doing" (Luke 23:24). To forgive, according to Webster's New Collegiate Dictionary, means, "To cease to feel resentment against an offender: pardon one's enemies; to give up resentment of or claim to requital for an insult; to grant release from payment for a debt."[1]

Corrie ten Boom, whose sister died in the Ravensbruck concentration camp, dedicated her life to talking about forgiveness. Years later after one of Corrie's speaking engagements, she came face-to-face with the power of forgiveness. She shared in her book *The Hiding Place* how she was shocked to be greeted by one of the SS guards she remembered from the shower at the processing center at Ravensbruck. He had been responsible for the death of her sister, Betsie.

"How grateful I am for your message, Fraulein," he said, "To think that, as you say, He has washed away my sins!" And suddenly, it was all there—the roomful of mocking men, the heaps of clothing, Betsie's pain-blanched face. His hand was thrust out to shake my hand. And I, who had preached so often the need to forgive, kept my hand at my side.

Even as the angry vengeful thoughts boiled through me, I saw the sin of them. Jesus Christ had died for this man; was I going to ask for more? Lord Jesus, I prayed, forgive me and help me to forgive him.

I tried to smile. I struggled to raise my hand. I could not. I felt nothing, not the slightest spark of warmth or charity. And so again I breathed a silent prayer. Jesus I cannot forgive him. Give me your forgiveness.

As I took his hand, a most incredible thing happened. From my shoulder, along my arm and through my hand a current seemed to pass from me to him, while into my heart sprang a love for this stranger that almost overwhelmed me.

And so, I discovered that it is not on our forgiveness any more than on our goodness that the world's healing hinges, but on His. When He tells us to love our enemies, He gives, along with the command, the love itself. [2]

It is not through our own strength that the power of forgiveness transforms relationships, but through the power of Jesus. God's purposes are accomplished by each act of forgiveness we give to another, and neither person

Forgiveness Sets Us Free

is the same. "Judge not, and you shall not be judged. Condemn not, and you shall not be condemned. Forgive and you will be forgiven" (Luke 6:37).

In 1955 Martin Luther King told his congregation in Montgomery that peace and forgiveness rested in their hands. In the book *Strength to Love* King wrote:

> Let us be practical and ask the question, "How do we love our enemies?" First, we must develop and maintain the capacity to forgive . . . He who is devoid of the power to forgive is devoid of the power of love. . . . Forgiveness is a catalyst creating the atmosphere necessary for a fresh start and a new beginning.[3]

Martin Luther King's example of forgiveness was Jesus on the cross. His family carried on this example by holding a service of forgiveness for James Earl Ray, who killed Rev. King.

Why not just cut the people out of our lives who have hurt us? Jesus has pointed us to a better way—a way that releases guilt and gives mercy. Mahatma Gandi, who was one of Rev. King's inspirations, said, "The weak can never forgive. Forgiveness is the attribute of the strong."[4] Could it be that we never really get over devastating wounds until we forgive?

Forgiveness is a journey that does not happen overnight. Someone who is deeply hurt cannot immediately forgive, nor would it be honest to do so. The sooner we can move toward forgiveness, the sooner our burden of pain will begin to lift. In his book *Forgive For Good* Fred Luskin describes three reasons our grievances become so intractable. 1. We tend to take things too personally, making them all about *us*. 2. We find someone to blame to off load our bad feelings. 3. We formulate a "grievance story" that can become our identity.[5]

Let's consider possible steps toward forgiveness. Make a short list of those who have harmed you. Then chose one circumstance where you would genuinely like to offer forgiveness.

- First, *acknowledge the pain*. You have been wounded. Take seriously the depth of your hurt. Write down a description of your thoughts and feelings, and verbalize them to someone. Rarely does forgiveness come if you skip this step.

- Second, *pray*. Ask for God's help in turning your heart toward forgiveness. To forgive is a choice that offers the wonderful gift of grace. You will be showing a deep love that keeps no record of wrongs. It is hard to hate someone when you pray for that person.
- Third, *determine a statement of forgiveness* that is appropriate for your situation. You may never have the opportunity to speak to the person who offended you, like in my case with my rapist. But I acknowledged my desire to forgive him before God. Forgiveness is not a feeling, but a choice. We may not *feel* like forgiving. We forgive because we have been forgiven and the slate washed clean forever.
- Fourth, *decide if there is any action you might want to take*—such as making a phone call or planning to see the person who has offended you—when you are ready.
- Fifth, *accept that forgiveness can't be "conditional"* on other people's responses. The other person may not respond positively, and you may never hear, "I'm sorry I hurt you." They may not be available or they may not even be alive. Forgiveness does not justify what others may have done to us. It does not condone it or mean we permit them to do it again. Nor does it always lead to a reconciliation that renews the relationship. It is not up to you to change them. The only person we can change is ourselves.
- Finally, *trust* that you have done your part and believe that God has already received your honest, good faith act of forgiveness. Remember you are covered by Jesus' act of forgiveness long, long ago.

It is easy to let go of the "little stuff," but some wounds or offenses are so deep that you may need to work through this process over a longer period of time. I said my prayer of forgiveness for some time, then one day, I realized the bitterness was gone and deep healing had taken place.

A real miracle occurs when hearts change through forgiveness. Ezekiel describes it this way: "I will give you a new heart and put a new spirit in you. I will remove from you your heart of stone and give you a heart of flesh" (Ezek. 36:26). We do what we can do, but ultimately it is not by our power alone, but through God's Spirit that the broken places in our lives can receive healing and wholeness through forgiveness.

Forgiveness Sets Us Free

Gracious God, with your help I can:
forgive my neighbor's rudeness
forgive my spouse's infidelity
forgive my parent's mistakes
forgive my children's ingratitude
forgive the abuse I've endured
forgive unfairness where I work
forgive a friend's betrayal
forgive people who judge me falsely
forgive a nation's injustice to the poor
forgive a church's indifference to the needy
forgive our blindness to children who are starving
forgive the blindness to prejudice and hatred today
forgive myself for my own failures and inadequacies
forgive God for things I can not understand
forgive, and accept God's amazing grace.

(Anonymous)

The power of forgiveness told in the story of the prodigal son took on deep meaning in my life. The father who gave his younger son his inheritance must have watched every day in hopes that the lost son would return to him. When the father saw his son from afar, he ran to throw his arms around him and kiss him, a sign of his enduring love. Before the son could explain how he had wasted his life, the father called for a robe to dress his son, a sign of honor. A ring was placed on his finger, a sign of redemption (from Luke 15:31–32).

It is hard for me to truly comprehend what God, the Father, did for me as he answered my prayer to offer forgiveness, after my meeting Pat Patterson (described in Chapter 9). Although Pat had spent time in prison for whatever horrific thing he had done, I did not have to fear him. His transformation led him to become a new creature. This realization propelled me to leave the dinner, fall on my knees in that bathroom, and surrender my pain. I prayed that night, "I forgive the man who raped me and I will pray every day that someone will talk to him about Jesus so that I will spend eternity with him." I forgave this man, like the father forgave his prodigal son. This act of forgiveness was what set me free from great pain and brought new healing.

Twenty-one years after I was raped, I was lying in the hospital unable to speak, move, or respond. It is hard for me to fully put into words my experience, but that night as I experienced a touch of heaven, I saw the man who raped me as a transformed person. I will never forget the look of remorse on his face for hurting me, and the tone of his voice as he said, "I am the man that raped you, and I would not be here except you prayed for me and forgave me."

How he turned to Jesus I will not know this side of eternity. All I know is that our Lord is willing to go to the ends of the earth to forgive everyone— even those who have committed hideous crimes. What I believe is that God the Father must have opened his arms and embraced this prodigal son for the sake of his own Son, Jesus. God's desire is that none shall perish and that all shall find their hope in Jesus. I believe that when we forgive others, it enables God to work good in our lives.

We may forgive, but we often find it hard to forget. When we experience another hurt, the old wound is often opened up again. It is like a fire that has embers still burning and the ashes are left. Just as a little wind can kick the embers into a blazing flame once again, a hurtful word from someone who has hurt us can flame the pain in our hearts once again.

I illustrate this at retreats with "flash paper" that vanishes into thin air when touched by a match. It demonstrates how quickly and thoroughly God releases us from pain that may have kept us captive for years. I offer all present an opportunity to write on their own piece of flash paper the name of a person they would like to forgive. They then place the paper in a bowl and with the strike of a match, in an instant, there is not a trace left. I recall one woman who just burst into tears when she saw her paper disappear. Then she began to laugh out loud as if the bitterness she had held was finally over. She exclaimed, "It's gone, it's gone. I'm free from this at last!"

When God forgives, he forgets and our sins are removed: "As far as the east is from the west, so far has he removed our transgressions from us" (Ps. 103:12). Often we find it is hardest to forgive ourselves. Jesus wants to take upon himself any guilt and shame that we carry. Forgiveness is the transforming gesture that brings us back and removes the barriers between us and the presence of the Divine.

We can look to the cross for healing and live in expectant hope that we are forgiven. Through prayer we can take our problems and suffering to the cross. The cross is a place of great sadness, but also great joy. Here Jesus bought new freedom for our lives by giving his life in total forgiveness for our sins.

JESUS' LAVISH LOVE BRINGS HOPE AND PEACE

"Surely, He took up our infirmities and carried our sorrows. He was wounded for our transgressions. He was bruised for our iniquities. The chastisement for our peace was upon him . . . By his wounds we *are* healed" (Isa. 53:5). The first part of the Scripture is in past tense but this healing by Jesus' wounds is in the present tense and is meant for us now—today! It is amazing to think these words were written eight hundred years before Jesus read them on the scroll in the temple of his hometown, and was almost stoned for saying, "Today this Scripture is fulfilled in your hearing" (Luke 4:21). The Bible from Genesis to Revelation is the story of Jesus, and each of us has our own story.

I attended a three-day intensive healing prayer retreat with my friend Trip Sizemore, who described the power of the cross. He explained in a way I had never considered before that "The cross is so huge that it stretches up to the throne of God and across from the beginning of time to all eternity. It is not like the little cross we wear around our necks. What Jesus did on that cross has the power to heal and transform lives today."

This became a reality in my life when I had my near-life experience. As I saw Jesus dying on that cross, I saw the horror of his death and yet the amazing love in his eyes as he looked down on me. This changed my life forever. In that moment the burden of guilt, shame, and fear that had dominated my rape experience melted in the light of this unconditional acceptance and adoring love. It was as if God was saying, "Look what is possible when you respond with love, forgiveness, and surrender."

Bountiful love poured out of Jesus and burned into my soul. I felt the magnitude of his love in the midst of unbelievable suffering and realized this was available to me and to everyone. In that moment on the cross, Jesus was both victim and victor. Through his death, I too can move from victim to victory in Christ. I give him my burdens, shame, and pain and in a *great exchange*, he gives me new peace, hope, and happiness. Jesus' love permeates the whole universe, both now and forever. To grasp this allowed me to release my own pain and suffering and find new freedom.

Jesus' death sets us completely free from the pain of our past, our need for forgiveness, and our anxiety for the future. His death has cosmic significance. The work of the cross works today! Paul said, "For I determine not to know anything but Jesus Christ and him crucified" (1 Cor. 2:2). He talks about the riches of the glories of this mystery, "Christ in you, the hope of glory" (Col. 1: 27).

There is a present reality of the cross. Its healing power is alive today for women that are bruised, for children that are fearful, for families that are broken. We cannot get around the cross. As we fix our eyes on Jesus and not ourselves, we can access the power of his suffering and abundance of his grace.

God might say to each of us, "Did you not think I would take care of you, embrace you in your pain, forgive your sins, and restore your joy?" When we experience deep suffering in our lives, we feel that there is no way we can ever find true peace, love, and trust again. But if this love is actually available to us at all times, in every moment, we need not be so lost. We can access this presence of love through forgiveness and unconditional love.

SUE'S STORY—THE POWER OF FORGIVENESS

At a Virginia Student Leadership Forum on Faith and Values, I took forty college women to visit the Woman's Correctional Facility in Goochland, Virginia, for their community service project. I had spoken with the chaplain of the prison and arranged a tour and an opportunity for several of the inmates to personally tell us their life stories. Sue Kennon was one of those who shared with us that day and my heart was bound to Sue's as a sister from that day on.

Sue explained how she had been sent to prison in 1987. Several years before, her husband had died tragically. She was pregnant with their first child, and this incident sent Sue off the deep end. She began using prescription drugs and became addicted and deeply depressed. Then she turned to heroin and began stealing to support her habit and her family.

"In my opinion," Sue wrote in a letter, "the worst addiction is a maintenance user. You believe with all your heart that you cannot function without your drug. You only take enough to appear 'normal,' whatever that is. No one knows except a few contacts that you are an addict. . . . With the addiction comes shame, guilt and self-hatred. Addiction presents you with a contradiction of self. You don't have a clue who you are any longer."

In May 1987 Sue used a toy gun to commit her first armed robbery at a clothing store in Portsmouth, Virginia. She desperately needed the money to support her drug addiction. Two subsequent robberies followed, also at clothing stores, again with a toy gun. Although she stole less than five hundred dollars in total, the impact on her victims was serious.

In June Sue walked into a pharmacy in Suffolk, Virginia, jabbed a long-barreled revolver into the pharmacist's ribs, and demanded drugs. She stated she wanted to use the drugs to take her own life. The pharmacist, Chris Jones, feared for his life. He did not know Sue's gun was broken. He drew his gun and shot her in the shoulder. Wounded, Sue dropped her belongings and ran out to a nearby field. She suddenly stopped and then ran back toward the pharmacist, begging him to end her life.

Sue was deeply troubled and had fallen into brokenness and despair even to the point of wanting to die. God used the pharmacist, her intended victim, to spare her life by wounding her, and thus preventing her from killing herself.

God loved Sue even when she hated herself. Sue needed much healing, but after many years in prison, God restored her hope and redeemed her love and self-worth.

She told the student leadership girls at the prison chapel, "I will always remember that field. My face and shoulder were covered in blood. I turned around to the pharmacist and begged him to kill me."

Sue's three robberies in three different jurisdictions in Virginia and a fourth, an attempted robbery, put her under the three-time loser law. This meant no parole. She was given a total of forty-eight years for her crimes. When she first arrived at the Goochland woman's prison, she was put in solitary confinement, even though she had never before served any prison time. Sue told the girls, "Unless the law changes, I will be in prison until I am sixty-three. The only thing saving my life is my hope to have an opportunity to get my education."

Sue continued, "I am the first woman in Virginia to finish my bachelor's degree while in prison, and now I am working toward my master's degree in psychology. I want to give hope to other inmates that they can better themselves while even behind these bars."

I prayed for Sue and the other inmates as our friendship deepened. I returned to the prison for Sue's graduation ceremonies. Tears filled my eyes, as I was so proud of this woman who had overcome so many obstacles. Sue acknowledged she had done wrong, had asked for God's forgiveness, and sought God's plan for her life. Even when her life seemed hopeless, Sue prayed that she would be free again, both from prison, as well as the prison of her heart.

Paul and I contacted three successive governors on Sue's behalf. In 1992 Delegate Marian Van Landingham of Alexandria introduced a bill that would have allowed the corrections department to review the three-time loser classification called the Sue Kennon bill. Paul and I later met with members of the parole board and told them of our personal experience with Sue and her remarkable story and amazing transformation.

We hoped she might to be considered for pardon, or at least be given a parole date and taken from under the three-time loser law. Sue continued her education and when I visited her we would pray together for the impossible to be possible through God.

Finally some of the members of the parole board agreed to go out to Goochland and meet Sue and another prisoner under consideration. I was so grateful when I got a call and they said, "Yes, Sue not only would be freed from under the three-time loser law, but she would actually soon be set free." I cried with Sue's parents and her daughter, whom I had come to love. God had done an amazing miracle and we rejoiced.

Once out of prison, Sue continued her education and ultimately earned her master's degree in psychology from Virginia Commonwealth University in 2001. She began working for the Department of Corrections on a program to help the children of inmates through addressing prison-related parenting issues. In May of 2006 Governor Tim Kaine presented Sue Kennon with the

Forgiveness Sets Us Free

Governor's Award for State Employee of the Year for Innovative Programs for her outstanding work. His announcement said:

> Ms. Kennon turned a personal setback into a mighty triumph for not only herself, but many others who have been in her circumstances. Ultimately, her work has benefits that are far reaching and of great value to the entire Commonwealth of Virginia.[6]

The wonderful thing also has been the reconciliation between Sue and the pharmacist, Chris Jones, now a member of the Virginia General Assembly. For years Sue had longed to have forgiveness from Chris. Although she felt she did not deserve his forgiveness, she desperately needed this precious gift in her life. After receiving her freedom from prison, Sue wrote a letter to ask Chris if she could come visit him. Chris, who already had forgiveness in his heart, agreed to meet. When they met, it was a time of true redemption. Chris believed Sue's sincere desire for forgiveness, and saw her humble and transformed heart. Chris' forgiveness set Sue free after so many years of shame.

A year later Chris and his wife, Karen, gave a painting to Sue as a sign of their reconciliation and new relationship. It was inscribed with the verse "Forget the former things; do not dwell on the past. See, I am doing a new thing! I am making a way in the desert and streams in the wasteland" (Isa. 43:18–19). In this heartfelt act of forgiveness came the fullness of freedom from guilt, shame, and despair for Sue and a deeper peace for Chris and his family.

I, too, have seen firsthand the power of forgiveness and have known the healing balm of this precious act of forgiveness that brought new life to Sue.

One of the most beautiful stories of a journey from fear to faith to forgiveness to freedom is Sue's story. God reached out and restored her life. In his mercy he forgave her and set Sue free to use her own journey to help so many others behind bars redeem their relationship with their own children.

CHAPTER 20

Living Out The Golden Rule

I carry a little marble with me that has the map of the world engraved on it. Often I will caress it in my hand and say a prayer for people that have touched my life. I am reminded that God has them, and each of us, in the palm of his hands. Although I fall short, my desire is to live in harmony with all people—to live a reconciled life.

Throughout my life I have had the opportunity to witness the remarkable diversity of people around the world and I have seen how their lives have been transformed by love. The words of the Golden Rule challenge us to "Do unto others as you would have them do unto you." Cultures, backgrounds, even religions may be different from our own, but we can live out the Golden Rule and come to treat others as we would want them to treat us.

The following stories are of people from other lands who live with the day-to-day reality of fear, but have chosen to trust God and be sustained by their steadfast faith. These individuals are an inspiration to my life, and I believe they also will inspire you.

Fear to Freedom

CHINA PASTOR PRAYS FOR THE WORLD

I came to care for the Chinese people through the many trips I took to China as president of Friendship Imports. In 1999 I began working for International Cooperating Ministries (ICM), where one of my responsibilities was to help lead and host "vision trips." During twelve such trips to China, Viet Nam, Cambodia, Cuba, and India, we visited churches in the building process, participated in church dedications, and encouraged our in-country partners. This was an experience of a lifetime where I saw the reality of people around the world that have walked their own journey from fear to freedom.

Founded in 1988, ICM has built or has under construction some 3,500 churches in fifty countries (www.icm.org). The ministry works with seventy national partners to fulfill the mission of "Nurturing believers and assisting Church growth worldwide." After each church is dedicated, the congregation agrees to plant five additional daughter congregations over the next three years.

This remarkable ministry grew out of the vision and friendship of successful businessman Dois Rosser and a gentle, soft-spoken pastor, Dick Woodward. Dick suffers from a rare degenerative spinal cord disease that has left him a quadriplegic so he works from his home with a computer that responds to his voice.

Dick developed the Mini Bible College, a survey of the entire Bible that is broadcast worldwide in twenty-six languages. ICM also provides Mini Bible-teaching material for small groups across the world through packages that include leader's guides, student workbooks, and a solar-powered digital audio player. In Dick's physical weakness, God has shown his power. Dick always says, "God uses ordinary people to do extraordinary things through God's amazing power and provision."

I returned to China in 2000 on an ICM vision trip and was amazed that this country was more open to faith, even though practicing faith can still bring persecution to believers. In spite of the dangers these people face every day, we attended church dedications and saw great joy as people sang and worshiped. I recall visiting the pastor of a small house church whose home was divided by pieces of fabric into three small rooms. The pastor's wife prepared for us pomegranates and tea with loving hospitality even through they had little means.

The main focus of their home, however, was a huge map of the world that filled the whole wall. The pastor said, "Here, each day we pray, not only for China, but for all the world to know Jesus. Yes, daily we pray for you in America!" We were humbled by our time together and I was pleased ICM agreed to build a church for this pastor and his congregation that will transform the entire community.

Our last day in China, my friend Roger Allen led our devotions on the Great Wall. We were all deeply moved as we prayed that God would continue to open the doors to China for people to express their faith. ICM has partnered to build nearly three hundred churches in China, and continues to encourage the growth of faith in this amazing land.

ON A MOUNTAINTOP LEPERS REJOICE

I will never forget a trip to India where we visited a leper colony. ICM had provided funding for a church five years before. The lepers built the church by carrying each stone up the hill with hands that had few fingers. As we walked up the steep hill to the church, I encountered my first leper and experienced a moment of apprehension because I did not know what to expect. Seeing his joy, I relinquished my fear.

The lepers' hands looked like nubs, and yet they held them together in worship as they shouted, "Halleluiah," which is the same word in every language of the world.

We heard how thirty lepers had been left on this isolated hill fifteen years before with only straw to build huts and one well to sustain them. They were to make a living from milking their goats, and going one day a week into the nearby village to beg in the streets.

Imagine the fear and ridicule these lepers must have experienced. These were the forgotten, the untouchables—yet God, the Good Shepherd, knew them and did not forget them. About twenty lepers gathered on the hilltop and Bagyama, a young woman, reached out to me. I felt connected to her as we joined in praise on that mountaintop. I was amazed as the lepers sang praises to God with deformed faces, hands with no fingers, and feet with no toes. They rejoiced, singing, "Jesus is the Joy of my life."

Fear to Freedom

As we knelt together and prayed, tears ran down my cheeks. I was humbled as Bagyama knelt beside me and gently wiped my tears with the scarf from her sari. In that moment we knew each other as sisters in Christ from two different worlds. She was the wife of a leper, yet she had no outward signs of leprosy. Although some might have feared her touch, I felt no fear because an intimate touch of the Master's hand had brought us together.

As we were leaving, we hugged good-bye and again tears flowed as I walked down the road toward our bus. I heard her call out my name. I turned and we ran back into each other's arms. I saw she had her daughter with her whom she wanted me to meet. This precious daughter was lovely and appeared perfectly healthy. I will never forget that moment. I continue to pray for my friend Bagyama. What an example of courage in spite of unbelievable challenges, and faith in spite of fear.

We attended other church dedications in India and the joy of the people was contagious. God connected my heart to many devoted people such as Pastor P. R. Misra and his wife, Anju, who visit my home whenever they come from India. Also Ananthi, I greatly admire as a woman of great vision, who began a slum school in the midst of filth that has become a beautiful Good Samaritan School in Delhi to serve the poor.

CAMBODIAN ORPHANS SING OUT

Cambodia was ravaged by war and torn apart by the Communist forces of the Khmer Rouge. Under Pol Pot's destructive reign, which began in 1975, some three million people were killed and the devastated land was left filled with orphans. Our concern for these orphans drew nineteen of us with ICM to fly thirty-two hours from America to Cambodia.

Floodwaters covered hundreds of square miles as we entered Cambodia, so we could visit our first ICM orphanage and church only by helicopter. Early in the morning, we boarded an old Soviet helicopter that had two flat tires and rotors warped by the sun. We sat on loose plastic chairs. There was no back door, no way to close the windows. Our feet rested on an eight-foot fuel tank with a sign that read "No Smoking," as if anyone in their right mind would even think of lighting a cigarette near such a combustible liquid! I can assure you that the prayer life of our little group of nineteen Americans really increased as we took off!

Living Out the Golden Rule

When we arrived near the site of the orphanage, we could see the top of the cross. The pastor and children waved us down as a man hurriedly cut down a tree to create our landing site. Then we traveled in style on ox carts through the deep mud to the orphanage.

I will always treasure the image of this church. Precious children in blue and white uniforms with little American flags lined the way to the orphanage as they laughed and sang "This is the Day the Lord Has Made." I thought about how Jesus had said, "Let the little children come to me, and do not hinder them, for the Kingdom of heaven belongs to such as these" (Matt. 19:14).

Unfortunately, this area is called Land Mine Heaven because of all the active land mines still hidden in the ground after the war. We met five orphan boys whose father and mother had been recently killed as they worked in the field where their plow hit a land mine.

Many of these orphans could have become prostitutes or beggars, as Cambodia has one of the highest rates of child trafficking in the world. I came to adore two sisters that I would have loved to bring home. The pastor said these orphans were not for adoption because he prayed that they would become the future leaders of Cambodia.

That night in our hotel room, I saw a piece of paper on my bedside table that read, "Don't take the taxi girls to sleep tonight." Tears came to my eyes as I realized some of these beautiful young orphans I had held on my lap that day would likely have become these girls used for prostitution. Instead of facing this horror, these children will grow up with a hope and promise of God's love and provision as his precious little ones.

ICM has now built 105 church/orphanages in partnership with a group that finds widows to help care for the children, provides tutors for those needing extra help, and takes care of the ongoing operating funds. These orphanages house more than three thousand children. It is amazing that these church/orphanages have also planted several hundred more congregations throughout Cambodia.

IN CUBA, THE LIGHT OF THE WORLD SHINES

During seven trips to Cuba I came to love the Cuban people! Fidel Castro and now his brother have tight control, but the power of God's love is even stronger. Being able to proclaim Jesus' love in a place of worship is the people's greatest joy, even in the midst of so many years of persecution for their faith. During an eight-year window of opportunity, 230 churches were built in Cuba and they still spread that light of faith.

I will never forget deciding to dedicate a church in honor of my mother, who had recently died. We had met the pastor, Juan Rodriguez, and his lovely wife, Rosemaria, at their home when they were first praying for a church to be built. They had a large congregation that was meeting in makeshift quarters and had been praying for a miracle.

Rosemaria shared how their precious young daughter died the year before. Through a terrible loss, they clung to their faith. The Spirit was so real in their home as we prayed together. I decided to honor my mother by providing financially for this church and make Rosemaria and her husband's dream a reality.

A year later when we returned for the dedication of the Paso de Cuba Church, I brought candles for everyone to hold. At the end of this joyous worship service, I lit my candle from the altar candle and passed the light to the congregation. There was a burst of light that swept through the church as we sang my mother's favorite song, "Amazing Grace." My father, who was ninety years old, could not attend, but the photograph I framed of this congregation aflame with the light of Christ was a blessing to him. The portrait of my mom will always hang in this church and I will forever treasure this memory.

My son also came on this trip and I was so touched on Sunday when Pastor Ricardo Periora called Paul to the front of his huge church in Havana. Here was my twenty-year-old son pointing his finger in the air saying, "*Gloria a Dios*, Glory to God." I was grateful for this opportunity for us both to see Jesus through the eyes of these Cuban believers.

That night we went to a service held in the house church of Pastor Juan Cuevas. He is a visionary pastor and incredible ambassador for Christ. A year before, we had worshiped with Juan and seventy-five people packed into his small apartment.

On this second occasion we worshiped in the yard of Juan's apartment complex. His congregation had grown to over three hundred. Children hung from the treetops to celebrate and worship the Lord. The music was pulsating and the Spirit was strong. The service took place in a housing project of over a hundred thousand people and, despite persecution, Juan and his wife, Olga, served as salt and light for the Kingdom of God.

Faith was spreading so fast that the authorities began to restrict Juan's activities. We were all praying for their safety and that of all the believers, because the government was clamping down on any public expressions of faith. Today it is not even safe for ICM to return to Cuba.

In July 2006 I received an e-mail from Juan saying a miracle had taken place. Because of the Cuban government's religious persecution, Juan became increasingly concerned for his family, and began looking for a way to protect them. He decided to participate in a lottery conducted by the U.S. government, even though it seemed like an impossible dream. The winner of the lottery would have the opportunity to come to America and receive a green card. Juan and Olga e-mailed me that by the grace of God they had won!

The family arrived in Florida, each carrying one suitcase. The three children and Juan and Olga thanked God for the miracle of beginning a new life in America. They claimed the verse in Matthew "Therefore, I tell you, do not worry about your life . . . Who of you by worrying can add a single hour to his life? . . . But seek first his kingdom and his righteousness and all these things will be given to you as well" (Matt. 6:25, 27, 33).

The whole family came to Virginia to visit us and we celebrated Christmas in America, the land of freedom. Juan is now working for a school, taking English lessons and serving as an associate pastor of a Latino congregation in Florida. It had been a long journey from living in fear to living in freedom, but Juan's confidence in God never dimmed.

A HUG OF RECONCILIATION IN VIETNAM

On another ICM vision trip, I was powerfully touched by a moment of reconciliation experienced by Rusty Porter and his wife, Ginny. Rusty had been a bomber pilot during the Vietnam War and struggled with his emotions from that season of his life. Now we were back in Vietnam to build churches and restore hope to those who would worship there.

We did not realize what awaited us as we came to the site of a new church and met their pastor. The pastor shared his story of how his first church had been destroyed by U.S. bombers during the Vietnam War. The pastor's wife and two children had been killed along with other members of his congregation.

As tears flowed down both men's faces, Rusty and the pastor embraced each other. This one act was deeper and more powerful than any words they could have shared—one military man from America and one pastor from Vietnam, both affected by a war that tore the lives of men and women apart. Now through the love of Jesus, these two men were drawn together in a new bond of love and respect.

Rusty and Ginny pledged to provide the finances for the building of a new church building. However, the building of this friendship across a broad divide had already begun. They were living out the Scripture "Be kind and compassionate to one another, forgiving each other, just as in Christ God forgave you" (Eph. 4:32). In that one hug, two men embraced in God's love and we closed by singing the hymn, "Halleluiah."

SMILES BRING HEALING TO GAZA

When our son, Paul, was a sophomore in high school, I wanted to share with him a meaningful trip that would serve others. I admired the work that Operation Smile did around the world to bring smiles to the faces of children. Doctors, nurses, and volunteers travel to operate on children who have cleft lips and palates. Often they have been shunned all their lives.

In America a medical procedure to fix such problems is done at birth, but children in developing countries cannot get that kind of care. That's why the work of Operation Smile is so important. For Paul's spring break we volunteered on an Operation Smile trip to Russia, but the trip was cancelled. "Where else can we go?" I asked. I was delighted to learn that there was a medical team going to Gaza.

I thought how perfect because our son had never been to the Middle East or visited the Holy Land. I called my husband, Paul, and he thought I had lost my mind! "Have you read the morning news, Rosemary? Gaza is definitely not a safe place!" After some persuading, Paul finally agreed we would all go together. My husband's idea of an overseas adventure is staying at the Ritz, definitely not going to Gaza! However, he loves his wife and respects my deep concern for the poor in the world.

Living Out the Golden Rule

After a long flight we joined our Operation Smile team in Tel Aviv and traveled by bus to Gaza. We were shocked by the devastation in Gaza. I knew Paul must be wondering what in the world we were doing here. We arrived at the hotel to find the building was under construction and only the first floor had been completed.

Our anxiety was rising until we arrived at the hospital and our hearts broke open with love. We were overwhelmed by the need of so many adults and children who had been burned by the open cooking fires used in Gaza. There were also many precious children disfigured by cleft palates and lips.

I always worked in the recovery room on Operation Smile trips. I tried to comfort the mothers as I brought their children to the operating room. After surgery, the recovery room nurses stabilized the patients, and then I would monitor vital signs and comfort them as they came out of anesthesia. When I returned the children to their parents, I experienced their tears of joy. A cleft lip or palate can be fixed in fifty minutes, yet the smile of a normal face will brighten a life forever.

Our son worked in the pre-op area, caring for the children's needs and easing their fears. He and Paul were orderlies and volunteered for whatever needed to be done.

What a wonderful picture of the way the world should be. We had Christian, Jewish, and Muslim doctors working side by side. I became close to one Palestinian doctor who would pass the recovery room and say, "There is that lady that loves God." We talked about Jesus and the Qur'an, and he told me about how he respected Jesus as a prophet.

The last night of our trip, I promised a terribly burned elderly woman that I would stay by her side while she was in the operating room. I scrubbed and sat on a stool praying for her recovery. The Muslim doctor finished his last surgery and joined me with his Qur'an. We spent hours freely talking about our faiths and the many times Jesus appears in the Qur'an.

After the operation he drew a triangle and said, "You, Rosemary, are here at one corner as a follower of Jesus and I am here at the other corner as a follower of Muhammad. But the closer we come together, the closer we come to God at the top." We then prayed together for a world of peace and understanding. It was after one o'clock in the morning when I settled my patient into her room and prayed for her recovery.

Fear to Freedom

As a family we will always treasure that trip. We saw whole families move into hospital rooms, bringing their prayer rugs, hopes, and dreams for their children to have a new opportunity at life. It saddens me to think of the victims of the fighting in Gaza now filling that hospital where so much healing took place.

For our son, Paul, this experience opened his eyes to the world outside our borders and deepened his compassion for people in the developing world. He and I went on a second Operation Smile trip to Colombia and Bolivia his senior year in high school. As he was fluent in Spanish, Paul was a great help with translations and assisted the doctors in communicating with patients.

After graduating from Washington and Lee University, Paul went to work for Operation Smile. For over eighteen months he organized and helped lead thirteen medical missions in nine countries. Then for the next two and a half years, he served as Executive Director of Operation Smile United Kingdom and led the Op. Smile U.K. Foundation. We never know how God can use an experience in our lives to guide us and allow us to be a vessel of Jesus' love to those hurting in the world.

THE GOLDEN RULE—UNITING US IN LOVE

Recall a time when you were really hungry. Perhaps it was waiting for that special Thanksgiving meal with the family. Willie was a great cook and my mouth waters just thinking about her chicken and dumplings, buttermilk biscuits, and fudge pie with homemade ice cream and chocolate sauce. Oh, my! What made such a meal great was not just the fabulous food, but the way Willie put her whole self into preparing it with love. Our tummies *and* hearts were filled.

Five thousand men, plus women and children, sat on a hillside to hear Jesus preach and they all became very hungry. The disciples wanted to send them away for food but Jesus said, "You feed them." They brought to Jesus only two small loaves of bread and a few fish given by a boy in the crowd.

Jesus took them, blessed them, broke them, and gave them to be distributed to the hungry crowd. All were satisfied and the disciples gathered the leftovers. The crowd had come that day because they were hungry for something other than food. Jesus met their needs of the hunger of the heart, as well as the hunger of the body.

Living Out the Golden Rule

Jesus is the bread of life and he came that all might have abundant life. I believe that everyone in this world can see Jesus in one of these three ways: a holy man, a prophet, or Lord. For some Jesus is a man, but everyone would acknowledge he is one of the holiest of men that has ever walked on this earth. For others Jesus is a prophet, a wise man. In the Qur'an you read about Jesus the prophet. For me Jesus is Lord. But wherever we encounter Jesus and however we see him, we can come together in his name; feel his Spirit and presence, and be fed by his unconditional love.

Jesus truly lived out the Golden Rule. I believe people everywhere are hungry for what satisfies the heart, mind, and soul—kindness, respect, understanding, compassion, acceptance, and unconditional love. The Golden Rule calls us to show compassion and respect for one another, even though we may come from different cultural backgrounds or religions. There are so many things that can divide us in this world. War can divide us, politics can divide us, religion can divide us, but love is universal and brings us together. Diverse people can come together despite differences in race, religion, creed, and color through the Golden Rule.

Jesus expressed this rule through these two Scriptures: "So in everything, do to others what you would have them do to you, for this sums up the Law and the Prophets" (Matt. 7:12) and "Do to others, as you would have them do to you" (Luke 6:31).

Moses said, "Love your neighbor as yourself" (Lev. 19:18). In Islam, Mohammed said, "No one of you is a believer until he desires for his brother that which he desires for himself." Even Plato expressed this thought: "May I do to others as I would that they should do unto me." And Socrates said, "Do not do to others that which would anger you if others did it to you."[1]

"Marianne Willliamson's book, *Illuminata: A Return to Prayer,* concluded with a prayer in which she asked God to help us "find our way home" from pain to peace, from fear to love. . . ." She continues, "Ultimately, the choice to love each other is the only choice for the survivable future. . . . As we receive God's love and impart it to others, we are given the power to repair the world."[2]

What if we began to focus our hearts on finding more harmony in our lives and in our relationships with other people? It has been my experience that you can talk to anyone in the world, not about religion, but about the person of Jesus, and be received in an open conversation. The name of Jesus does not divide.

We come together in this Spirit each year at the National Prayer Breakfast, as people of all backgrounds and faiths gather. Here, I have come to be good friends with Dr. Mounzer Fatfat, Doria Charmand, and Eman Kaskas from Lebanon and Saudi Arabia. Through our relationship, four Lebanese students are now attending Christopher Newport University. These three friends came for a visit and I asked them to speak to my girls' fellowship about their love for Jesus.

Dr. Fatfat has served as a senior advisor for the U.S. State Department in Iraq, and has been working on the Middle East peace initiative with Ambassador Tony Hall and Cardinal Theodore McCarrick. Their hope is to bring together the leaders of the three Ibrahemic religions—Christians, Muslims, and Jews—to build bridges of respect and find common ground. In doing this they are living out the Golden Rule.

Fatfat explained to my CNU girls, "I am a Muslim, but I am also a follower of Jesus and I love Jesus. We can come together anywhere in the world in the name of Jesus, be welcomed, and find common ground. In a Muslim country if I talk about Christianity, people often cannot relate, but if I talk about the person of Jesus—how he lived and loved everyone unconditionally, people respond. In the Qur'an you will find the name of Jesus eighty-two times, and there is a whole chapter about the Virgin Mary, who is respected and honored. In the Family of Imran, Chapter 3:42 of the Qur'an, the angel said to Mary: "Mary, God has chosen you and made you pure: He has truly chosen you above all women of the universe."[3]

Later at dinner, my friend Eman shared about a young man from Lebanon that came to the United States shortly after September 11 to receive medical attention for an eye injury caused by a terrible accident. Before he visited America, his impressions of our country were very negative and he felt everyone would treat him badly, suspecting he was a terrorist.

He was surprised when he went to the hospital that people went out of the way to care for him. He was amazed that his doctor, who was Jewish, showed great concern for him even though he was Muslim. Test after test,

Living Out the Golden Rule

he was treated with respect, and the doctors and nurses tried to meet both his physical needs and his emotional concerns about losing the sight in the injured eye.

His heart began to change. This young man was touched by the way people smiled at him. Isn't it amazing the difference a smile can make! After he returned to Lebanon he said, "Although I didn't get to have the surgery on my eye, I assure you I have had surgery on my heart." The compassion of people had changed him so much that his mother asked Eman, "What have you done to my son!" Instead of eye surgery, he had experienced the *open-heart surgery* of moving from hatred to love. Kindness had touched his soul and brought on a new sense of well-being. This kind of *open-heart surgery* is at the core of the Golden Rule.

Norman Rockwell published a mosaic that was reproduced by Venetian artists for the fortieth anniversary of the United Nations in 1985. It was presented to the UN by Nancy Reagan. The inscription read: "Do unto others as you would have them do unto you." The picture shows people from all over the world lovingly holding each other's children.[4]

What would the world be like if we had respect and compassion for one another, and honored everyone with dignity? What if we were concerned about feeding the physical hunger of people, and also the hunger of the heart, soul, and mind? What would our individual lives be like if we committed to live by the Golden Rule? The diverse music of God's universe is beautiful—if only we would learn to sing along.

We should be like a flute through which the music of the Spirit, the breath of Christ, can flow.

Fear to Freedom

You Make The Music

You make the music
You are my song.
You play me like a flute
The wind of your spirit
Pulsing through my soul
I'm here, I'm here.
You make the music
All creation is your song.
You play the flowers' violin
And the mountains drum roll
Beats out in majesty
I am, I am.

You make the music
Forgiveness is your song.
Your grace, your mercy
Sweet melody, releases pain
Touches hearts
I'm free. I'm free.

You make the music
All humanity is your song.
Some black, some white,
Some red, some bronze
All part of your orchestra
We are one, we are one.

If only harmony could be our song.

CHAPTER 21

Hope For The Brokenhearted

I have felt broken at times, but I have come to understand tribulation and brokenness are part of life. It seems there is an epidemic of stress and lack of self-esteem. Sometimes people have asked me for advice in how to get through their difficult experiences. In this chapter I want to share some practical tools that were helpful to me, and I hope will also encourage your healing process. Remember, Jesus desires to heal us from our fear and pain, for God is in the business of redeeming what is broken.

We need a revolution of love—a revolution of forgiveness—and a revolution of restored dignity. For this to happen, it will require some changes in our old habits and ways of thinking. We look to the exterior things to make us happy and fulfilled—success, money, prestige, power, our spouses and friends. Inner joy, inner peace in our hearts, and a sense of purpose and passion in our minds will create a better future.

After my rape I studied the Gospel of Mark, focusing on the woman with the alabaster jar. Her heart had been changed by Jesus' unconditional love so she now gave all that she had in this act of love as she broke open her vessel of precious oil to anoint Jesus. I too had experienced great pain that had brought on feelings of shame and worthlessness. Jesus' love changed me from within, and I would never be the same.

Fear to Freedom

Perhaps it is this moment in the Scriptures that Jesus felt most loved, as this woman entered the room knowing every eye was watching her in judgment. However, she pressed on to show Jesus her love. She brought all she had that was of worth—an alabaster bottle of valuable perfume. She lovingly knelt in front of Jesus and cracked open the bottle, anointing him.

Jesus knew he was about to be abandoned, even by those who had walked with him for three years. When the critics began scorning this woman, Jesus did not permit her simple act of love to be ridiculed. "Leave her alone, Jesus said. Why are you bothering her? She has done a beautiful thing to me . . . I tell you the truth, wherever the gospel is preached throughout the world, what she has done will also be told, in memory of her" (Mark 14:6, 9).

What an amazing affirmation. How she must have felt when his love met her own. Jesus stood up for her, honored her, restored her self-worth, and empowered her. He vacuumed up every last trace of the ashes of failure, shame, and worthlessness in the deep resources of her heart. He replaced them with beauty and bountiful love that set her free.

Jesus also did something beautiful with my ashes. What he did for this woman, he did for me as I was covered with that blanket of love after the burglary of my house and later touched by his Spirit in the Prayer Room of the Capitol. I have also been given the privilege of hearing many stories of women who suffered abuse in their lives, children who have gone astray, students who have felt rejected, and dreams that have dimmed. Whatever the pain, we can turn to the one who brings light to these dark places.

Also be the kind of person that affirms others, and speaks a word of encouragement letting people know when they have made a difference in your life. I had the pleasure of spending time with Marci Shimoff, co-author of the women's books in the Chicken Soup for the Soul series as she introduced her latest book, *Happy For No Reason*, at a speaking engagement at CNU. I recall one story as she shared about the power of affirmation and love.

One day a NY city high school teacher held a "blue ribbon ceremony" for her students. She told each student what she most appreciated about them and acknowledged them by handing them a blue ribbon that said: "Who I am makes a difference."

She then gave the students an assignment of passing on three ribbons: they were to acknowledge someone in their life they appreciated and hand them a ribbon. Then they were to give that person the other two ribbons and ask them to pass them along.

Within a short time, word got back to the class about just how powerful this ceremony was. One father who had gotten a blue ribbon from an employee passed on a ribbon to his teenage son and told his son he loved him. Shocked, the boy burst into tears and told his father that he had been planning to take his own life because he thought his father didn't love him. Now, he didn't need to. [1]

Deeply inspired by this story, I decided to try something similar. I had some lapel pins made with the word *Joy*. I believe joy in the heart can impact our world for good. We should acknowledge the joy others have brought to our lives.

I gave one of my students the first pin attached to a gold ribbon that said, "Joy can change the world." I shared, "Beth, seeing the transformation in your life has been a great joy to me. I want you to know I appreciate who you have become, and how you have blessed my life." We embraced as she put on the pin and tucked away the ribbon. I gave her two other pins on gold ribbons to pass on to someone else that had made a difference in her life.

What would it take for us to affirm someone in our lives and express one specific thing about that person we appreciate? A touch of love can be transformational. I am continuing to pass out "Joy" pins, but you don't need a pin to pass on the joy. Perhaps you might want to make a few simple ribbons, try this yourself, and see the blessings.

Especially when you are having a bad day, a word of encouragement can brighten your spirits. Bad things do happen to good people—they've happened to me. I believe we may do a disservice to people if we imply, "If you really believe and are a good person, you won't have trials." In fact, Jesus warned that in this world there will be tribulation. His life and that of the disciples was witness to that. But, there is good news. God is in the business of redemption and restoration, healing and forgiving, comforting and guiding, and transforming and anointing lives. Jesus has the power to restore that which is broken even as he did on the cross. God can take what was guilt ridden and shameful and make it pure and flawless.

Fear to Freedom

Whatever our heart's cry—whatever our fearful and broken places may be—we can believe that the Spirit is with us in our pain. God can transform even our worst challenge into a life that can shine brightly and recapture joy. When something is shattered, it needs mending. How terrible it would be if we fell and hurt ourselves and our bodies never healed! Just as God provides a way for us to heal physically, God provides a way for us to heal when we are emotionally wounded. What would it take for you to have a "stress-less" life? The following are some practical approaches and tools that helped me in the healing process. I hope these eight tips might encourage you as you move from victim to victory. Always remember: *Guard your heart; face your fear; set your mind; lean on others; be gentle with yourself; live a grateful life; lighten up, laugh and love yourself; and, most importantly, surrender your pain to Jesus.*

One way to begin to cope with fear is to **guard your heart**. In truth you may have been anxious about many things, most of which will never happen. Fear deals primarily with what hasn't happened, rather than what does—it deals with what isn't, not what is—it deals mostly in the past and future, not in the present.

I had to guard my heart and not believe the lies. It was also helpful for me to avoid places or things, as far as possible, that triggered fear or played the old tape of pain. The enemy withers from neglect, but thrives on attention. You cannot withdraw and always avoid triggers, but try to identify small things like smell, touch, or a tone of voice that can set off your emotions.

Next, *face your fear* when you are experiencing great anxiety. It may seem a strange thought to turn toward something, someone, or some circumstance that is causing you grief and anxiety, but when you confront your fear, you find new ways to overcome your fear.

Fight or flight is a natural response that is often physically prompted, and usually multiplies the fear. Running can be the right response if you are in physical danger. However, running away from fear is often unhealthy. At Yellowstone National Park, the rangers post signs telling visitors what to do if you come upon a bear. "Don't run! Be calm. Don't look the bear in the eyes, but be perfectly still." Don't let anxiety overrun and control you. As with a bear, when you run, your fears will run after you.

Set your mind to get out of the cycle of fear. My brother, Gene, has devoted his life to helping people create healthy relationships and lead purposeful lives. He has traveled the world as a trainer to assist people in opening up their minds and hearts to new possibilities and to being personally responsible for their actions, thoughts, and beliefs. He has helped me develop my thinking by using ideas from modern psychology and personal transformational practices in conjunction with spiritual growth.

Below is an illustration of a *Fear Trap Cycle*. In the center of the rectangle is the word *victim*. An action or situation takes place that we interpret in light of what we *believe*. We are also influenced by past echoes from unhealed wounds. We may believe the lies about ourselves are true; "I am worthless, it is all my fault, I can never be free!" These work together to form an *automatic response*. The past fear we experienced reinforces the belief that the situation is fearful and the cycle repeats itself.

For the first year after the rape, I felt trapped by this fear. In many cases we can be unaware of when and how the beliefs were formed and even the fact that our beliefs are driving our experience. Unconscious beliefs lead to unconscious behaviors. The events and situations are not causing my reaction. But instead they are produced by what I believe and my past interpretations.

FEAR TRAP CYCLE

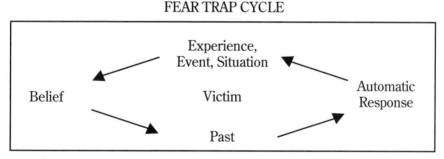

If I believe something is true, whether it is or not, it is true for me.

How I see a past situation and what I believe about an event mold my emotional response. For instance, if I believe the lie about myself that I will never be enough or that I will never be free from this painful event, it is difficult for me to be open to new possibilities. Those new possibilities might include acceptance, joy, a willingness to risk, or a fresh vision for the future.

The good news is that we have a choice in how we respond! We must distinguish between what we can and cannot change. The only person I can change is myself. The Serenity Prayer reminds us we must accept things we can't change, seek courage to change what we can, and find wisdom to know the difference.[2]

What we feel, think, and say has a direct impact on our mind, body and spirit. If your outlook remains negative, it will not only influence your life; but, did you know emotions can be contagious? If someone close to you always perceives everything as negative, how does that make you feel?

Sometimes a victim state of mind can actually attract further harm, because the negative thoughts of the victim make her believe she is unworthy of self-esteem and happiness. A continual victim thought process might be "I am fearful I am going to be raped again. I am fearful I am going to be abused and hurt. I will never be free." This attitude can actually make us more vulnerable to pain, as we are attracted to what we perceive to be true. It is time to consider changing our thoughts for everything we think *is not true.*

Marci Shimoff when she spoke at CNU, gave the following statistics: "According to research we have some 60,000 thoughts a day. An amazing ninety-five percent of these are the same thoughts we had yesterday or before. There is tremendous power in our thoughts and unfortunately, for most people, about eighty percent of their thoughts are negative. The negatives stick like Velcro and the positives slide off like Teflon."

During Marci's presentation, she gave us a wonderful demonstration of the impact our negative thoughts and self-talk have on our bodies through using a muscle testing experiment. Marci had two volunteers from the audience come on stage. She began by asking the young woman to hold out her arm from her side. Marci told her, "Now keep strong," as she tried to push her arm down. The woman's arm was able to resist and stay strong. Then she asked the woman to say out loud three times, "I am a bad person, I am a bad person, I am a bad person." This time when she put her arm out to stay strong, Marci was easily able to push it down. Then she asked her to say three times, "I am a good person, I am a good person, I am a good person." When the woman held her arm out this time, she could keep it strong when Marci tried to push it down.

Marci did the same demonstration with the second volunteer, a strong young man from the audience, and got the same result; saying he was a bad person made him weak, while saying he was a good person made him strong. She then used another example, having the woman say three times, "I can't do a good job" and then three times "I can do a good job." Again, the arms stayed strong with the positive message and went weak with the negative message. Marci said, "No wonder we often feel discouraged and weak—our negative self-talk actually creates bio-chemical changes in our bodies that weaken us."[3]

Marci's demonstration greatly impacted the students about the power of their negative self-talk. What if you determined to be positive for one whole day? Do not say anything negative—try not to even think anything negative, and when bad thoughts come, let them go and replace them with a positive thought—and see the difference.

The *Freedom Possibility Cycle* below opens up new possibility thinking and creative action that breaks us free from the *Fear Trap Cycle*. The healing process takes time, but we do not want to remain in a victim mindset. We can move toward a responsible and fulfilled life.

FREEDOM POSSIBILITY CYCLE

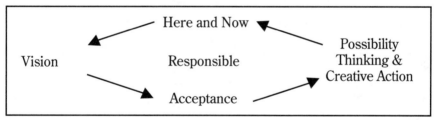

Instead of reacting automatically as we did in the *Fear Trap Cycle*, in the *Freedom Possibility Cycle* we operate from the *here* and *now*, in a way that is consistent with our *vision* for how we want life to be. We cannot undo the past and we cannot control the future. The here and now is where we need to live. This day is where we experience the fullness of life and come to appreciate life as a gift. This hour we have the potential to love and grow. This moment we can be in God's presence.

All transformation happens in the now. We are loved, accepted, and forgiven this very moment. The past is over and done. We may wish we could erase it, but it is written in black ink. Your past can, however, cease to control your future as we remember whose we are. We do not have to be possessed by debilitating fear. When we succumb to fear, we forget we belong to God and are not alone.

If we dwell on our fear or resist our fear, the fear persists. The more we focus on our fear, the more fearful we become. We can develop patterns of fearful thinking. There is no magic wand or formula to make the pain go away. We can't just say, "If I do this, I will be healed and healthy again." But with God's help we can learn to work *with* our fear and move toward living free with an attitude of personal responsibility and believing that it is possible. It is exciting to pursue new ways to turn our thinking around and consider fresh creative actions. A Chinese proverb says, "You cannot awaken a man who is pretending to be asleep."

For me, *acceptance* meant my acknowledging the truth about what occurred when I was raped, and how devastated I felt about it. I could not just pretend this abuse never happened, but had to accept that the pain was very real. Rather than pushing the agonizing emotions away, I faced them head-on. Denial keeps us caught in the cycle of fear, and hiding our pain can lead to further lack of healing.

A victim attitude or mindset is about avoiding or assigning blame. While this may be a natural defensive reaction or even true, it keeps us stuck when we're ready to move on. My brother, Gene, likes to say, "Blame comes in three flavors: blaming others, blaming circumstances (dwelling on reasons, stories, and excuses why things were the way they were), or blaming ourselves." We complain, "It's all your fault. Don't make me angry. Why are you making me so unhappy? I can't do anything right. I am not measuring up." The voices of condemnation are so loud. Yet we can move from our false self to our true self.

I would add a fourth flavor: blaming God. Blaming ourselves, however, is the most painful. When we are already suffering and upset with ourselves, it adds to the weight we carry. Instead of blame, I ask what I can do now to transform the way the past is impacting my life or others. It involves *possibility thinking* and a willingness to confront the question of how I am allowing the situation to negatively influence my life and my journey to Christ now. Everyday my iPhone display starts with the message, "I exist to radiate joy and help others in their healing journey to joy." This joy comes from the inside not from the outside. It is important we choose joy! Ask who do I need to be, and what do I need to do in the present moment? This attitude empowers us to break the cycle of fear.

Consider working through the *Breaking Free Questions* in the Devotional Guide. Identify the hurtful thought you are believing. Then move toward claiming your new *possibility statement* for today. My *victim point of view* was "Because I was raped, my life is ruined and I will always live in fear." My new possibility statement is "Having been raped, I now am a stronger, more compassionate woman dedicated to helping others move from fear to freedom."

FEAR TRAP CYCLE	FREEDOM POSSIBILITY CYCLE
Victim	**Responsible**
No possibilities	New Possibilities
Live in the Past	Live in the Present
No Choice	New Choice
Change Others	Change Myself
No Power	New Power
React	Act Now
Negative Experience	Positive Experience
Live in Fear as a victim	Live in Freedom and Victory

Do you have a *victim point of view* that may be holding you back? Ask yourself what needs to change; what can you do that will help you put what is behind you behind you. Consider setting your mind and surrendering your thoughts. Confront how your negative thoughts may be influencing your life and envision how you want to be *now*. We can start living the abundant life! It's time to move beyond fear and move on in your life.

I also learned how important it is to **lean on others** when you are afraid. In our lives, we need to find those friends who will hold us up until we are stronger to face our pain and troubles. Do you know some people who are just filled with "drama" every day? Surround yourself with people that encourage you to celebrate life. Remember you were made in love, for love, and to love others!

I recall one night when our son, at four years old, awoke during a storm and cried out to me. I went to comfort him and tried to assure him, "Paul, everything is all right. Mom and Dad are right in the next room and Jesus is here with you." Paul looked up at me with tender eyes and said, "I know Mommy, but sometimes I need to feel a little skin."

I got in his bed and held Paul the rest of the night. I'll never forget his wisdom as a child. We know in our hearts that the God who we cannot see is with us, but sometimes we need a friend who will be "Jesus with skin on." Find two people in your life who are willing to stand by you through thick and thin. Be committed also to be there for them and exemplify being Jesus to one another.

Reach out to get the healing support you need. Perhaps join a Bible study or meet with a pastor, teacher, or spiritual director. You may need to seek out a professional counselor, especially if you are experiencing deep depression and continue to live in fear.

Carleton Bakkam has been my spiritual director for fourteen years, and his wisdom and comfort have been a great influence on me. When we do not deal with problems, they often rear their ugly heads at a later time and cause even more pain. If you feel you need help, reach out and make that call today. There are resources in your community to help you face your fear.

Be gentle with yourself. Too often we get upset because we cannot seem to *just get over it*. This frustration can lead to more fear—the fear of failure to cope. I am thankful that the abuse of the rape and healing process I undertook changed me into the woman I am today.

I wish there were easy answers, but fear can be deep-seated. Healing is usually a process, a journey, and quick cures are rarely the best course. At first, I had to acknowledge little accomplishments each day. "Today, I had ten minutes of peace. Today, I did something for myself that took courage."

If you have been sexually assaulted, there may be intimacy issues that need to be worked out with the person you are dating or your spouse. Women may struggle for a time with physical touch that triggers their pain. Trust and anger issues may come up. Wounded women may find they are even angry with God and have difficulty trusting God's goodness. It is all right to allow yourself to be angry when you are in deep pain. God is big enough to meet you where you are and restore your broken heart.

Don't let what happened to you steal your potential for love. If you are not married, future relationships may be complicated by your experience.

Hope For the Brokenhearted

Be careful not to attract the same kind of man who hurt you. It is strange, but women that have been abused often are like a magnet that draws hurtful men to them. Be thoughtful in choosing the person you want as a spouse. It may take time, but be willing and risk trusting and loving again.

Live a grateful life and think about the good things. Find something to be grateful for even in tough times. Begin to be thankful even in the midst of fear. Put on your favorite music and sing along. Go out and do something that makes you happy. Keep a gratefulness journal.

Don't you find people who live life with passion and have a grateful heart inspire you? Such a young woman was Rebecca Ehehalt who died at the age of twenty-four, having been born with Williams syndrome, a rare genetic disorder characterized by learning disabilities and cardiac problems. Her parents shared, "Rebecca's most remarkable qualities of unconditional love and living the dream that 'all men are created equal' captured the hearts of those with whom she came in contact. Her smile, sincere honest affection, innocence and exuberant zest for life, taught us the true meaning of existence. Becky lit up the world and everyone she met with genuine and boisterous laughter. 'Do unto others as you would have others do for you' was Rebecca's way of life."

Rubbing a small pebble gave her comfort to face her trials and as a token of her love for life, stones were passed out at her memorial service. Suzie Ehehalt, her aunt, said, "Becky's smile and zeal for life had the uncanny ability to lift the weight of the world off your shoulders. I tried to adopt her philosophy that a smile can cure almost anything."

Passion comes from within and Becky unleashed her passion and love on each person she met. Although she faced some very difficult challenges in her life, Becky kept active in Special Olympics and Young Life and made the impossible seem possible. Her mom told me, "Becky welcomes the new opportunity to be an official Greeter of Heaven."

Becky is a witness to a life full of passion and joy in the midst of difficult circumstances. Worry and anxiety only make life more difficult and keep us from living in the present. Don't worry about the things you *don't have*. Be grateful for what you *do have* and ask God for whatever you need. Trust God's strength and rest in his provision. The apostle Paul's passion was for Jesus. He gives us in Philippians an understanding about the conditions to receiving peace: "Rejoice in the Lord always. I will say it again: rejoice! . . . Do not be anxious for anything, but in everything, by prayer and petition, with thanksgiving, present your requests to God. And the peace of God, which transcends all understanding, will guard your hearts and minds in Christ Jesus" (Phil. 4:4, 6–7). Paul then closes in verse 13, "I can do all things through him who gives me strength" (Phil. 4:13). That same strength, peace, and passion is available to each of us today.

Lighten up, laugh and love yourself. We are not perfect and God does not expect us to be perfect. Life is going to throw us some curveballs. Live life with a lighter touch. Allow yourself a good laugh. Let loose the joy inside of you.

Fear struck my friend René's heart seven years ago when she was diagnosed and had surgery for breast cancer. Since then she has poured her emotional healing into being there for young women dealing with cancer. She has developed a support group called "Beyond Boobs." These women did not want to be defined by their status as breast cancer victims or to focus on outward appearance, but instead to find the power and courage to live life to the fullest despite their illness.

Beyond Boobs, Inc., has become a non-profit that produces a calendar each year sharing their journey and raising awareness of life-saving early detection. www.beyondboobsinc.org. René appears in her "Good Health Fairy" costume—a flashy prom gown, tiara, and pink tennis shoes to bring the light touch. She believes a merry heart does good, like medicine!

Laughter

You would be so serious
But I desire to hear laughter
You would be so worried
But I desire you to let go.
It is time
Come my *Beloved*
Play in my fields
Roll in my grass
Dance in my garden.

Hope For the Brokenhearted

Let the joy of my love
Bring laughter to your lips
Joy to your heart and
Happiness to your soul.
I am waiting
for a good laugh!
I started laughing
And I could not stop.

I hope these practical tools are helpful, but the most important step is to **surrender your pain to Jesus**. He is the Shepherd who will leave the ninety-nine to come looking for you when you are lost. He can lift you above your circumstances, place you upon his shoulders, and carry you to safety. It may not be as fast as you like, or the way you had planned, but God is faithful!

All of us have times when we feel like sheep that have gone astray. God doesn't always save us from the circumstances—to the contrary, my life still has painful events. But he can see me through these challenges as I transcend my limited ideas about myself and remember my true spiritual nature as a child of God. You can trust God even when your feelings rob you of peace.

Jesus sent his Spirit as comforter, provider, and guide so he could be with us at all times. "But the Counselor, the Holy Spirit whom the Father will send in my name, will teach you all things and will remind you of everything I have said to you. . . . Peace I leave you; my peace I give you. I do not give to you as the world gives. Do not let your hearts be troubled and do not be afraid" (John 14:26–27).

Another way to help you surrender pain is to claim a Scripture on fear. Memorize it and repeat it often. I still carry the little card in my wallet I was given by Ann Kimmel with God holding the little child. It has the Scripture Isaiah 49:15, about how God holds us in the palm of his hand. That was thirty-three years ago and I have given out hundreds of these cards to others! Check the Devotional Guide for some Scriptures you might want to consider making your own.

Give yourself the grace to know that you do not have to have it all together. Jesus is not asleep as storms hit. Peter found this to be true when he

Fear to Freedom

saw Jesus walking on water toward the disciples' boat and came out on the water toward them. As long as Peter kept his eyes on Jesus, he overcame his fear. But as soon as he looked at the waves, he began to sink. Jesus stretched out his hand to save Peter. We can be assured, Jesus' strong hand is there today to reach out and lift us out of our fear if we will call out, trust, and keep our eyes on him.

CHAPTER 22

A Hidden Tragedy

B rokenness can be found in many forms, yet sexual violence has deeply touched my heart because it is often a hidden tragedy. As a past victim of sexual abuse, I want to make the prevention of sexual violence one of our nation's priorities. It is important that women know the extent of this crime and cry out enough is enough! These victims are caught in the cycle of fear. Their freedom has been stolen by those who have taken advantage of them. Where is the victory for this type of victim—the silent sufferers in this shadow world?

I am passionate about combating these crimes against our children and women, and I became more deeply involved when I served on the Youth Internet Safety Task Force led by Virginia's former Attorney General Robert McDonnell. The statistics are frightening—we need to raise awareness— yet this is a subject difficult for people to discuss. The report on human trafficking recorded by a Congressional Research Service indicates:

> Trafficking in persons (TIP) for the purposes of exploitation is believed to be one of the most prolific areas of international criminal activity. According to the most recent Department of State estimates, roughly 800,000 people are trafficked across borders each year. If trafficking within countries is included in the total world figures, official U.S.

estimates are that some 2 to 4 million people are trafficked annually.

As many as 17,500 people are believed to be trafficked to the United States each year. Human trafficking is now a leading source of profits for organized crime syndicates, together with drugs and weapons, generating billions of dollars.[1]

We often think of sex trafficking as a problem in developing countries. Unfortunately, there is much smuggling across our borders that involves sex rings of both children and adults.

Secretary of State Hillary Rodham Clinton said in her remarks at the release of the 2009 Annual Trafficking in Person's Reports (TIP):

> Around the world, millions of people are living in bondage.
>
> This is modern slavery, a crime that spans the globe, providing ruthless employers with an endless supply of people to abuse for financial gain. Human trafficking is a crime with many victims: not only those who are trafficked, but also the families they leave behind, some of whom never see their loved ones again.
>
> Look, our goal is simple: We want to end trafficking. We want to end this modern slavery.[2]

I learned firsthand of the precious children in Cambodia that are stolen and sold into sex trafficking and manipulated by pimps to live a life of horror and shame. The human sex trafficking going on both at home and around the world is one of the international challenges of our time.

Christine Dolan, who previously was a professional journalist with CNN, has dedicated her life to combating this terrible crime. She calls this outrage against children around the world a "Shared Global Shame." Cynthia told me about a time when she went undercover as a prostitute in a case the police were investigating internationally. She met with eight children who were captured from their abusers and secured in a safe house. Christine asked the girls if any of them would be willing to tell her their story. First, there was complete silence. Then one young girl with sad eyes finally responded, "No one wants to hear my story, no one cares, I am nothing."[3]

A Hidden Tragedy

Years of being used and abused sexually had stolen this girl's joy and also her identity. She not only felt she was nothing to anyone else, but something inside of her had been crushed and had died as well. My heart breaks for these children who have lived in terror. The girls in this case were now physically free, but this was just the first step in their healing process.

These children and so many women like them caught in the horror of sexual abuse must next break free from the horrible memories and flashbacks that continue to ruin their lives. These terrible thoughts come not only from the abuse, but the lies they have believed that they are nothing but worthless and nobody cares about their pain.

It is important that we increase the awareness of this hidden tragedy. It is very troubling to hear about such abuse internationally. However, it is extremely devastating to see the sexual violence going on in our own streets—in our communities—with our children.

I spoke with Mike Wagner, who co-authored with Alan Johnson a powerful article in the *Columbus Dispatch* about sex trafficking. They wrote, "A new word for prostitute: Victim. Naïve and vulnerable girls lured by slick-talking pimps are drugged, beaten and held hostage for sex. They are our children, and they are the latest casualties of human trafficking. The U.S. Department of State estimates that 15,000 to 18,000 women and girls are trafficked in the U.S. each year. Up to 300,000 may be at risk because they live in poverty, have a family history of abuse or are vulnerable for other reasons."

Andrea's heart-wrenching story is becoming all too commonplace.

The rusty black Chevrolet crept slowly down W. Broad Street until a stranger waved it to a stop. The man handed the driver $50 and climbed into the back seat beside a cute young woman with brown hair and brown eyes.

Before sunrise, about 20 more strangers would do the same.

Andrea, barely 18, pleaded to the driver to let her go. Three other women, who had taken her in from the streets, introduced her to the man she didn't realize was a pimp. Soon, he was beating her and threatening to kill her and harm her family if she didn't continue prostituting in the back seat of that car.

Fear to Freedom

Two weeks earlier, she had been sitting in English and math classes in high school. She left home after graduation to get out on her own, and the first people she met lured her astray.

"And just that fast, Andrea was trapped in an ugly underworld with no clear escape. 'I wanted out,' she said. 'But he told me they owned me now.'" Thankfully, an undercover cop helped Andrea regained her freedom. The article explains:

He was just another man, just another trick for Andrea. She had seen hundreds of men during the summer of 2008. Any attempt or even hint of running away prompted beatings and more threats. So with her pimp watching from nearby, she routinely offered men oral sex for $20. But this particular guy wasn't another john; he was an undercover Columbus cop. He arrested the teenager for solicitation and, without pity or coddling, booked her into jail.

The police record lists Andrea's address as "streets of Columbus." "I know I would be dead if he hadn't arrested me that night," Andrea said. "I was just a crack-addict hooker he was pulling in off the streets, not a victim. But that's what gave me a chance to get my life back."

Gone is the girl in the senior-year photo with the rose-colored skin, innocent smile and ambitious eyes. Almost a year removed from life on the streets, Andrea's body is fragile. But what remains of her spirit fends off the demons when her mind wanders to the past. "I have flashbacks, awful flashbacks," she said. "I am trying hard to be normal again, to have a decent life. No matter what people think of girls like me, no matter if they see us as victims or not, there are more still out there that need help."[4]

I know what it is like to live with flashbacks of terror, but I cannot even imagine the pain and suffering women and children endure, who have been lured into such sexual violence. It is frightening to see that our children can be vulnerable to such a hideous crime, especially those who are runaways. The FBI reports:

> One point six million children are estimated to run away from home each year, and it is estimated that approximately 40,000 of those children will have some type of involvement in or brush with sexual trafficking. A large percentage of these children left home because of physical, sexual and psychological abuse. These runaways become a prime target for sex offenders, pornographers, and pimps. . . . Prostitution is a continuation of the victim's sexual exploitation, not the beginning.[5]

It is not just runaways, but innocent, vulnerable women who are lured into this trap of shame and fear. I have come to admire Theresa Flores, who said to me, "The wounds will heal, the scars are forever." A victim of devastating abuse at the age of fifteen, Theresa is now dedicating her life as an advocate for abused women and developing Gracehaven, a safe house for underage victims of sexual exploitation in Ohio. "I have two daughters myself, and I don't want one girl to go through what I did," she said.

Here is a woman who had the courage and determination to heal from excruciating pain and use what was meant for evil, for good in the lives of others. Here is a woman with the compassion to help others heal, who understands their shame and is willing to walk alongside broken teenagers as they seek to find wholeness and peace in their lives.

Here is Theresa's story:

An older boy at her private school, who took a special interest in Theresa when she was a freshman in high school, wove an evil web of deceit. What began as an innocent infatuation with this young man, led to a night of horror. He offered Theresa a ride from school to her home in an affluent Detroit suburb. Home, however, was the last place he intended to take her.

Instead his calculated crime took her to another house where she would experience a nightmare of abuse. Theresa was drugged, raped, and photographed to blackmail her into two years of sexual abuse with hundreds of men. This man and the photographers, his cousins, demanded she earn the pictures back night after night, slipping her out of her home to a car that deposited Theresa to her forced prostitution. The trap of fear was set. He said to her, "I own you!"

"I can't describe to you the feeling of terror. No one should ever expe-rience that kind of fear. I had no idea what I was going to have to endure that night, for how long, or if I was going to come back home," Theresa ex-plained. "Although these ruthless men controlled me physically, mentally, and emotionally, the only thing I had was my faith in God. They could not take that away. That is what got me through."

As Theresa has turned her fear into freedom, she now is using her story to fight back for others to be set free. May her own suffering give hope to those that are hopeless that they too can move from victim to victory.

The Internet and pornography are often tools used to facilitate these invisible crimes, and enormous profits are being made. Enough Is Enough (www.enough.org) is an organization, led by my friend Donna Rice Hughes, which is dedicated to making the Internet safer for children and families. In 2006 worldwide pornography revenue was $97.06 billion. Of that, approxi-mately $13 billion was in the United States (Internet Filter Review, 2006). Donna spoke passionately, "Our kids are bearing the burden of this explod-ing industry, and it's estimated that seven out of ten children accidentally encounter pornography online, and one in three have used pornography intentionally because of its addictive nature."

Additionally, predators are utilizing pornography to seduce and groom children online. Predators will target children on the sites kids most often visit, like social networking sites, or through chat rooms or instant mes-saging forums. Donna shared, "An once of prevention is worth a pound of cure. According to the Department of Justice, one in four girls and one in six boys will be sexually victimized before adulthood. Parents are the first line of defense. That's why Enough is Enough, in partnership with the U.S. Department of Justice, developed the Internet Safety 101: Empowering Par-ents Program. The four-part DVD teaching series and workbook are filled with compelling stories and current information to help parents become more aware of these growing problems and to equip them to protect their children on all Internet-enabled devices."

I spoke with Daniel Homrich from Meet Justice who shared with me the following Atlanta statistics according to the Mayor's Report "Hidden in Plain View," and the Shapiro group researchers. "The number one site for

A Hidden Tragedy

prostitution in Atlanta is Craigslist where the prices for erotic services are measured in 'roses.' There are 400–500 listings for erotic services per day on Craigslist. Eighty percent of adult prostitutes begin between the ages of twelve to fourteen. In the state of Georgia alone, approximately 250 girls are recruited into prostitution on a monthly basis and conservatively, one in three are victims of childhood sexual abuse."

My eyes have been opened to the extent of this very challenging problem that is a threat to our children. I have become friends with Elizabeth, who shared this compelling story and the lessons learned from this terrible tragedy. She is a great advocate for victims and has developed a safe house in Atlanta. Elizabeth and Theresa are courageous women who are willing to stand in the gap to provide a safe place for those that feel there is no escape.

Elizabeth shared, "These women are not all runaways, but are innocent women who are preyed upon in bus stops, schools, shopping malls, and on the Internet. The pimps often use beatings and drugs to destroy what's left of self-esteem, as they demand their victims 'Go make some money.' Caught in this cycle of fear, their world becomes a web of lies. Their identity has been stripped, conditioned, and controlled for profit."

Elizabeth told me this story of redemption called "Lessons," about Meredith, a young woman abused as a child, caught in a game of survival in the sex-for-sale industry, and how she found freedom and found Christ. Here is Meredith's story:

LESSONS

1991: Nine-year-old Meredith and her dad are on the way to take her to elementary school when he quickly turns off the path. "Oh no," she thinks, "I'm going to be late again." As they pull into the apartment complex she sighs and assumes the familiar routine as they walk inside.

"Stay right here," he tells her, as her small feet hang over the tattered couch, "and wait until I come back." Handing her twenty dollars, he disappears into the back room with a woman who is not Meredith's mother. Unfamiliar sounds permeate her ears and she is exposed to sexuality before she even enters double digits. Walking out, he grabs the money from her and tritely tells her it's going into her college fund. She never sees it again.

Lesson Learned: Everything has a cost, and things that don't quite seem right can be justified with a few dollars in hand.

Fear to Freedom

1994: Meredith is now twelve. Her dad continues to take her along on his affairs, only now, she is included. Dropping her off at a male friend's house one day, he tells her to "be good for John." Within moments, her innocence is lost. For years following, her dignity is continually destroyed.

Lesson learned: My body is a tool to make other people happy. Sexuality is not sacred and my purpose in life is to leverage that sexuality to gain approval, acceptance, and material things. Wanting to please Daddy means pleasing other men, no matter how much I hate it.

1996: Overwhelmed with shame but tired of living in continual abuse, Meredith breaks the secret to a friend outside the family. Instead of being restored and cared for, her family sends her off to an orphanage and her father has washed his hands of her.

Lesson learned: Telling the truth is bad. Bringing abuse into the light leaves me alone and abandoned.

2000: Meredith left the orphanage and is working toward her cosmetology license. With no support, she makes her living by "escorting" high-end clients. She makes a thousand dollars a night to do whatever they tell her to do. Some of them beat her and force her to perform illicit sexual acts. Deep down in her heart, she is desperate for someone to affirm her for who she is, not just what she can do for them in their moments of lust. She slips into prescription drug abuse to numb the pain.

Lesson learned: Life is a continual game of survival. Value is not inherent. It is dependant on the giving of your body. Nothing is your own. You don't have a place in this world—you are aimless.

2004: Without hope, Meredith is now under the control of a pimp and working for an international sex trafficker. Desperate to do less work and still survive, she begins to work with her trafficker to recruit other girls. Her disdain for her actions increases, and she begins to lose all hope in humanity, including herself.

Lesson learned: The only way to make it in the world is to be exploited and exploit others. There is no true, self-sacrificing love to be offered or received.

A Hidden Tragedy

2008: Meredith made the choice to escape from her trafficker, move to Atlanta, and work in a strip club to make ends meet. She is desperate to get a better job, find new friends, and start a new life. Here her path intersects with Elizabeth as she reaches out with compassion, listens to her story, and asks her about her dreams and goals in life. Meredith begins to have hope, and opens up to trust Elizabeth.

Lesson learned: Maybe there are people who actually care about me. My life is not worthless, and maybe I actually could pursue some of the dreams I had as a little girl.

2009: Meredith is placed with a job, but she relapses. Elizabeth reminds her of the truth that nothing she has done or will do can separate her from the love of God. She tells Meredith that she has value, and her road to recovery will take time, but she has people who will hold her hand and walk with her along the way.

Meredith takes a step of faith and decides to enter into a detox treatment center. She walks to Elizabeth's car and sees a pile of letters of hope written by the ministry volunteers. She reads them, looks up at her with eyes so full of pain and hope, and she begins to weep. Between sobs, she whispers, "This is real, Elizabeth. This is real. People really do care about me. I'm a believer now, I'm a believer."

Lesson learned: I am not a throwaway. I am not abandoned. God is with me even now, and so are the people He's placed in my life to walk with me through the hard times. These people do not even know me, but the God they know has led them to love me in a way that I can't fully comprehend, but I know it's good.

Evening of Ash Wednesday 2009: Meredith is sitting in a white room waiting to be transferred to the detox center, with nothing but her purse on the floor. All items have been stripped from her, as she is on suicide watch. As Elizabeth sits with her, they talk about the significance of Ash Wednesday. "It's a time where people recognize their brokenness and take a season to remember what God has done for them," Elizabeth explains.

She read to her part of Isaiah 61: "He has sent me to bind up the brokenhearted . . . To bestow on them a crown of beauty instead of ashes, the oil of gladness instead of mourning, and a garment of praise, instead of a spirit of despair . . . Instead of their shame my people will receive a double portion, and instead of disgrace . . . everlasting joy will be theirs" (Isa. 6:3, 7).

She doesn't know if she's listening or not but later Elizabeth receives a text message. "The hospital staff is transferring me to the detox center now. I am really doing it, Elizabeth. I am excited about my new life. And God? God is making beauty from my ashes."

Five Months later:

Meredith got into a program, is working two jobs, and meets with her mentor and counselor regularly. She accepted Christ and Elizabeth keeps encouraging her about the role of the Holy Spirit in her life. She told Elizabeth about how a woman at church had said to her, "You are absolutely blooming!" Meredith shared with Elizabeth, "I guess you were right when you said God plants the seeds of hope in our hearts then he helps them grow."[6]

My heart breaks for women like Andrea, Theresa, and Meredith, and I am grateful that there are people like Elizabeth dedicating their lives to helping women with such brokenness as they begin the healing journey to wholeness.

I am in the process of discovering what my role may be in helping to transform the ashes of a young woman's life into the beauty and dignity she was created to experience. Working with two other victims, we are developing a healing intensive program called "Victim to Victim," which I hope will offer both practical tools and new hope for healing for those who have been raped. Our retreat house called "The Eagle's Nest" on the Chesapeake Bay will provide a wonderful setting for women to seek healing for their hearts and peace for their minds. Perhaps there are ways to also reach out to children and young women who have been abused by sex trafficking. My heart is especially burdened for young girls in our country who have been so affected by this hidden tragedy.

The next chapter tells the powerful stories of young women who have struggled with rejection, rape, panic attacks, and eating disorders. Each has come through these challenges and found new purpose, passion, and vision for her life. We do not have to live in despair whatever difficult circumstances come our way, but we can trust in God and take ownership for a better future filled with hope for the brokenhearted.

CHAPTER 23

Beloved, Even When Broken

God loves each of us in our successes and in our failures, in our challenges and our joys and even in our shame and woundedness. Yes, we are God's beloved even when we are broken. Many have said, "There is nothing you can do to make God love you any more and nothing you can do to make God love you any less." If we can grasp this truth and receive this awesome love, our relationship with God and others will never be the same. This love is here for everyone, everywhere. This love is for you.

This is the truth that filled my heart after my near-life experience. I finally got it—I was loved. I was God's beloved. Jesus knew my name. Somehow, as crazy at it might seem, I understood my life mattered to God. This divine love was in me, part of me, and around me in everything. Not even death could separate me from this love.

You are loved. Trust it. Receive it. Believe it. "And now these three remain: faith, hope and love. But the greatest of these is love" (1 Cor. 13:13).

Sometimes we think this life is all about me; how good I am, who I please, how successful I am, how "in control" I am. It's not. This life with all of its challenges and joys is all about the love relationship with a divine presence who wants to share every moment. The good, the bad, and the ugly are all part of this dance of life. When we surrender our pain, God sends Jesus to lead us in a dance of healing, through his Spirit, to a new place of faith, forgiveness, and freedom. Are you willing to dance as God's beloved?

My experience of being saturated with love in the hospital happened just after Paul and I came to Christopher Newport University. I think God was preparing me for the work he had for me to do with young women. Paul and I believe we have been placed at CNU for a purpose. Paul feels that all the other wonderful experiences of his public life were to prepare him for this time.

Over the past fourteen years, the university has gone through a period of dramatic transformation and has quickly taken its place in the ranks of America's finest liberal arts schools. Applications have exploded by eight hundred percent, SAT scores have soared by more than two hundred and fifty points, and the beautiful campus now has spectacular facilities. In 2008 *U.S. News and World Report* named CNU as one of America's "schools to watch." CNU was ranked number seven among all the national liberal arts schools for making the "most promising and innovative changes in academics, faculty, students, campus and facilities."[1]

Although the CNU story is exciting, the most important thing for Paul and me is our personal involvement in the lives of our students. We know hundreds and hundreds of students not only by name, but we also know their dreams and hopes and where their hearts are breaking.

I believe I was brought here to walk alongside those who are brokenhearted to help them find new freedom in their lives. I have had the joy each year of leading three groups of students on campus. We have annual retreats on the topics of Living as God's Beloved, Fear to Freedom, and Beauty for Ashes.

More than anything, I want these young women to understand that they are loved by God. The trust factor is also so important. I ask them, "Give me an opportunity to earn your trust." I am very protective of my girls, and treat their vulnerability as a gift. These are some of their stories, told with their approval and in a way to protect their identity. I am thankful these women wanted to have their stories heard that others might be blessed by their healing.

Beloved, Even When Broken

I stand amazed at the transformation that takes place during four years of college. I recall one of my girls, Jennifer, as a freshman was gripped with fear in her life. At one of our retreats she shared some of her own story.

> In middle school I felt people were saying, "Look at that loser. She doesn't have any friends." In high school, I felt girls ridiculed me and made fun of me. I felt so alone. My health began to break down and I was anxious all the time.

> I thought, "It is better to be unknown, than known and not wanted." I led a sheltered life growing up. Then as a college freshman, I let go of some of my beliefs and values. I changed what I wore and how I talked. I began going to parties and drinking. This was the first time I felt real attention from guys and I desperately wanted to fit in.

We fear rejection so much that we will do anything to avoid it. Young people feel pressured to find a way to fit in or find a way to hide. Too often, especially in college, drinking becomes a way to feel accepted by your peers. A few drinks can sometimes lead to a dependence on alcohol to face life and cover up insecurities. We want so desperately not to be lonely that we settle for less than God's best for us.

Jennifer went on to share how she was broken and lived in fear after she was raped at a party her freshman year. It was a painful journey as she fought to regain her self-esteem. She explained:

> I had low self-esteem before I was raped, but it was worse afterward. I thought my life was ruined forever. Through getting involved in InterVarsity, I began to heal. I learned how I was created by God in his image. I was loved as his child, even in my brokenness. This helped me regain my self-esteem.

> I came to realize my worth did not come from being in a relationship or having friends, but it came from God. I do not lose worth because of things that have happened in my life. I can turn to Jesus and seek his strength in challenging times.

191

Fear to Freedom

Through the help of friends and the mentoring she received, Jennifer was renewed in her faith and ultimately began to walk in forgiveness and freedom. I would have never dreamed during her freshman year that this young woman would enter seminary after graduation. Now she uses her story to help others who experience fear and rejection to open their hearts to the one who can truly heal and forgive. This young woman's story and so many others like hers are the reason that I came to believe I should share my own journey.

Lori Bickham Throupe, another dear friend and CNU graduate, is a gifted teacher and visionary who shows wonderful leadership skills in Bible studies and retreats. She has recently formed Beloved Ministries with three other CNU graduates. Their vision is to see college women changed by the reality of knowing that they are fully loved by God.

Henry Nouwen wrote in his book *Life of the Beloved*, "To know God is to know that we are *Beloved—Beloved* before our birth, beloved regardless of our successes and failures, and beloved even in the midst of great suffering and anguish." Henri Nouwen uses these four words: *taken, blessed, broken*, and *given* to describe our love relationship with God.[2]

Lori developed her own definitions to share with students and to use on retreats. (See Devotional Guide for scriptural references.)

Taken—To be accepted and acknowledged for all that we are and all that we're not, redeemed, and chosen to be used for glorious purposes.

Blessed—To have value placed on us, acknowledged and affirmed through someone expressing appreciation for us through words, time, and gifts.

Broken—To be torn apart in order that the value, beauty, and glory placed in us might be revealed and seen by others.

Given—To have received such great value and worth that we're given as an extension of what we've received and used to fulfill and satisfy others through the power of God, *Christ in us*.

The following are life stories of four young women: Amanda, Martha, Rachael, and Katherine, each of whom has experienced being deeply broken and then restored as God's beloved. They have experienced what it means to be taken, blessed, broken, and given.

Beloved, Even When Broken

TAKEN: FOR HIS GLORIOUS PURPOSE

Amanda's life exemplifies what it means to be taken. She was a shy but outstanding student. Few knew of her struggle with agonizing childhood memories of being abused at school. She became increasingly unhappy with her weight, and hurtful remarks from her peers deeply wounded her self-esteem. The pain became too much, and the desire to control something in her life was so strong that as a tenth grader, she secretly cut her arms, legs, and wrists. Amanda explains:

> The progression was slow and took a year or so as I became bolder and more desperate. It was like a drug—I got temporary release from my pain but had an ever-growing addiction. It was like needing a fix. I needed more and more to satisfy my urge. I used cutting to cope with overwhelming emotions that I didn't know how to express. I used cutting to deal with everything, to keep myself alive. While absurd, it was the thing that I relied on to keep me going.

Her mother noticed something suspicious when she was in high school and asked her about it. She just got better at covering it up, and her mother never brought it up again. Amanda hid her problem and hoped it would just go away. It rarely does.

> For six years, the idea of suicide had floated in and out of my mind. Finally one night I wept and cried aloud to God to make it stop. I wanted desperately for those thoughts to go away. As in Psalm 118:5, I cried out to the Lord in my anguish and he answered by setting me free.

> That night I experienced the sweetness of God in a powerful way. As I sat there crying in the rain, I threw my hands up because I knew God would have to be the strong one. The weight of my desire to die was lifted. I haven't been suicidal since that night. That option went away.

After Amanda entered college, this pattern of fear was still causing her to break down and hurt herself. She found good fellowship, became involved in a campus faith-based ministry, and recommitted her life to Jesus. She had a wonderful former Sunday school teacher who remained her mentor and confidant, and she got into counseling to fight the thoughts of self-injury. Finally at a "Fear to Freedom" retreat while hearing about the woman with the alabaster jar, Amanda had a breakthrough. She said:

> I finally realized I was destroying a woman loved by God—a woman Jesus died for. The depth of Jesus' love for that woman, for me, was enough to redeem even the ugliness of my shame. In this place of intense brokenness, I could hear his voice more clearly. Jesus called me *Beloved Daughter.*
>
> I left that weekend knowing I was forgiven by the grace of God and empowered by his love. I would push forward. I was ready to fight. I knew that it would be an intense struggle, but the cutting had to end, because I could not continue to destroy one that God loves that much.

Amanda found in music a beautiful outlet that helped her express herself. "It was a way of using my body, which I had been destroying, to encourage other women to come together and worship God." She would lose herself in her music and found new release from her fear and pain. She began writing songs and started a music group whose members were committed to supporting one another.

For Amanda, music was a way of actively and intentionally worshiping the Lord. A Scripture encouraged her: "Do you not know that your body is a temple of the Holy Spirit, who is in you, whom you have received from God? You are not your own; you were bought at a price. Therefore honor God with your body" (1 Cor. 6:19–20).

I sat with Amanda and a friend on the banks of the James River a few days before her graduation from CNU. We celebrated the one-year anniversary of her not cutting herself! With great joy we thanked God for taking Amanda in his strong arms and setting her free! She started seminary after graduation and ultimately desires to work in overseas missions and help others who are deeply wounded. Amanda was taken as God's beloved—accepted, redeemed, and chosen to be used for his glorious purposes.

Beloved, Even When Broken

BLESSED: BY THE AFFIRMATION OF A FRIEND

We are not only to be blessed but to be a blessing to others who are hurting. Martha, a student from Northern Virginia, got the news that her grandmother had died suddenly. She began to feel panicked, as if her heart was about to stop. She could not even remain at the funeral service that celebrated her grandmother's life. Martha became so frightened she asked a friend to take her to the emergency room as she was convinced that she was in danger of dying. The doctor diagnosed a classic panic attack. Fortunately her heart was healthy.

Over the next two weeks the panic attacks occurred three more times. On each occasion she went to the emergency room and was reassured that her heart was fine. Sadness, confusion, and fear began to set in and compound her panic. "How do I stop this? How do I get free from this fear?" she cried out.

One of my older students, Emily, had suffered from panic attacks in college and she reached out to Martha and shared her own struggles in the hope it would comfort and bless her. Emily said:

> When you have a panic attack, the thoughts and feelings of terror and physical reactions are so real they are true for you, even if you logically know you are not in physical danger. When I felt the anxiety coming, my heart would start pounding and my palms began to sweat. The fear is real and it is difficult to break free from these panic attacks. Please, try to be gentle with yourself, Martha.
>
> My mom could look at me and see the anxiety coming in my eyes. She would sometimes just hold me close and comfort me until the panic subsided. It was like a tsunami wave would hit me with full force when I least expected it. It helped me to talk to someone when I felt an attack coming. Feel free to call me night or day. Also if you think a counselor would help, don't hesitate to get support. Reaching out to others really helped me.
>
> Sometimes it is thoughts from our past that may be causing a panic attack that is being triggered by something going on now. Perhaps something in your younger days may have

been triggered by the death of your grandmother, and this helped ignite the fear. Be encouraged. You can get over this. I truly believe you can. I will pray for you for God's healing.

Martha was encouraged by Emily's advice. She determined not to let these panic attacks steal her joy in life but to live life as a blessing. She got some help from a counselor to learn to deal with the panic attacks and find ways to calm her racing heart. Martha realized holding on to fear does no good. Friends like Emily and her family, were a real blessing, and Martha gained new courage to meet each day without fear.

BROKEN: BUT REDEEMED BY GOD

One of my girls, Rachael, found that in the midst of being deeply broken she was loved by God. God brought her through her brokenness and strengthened her love for Jesus. Through the years fear often gripped Rachael's life as she journeyed from fear to faith to forgiveness to freedom. Now, working in higher education, she uses her past pain to help others. Rachael shares her story:

> Throughout my life I have had a horrible relationship with men. My own father died November 17, 1981, when I was five weeks old. He was on deployment as a military pilot and went down in a plane crash. He never once held me in his arms and I would never know his love. My mom later remarried, so I had a new dad. Yet, a devastating trauma changed everything.

> It was the spring of 1990. I was eight years old playing in our backyard under our fig tree around the picnic table when my life changed forever. Suddenly, this eighteen-year-old high-school guy from the neighborhood showed up from nowhere and came toward me. I recognized him as Sam, the boy who lived in the red house around the corner, so I was just surprised. Then he grabbed me, threw me onto the picnic table and did terrible things to me that I could not understand.

> I was so confused because my daddy was in the front

yard mowing the grass. I screamed, "Daddy, Daddy, help me!" But he never came. I ran into the house when the guy left and felt horrible. I did not know how to tell anyone what happened, so I kept it a terrible hidden secret. I felt sick, ashamed, guilty and so angry with my daddy for not saving me. Still, the smell of cut grass brings me back to that horrible day when Sam raped me.

As I grew up, I became angry with all guys in general and my fear translated into the need to control. I had to have the upper hand with guys so my heart would not get hurt. I didn't trust anyone.

During college Rachael developed a strong desire to control something in her life and that's when the bulimia started. She couldn't control her life, but she could control what she put in and out of her body. As she became obsessed with food, she moved deeper into the pit of depression. She thought, "Maybe if I look better, I will be valued and loved more. Maybe if I am thinner, someone will really care for me." She shares, "I got a high from throwing up and it was a sense of cleansing; a purging from all the bad things that were happening in my life." Then the unbelievable horror happened. Rachael recalls:

One beautiful spring day near the end of my sophomore year. I stopped by Target to shop for something. I suddenly looked up and saw a man who looked just like the person who victimized me as a child of eight. I told myself, "This could not be the same person; this could not be Sam!"

In a panic, I ran to my car and tried to put my key in the door. But when I looked up, he was standing behind the car. One good look at him smiling at me in that evil way, and I was completely terrified. It was him! It was Sam! I somehow got in my car, locked the door and took off, watching him in my rear view mirror still standing there.

I rushed to my apartment, locking the door behind me. I was huddled in my bedroom with a blanket wrapped around my shoulders and my knees pulled up to my chest trembling when I heard the splintering of wood. I started to get up but all I remember is being knocked over by a green book that smashed my face. I must have gone completely out, because the next thing I knew was my roommate, Sarah, was standing over me. She kept repeating, "Oh my God. Oh my God," as she pushed over the side table that was on top of me.

Her roommate called me and I rushed over and held Rachael close until she was strong enough to face our going to the hospital together. I recalled my own night of horror and after we left the hospital, I took her home with me for the night. Over the next couple of weeks we met several times with the police. They circulated a sketch Rachael had done, but Sam was never caught. She finished some of her exams and got extensions on others. Rachael explains:

I hoped Sam had finally disappeared from my life for good, but I was still traumatized. The bulimia got much worse and began to control me, instead of me controlling it. This is a rampant disease and it is not about the food, but how you see yourself and your lack of self-esteem. This evil had its power over me and was destroying me from the inside out. My doctor finally said to me, "If you don't stop this, you will have a cardiac arrest or cancer of the esophagus. You are already down that road." The disease had power over me. I tried to stop, but I could not.

At the end of the fall semester of my senior year, I got a call that Sam had been arrested in Indiana. He had been stalking women for years, and was finally caught and imprisoned. I learned the police had identified fifty women in three states that had been his victims; all petite blonds similar to me who he had abused.

Sam was sentenced to three consecutive life sentences of fifty years each. Finally this man was out of Rachael's life. She was safe and did not have to always look over her shoulder in fear. The most immediate challenge was dealing with the bulimia. She got help with her eating disorder and spiritual counseling to deal with the fear, self-worth, and bulimia issues. Rachael explains:

> Looking back, I began to see God's protective hand in my life as I deepened in my faith. Jesus became real to me. The transformational moment in my life came during a Christian counseling session. I went back in my memory and experienced again much of the pain from my past. Then I heard the Lord's voice saying, "You do not need to do this to be loved."
>
> Next, I had a vision of my wedding day and everything was white; the church, flowers and steeple were white, and I was dressed in all white. I knew at that moment that this is how God saw me—pure, white and forgiven. The only color was the red of the carpet down the center aisle of the church. This seemed to represent Jesus' blood that had covered me and made me pure forever in his sight. Yes, I had been deeply *broken* but somehow, Jesus had taken me, even in my *brokenness* as his bride.
>
> For the first time, I believed I deserved his love. I was worth Jesus giving his life for me. This moment completely redefined my relationship with Christ. I realized that there was nothing I could ever experience that God could not pull me through. I felt a peace like never before. I occasionally go back to that moment to relive that incredible presence of God's love and compassion for me.

My friend Rachael now is married to a wonderful man, Michael. When she told him about her past pain, he responded, "How did I get so lucky to find someone so amazing that can overcome such things in her life?" Rachael works at a university and plans to get her doctorate. She said, "I want women to know that God's healing from brokenness is real. It is not just something you read about. My own healing brought me from ashes to a new joy on my journey from fear to freedom." Evil had broken her as a child and again as an adult through the abuse she endured, but Jesus came to take her brokenness away.

Fear to Freedom

GIVEN: "MY SUFFERING MADE ME WHO I AM TODAY."

This last story shares how my friend, Katherine, had the courage to face her fears and challenges with anorexia. She now gives her life and all she learned from her pain to help heal others. Katherine confidently says:

> There is a difference between disordered eating and an eating disorder. Many young women struggle with a pattern of not eating properly. This may lead to an eating disorder that begins to control one's life and has physical symptoms: chemical changes in the body and, often, deep depression. In society there is so much focus on beauty and controlling your weight. Young women can easily get caught up in a lack of self-esteem and a harmful cycle of control.

Katherine was diagnosed with anorexia during her first year of college. Her problem became severe and the depression so intense that she withdrew from the school of nursing at her university for a semester to get the help she needed. Katherine explains her problem:

> The illusion is that eating disorders are about food and weight. In actuality, it is not about the number of calories consumed, the numbers on the scale or about food. For me, it was about not loving myself and, therefore, I could not receive love from other people. I thought I was controlling my food, but in truth, my eating disorder was controlling me. That is not freedom. You are bound—it controls you! Ultimately, you have to choose healing and life for yourself.

Anorexia is a symptom of an underlying problem that can be psychological, mental, spiritual, and emotional in its impact. Katherine's problem began when she was homesick her first semester at college and many changes were occurring in her family. Katherine shares her feelings:

> I felt so out of control of all the changes in my life that I began focusing on those areas in my life that I could control, such as what I was eating. This made that aching hole inside me go away for a while at least. I isolated myself and tried to convince myself that I was happy and that I enjoyed life.

Beloved, Even When Broken

Then the walls came tumbling down . . . my life was a tangled web of lies, confusion and illusion. Friends came to visit me at school and began to ask questions. My mom came demanding that I eat. I was hard on myself already, so when I attempted to live up to their expectations, I failed miserably.

I had this constant fear of being fat. Out of desperation, I cried out that my life was breaking apart, slipping away from me. I thought I had it under control, but it was only an illusion of control that masked utter and complete chaos.

Katherine wrote a letter to herself five years after her diagnosis of severe anorexia and talked about her anger:

My fear increased as I lay in my bed at night wondering if I would wake up; if I would live to see the next day. I was angry with God, angry with my parents, angry at the pain, angry because the world was not kind. I remember feeling that any prayer I prayed felt like empty words. I remember feeling helpless and hopeless.

My parents did everything right. They taught us to pray and to read the Bible. They loved God, each other and us very much. But I could not get better for family, teachers or friends. I finally had to answer the question myself, "Do I want to get well?

Words others spoke to Katherine offered courage and hope. One friend told her, "You will never be able to give and receive love if you cannot love yourself. One day you will experience joy again. If you can't believe it, or have lost hope, cling to the hope that I have for you." A common underlying problem of a woman suffering with an eating disorder is insecurity and not loving herself. It is difficult to love yourself without God getting involved. You cannot love God without having a deep experience of the goodness of yourself.

When Katherine went back to her university, she had to heal old scars and work through the horrible memories of loneliness and isolation. She always imagined herself in a dark damp dungeon where she had shackles on both of her arms. She felt she deserved this dungeon. This was the world she knew. Finally one morning Katherine felt the Lord say to her, "Come on out. You do not have to stay in there. Come and play. Come know my joy."

The most freeing thing for Katherine was finally to believe she could be in the presence of the Lord in the midst of her struggles. In her senior year Katherine's joy began to return. A friend once asked her, "What if your struggle with food is really a gift rather than something you are doing wrong?" Katherine began to consider this idea of her struggle as a gift, saying:

> Perhaps the best gift is I can choose to live life trying to just get by on my own, or I can run with my whole trembling self into the presence of a loving, mysterious and merciful God who wants to be with me and who loves me no matter what.

> I am thankful because through all the suffering, I have become who I am today. I am now able to experience a kind of joy that I've never been able to experience before. Somehow, I believe that joy and suffering are linked, and that joy is made possible by the suffering. I am in awe of all that the Holy Spirit has done in my life.

Katherine is now a registered nurse giving back what she learned to help others heal. What a powerful testimony of God's grace and redeeming power. We may have broken dreams, but God can mend our hearts. May God continue to use women like Jennifer, Amanda, Martha, Rachael, and Katherine, who have faced brokenness to help others see light in their own darkness. Brokenness *taken* into the Master's hand can be made into something truly beautiful, and then be a blessing when *given* to heal others and make this a better world.

Beloved, Even When Broken

Hear My Cry

Oh Lord, hear my cry
Take away the pain inside.
Take my anger and my fear,
Hold me in my lonely tears.
The nights I'm broken all in two,
I need you Lord to see me through.
I need you just a hand to hold
Help me God to be more bold.

I know that you are somehow here.
I believe you're near and trust you care.
I want to let go and surrender all,
To feel your comfort when I fall.

Safe within your loving arms,
Secure within your tender heart.
Strong again your hand in mine,
Free to soar and dance again.

CHAPTER 24

Join the Journey To Joy

I have shared my life with you as well as some tools that helped me deal with my fear. Now in this last chapter, I want to challenge you to let your brokenness be used by the Lord to help someone else. This book was inspired by two questions. First, "What if you did not have to be so afraid?" And second, "What if you could help someone else not be so afraid?" You can succeed on your healing journey from fear, to faith, to forgiveness, to freedom and live your life, not being so afraid.

Through the Holy Spirit, Jesus does the work of God only he can do, then he calls on us to do our part. There comes a time when we need to begin to focus outward, not inward. Do we have enough love to help unbind those in fear and bear witness to what God has done in our lives so that the darkness does not overcome the light? Are you willing to be *salt and light*? Your light might be just what someone needs to see her way out of a time of darkness. Salt brings out the best in things. Your pain and the story of your own redemption may be the balm desperately needed to empower someone else to believe that she too can live free.

205

Fear to Freedom

My husband at our 2009 CNU Honors Convocation said:

I hope you will make your life a great adventure. Empowered by great dreams, I hope you will live each day with passion—a commitment to excellence and to something more important than yourself.

There are great causes that we should be willing to die for. But happily few, if any of us, will be called upon to make that kind of commitment. Rather, I urge you to find something that you are willing to really live for.

In the words of Max Lucado, "There is a rawness and wonder to life. Pursue it. Hunt for it. Sell out to get it. Don't listen to the whines of those who have settled for a second-rate life. On one side there will always be the voice of safety. Build a fire, stay inside, warm and dry and safe . . . Or you can hear the voice of adventure. Instead of building a fire in your hearth, build a fire in your heart. Follow God's impulses. Adopt the child. Move overseas. Teach the class. Change careers. Run for public office, make a difference."[1]

To take what we've learned and invest it in others is another step in the healing process. God invites us to join him in changing the world for good. We do that one person at a time through his strength, not our own. "Those who wait on the Lord will renew their strength. They will soar on wings like eagles; they will run and not grow weary, they will walk and not be faint" (Isa. 40:31).

When my family lived in Williamsburg, there was an eagle's nest behind us and I began to research and read about eagles. Dick Woodward wrote a truly inspiring booklet called *As Eagles* that compares the way of the eagle to the way of the follower of Christ.[2]

An eagle is faithful and chooses a mate for life. An eaglet must be taught to fly, unlike other birds, and when that time comes the mother eagle literally bumps him out of the nest. "Mom, I'm going to die!" the little bird screams. Then the father swoops down at record speed, catches the baby on his wings, and places the little one safely in the nest. "Whew, must have been a mistake," the little eagle says thankfully. Time and time again she boots the little ones out of their comfort zone because she knows what the eaglets don't know: "They were meant to soar!"

Sometimes circumstances in our life push us out of our comfort zones. Our Savior can rescue us from the storms of life and place us back in our nests. Then instead of *staying under* our circumstances we can *rise above* our circumstances not only on our own effort, but through the Spirit. Like baby eagles we were made to soar! If we try to soar only through our own strength, we will soon burn out. To be useful to God, we must be willing to rely on him to teach us to soar "as eagles."

Could we dare to be part of Christ's plan of reconciling men and women to love one another and stand in the gap? Could we dare to be the leaven for the loaf or be the tiny mustard seed of faith that would provide hope for tomorrow? Could God be calling us to be his hands and feet?

In Italy there is a statue of Jesus that was destroyed during World War II. Several sculptors in the community worked to put the beautiful statue back together except for the hands, which were completely demolished. They left Jesus without his hands and the statue stands today with this message, "He has no hands but our hands." Likewise, Teresa of Avila wrote:

Christ Has No Body

Christ has no body but yours,
No hands, no feet on earth but yours,
Yours are the eyes with which he looks with
Compassion on this world,
Yours are the feet with which he walks to do good,
Yours are the hands, with which he blesses all the world.
Yours are the hands, yours are the feet,
Yours are the eyes, you are his body.[3]

What ignites your heart? What adventure is God calling you to? It is important you get in touch with your passion, because this world needs people who have come alive and want to respond to God's purpose. You are here for a reason. Your passion will fuel your vision. Think creatively—out of the box! What excites you and makes you come alive? I believe your joy can create a better world.

As I shared in the beginning of this book, I believe God has given me a passion for three things: to live in God's presence, to love and forgive everyone, and to inspire and empower others to live free from fear! Themes found throughout this book have directed my life and I hope will challenge you to identify your purpose. Then look for eagles who will inspire you to passionately soar and elephants who will hold you up when the going gets tough.

God desires to walk with each of us in a love relationship. We were made by him, in him, and for him; and we can find healing through him. He created us and he knows who he has made. He knows our potential, our gifts, and the beauty that lies within each of us. He invites us to be part of his plan—to become who he made us to be. But to discern his invitation, we need to seek God's presence. Ask, "What is your agenda? What is your best for me, Lord?" Ask God to fill you with the knowledge of his will through wisdom and spiritual understanding. Our prayer for our children has always been, "Lord, make Mary Katherine and Paul III the woman and man of God you would have them to be."

Sometimes we don't recognize God's fresh invitation—his new blueprint. We can each be part of his plan if we agree to be available and trust his provision. God has prepared in advance the work he has prepared for us to do. Lance Wallnau, an outstanding spiritual communicator, described at a retreat how God invites us to be part of his larger purpose.[4] I have expanded his ideas into this description and following illustration.

CYCLE OF GOD'S CALLING—THE PURPOSEFUL LIFE.

1. *Relationship*—We develop a love relationship through spending time in prayer, the word, and fellowship.

2. *Invitation*—Out of this relationship, God issues us invitations throughout our lives to be part of his plan.

3. *Prayer*—We must pray to discern his invitation, even though we may have some fear of inadequacy and questions. Look up not in!

4. *Surrender*—We can choose whether to accept or not. "OK, I'm in. I surrender to your agenda."

5. *Adjustments*—If we say yes, there may be some necessary adjust-

ments. We may not have the right tools or resources. Time constraints and old baggage may not fit into God's plan. We may need additional education or training to meet the next challenge.

6. *Blessings*—God's provision and blessings bring favor.

7. *Transformation*—As we trust, God does the transforming through the power of the Spirit.

Cycle of God's Calling
The Purposeful Life

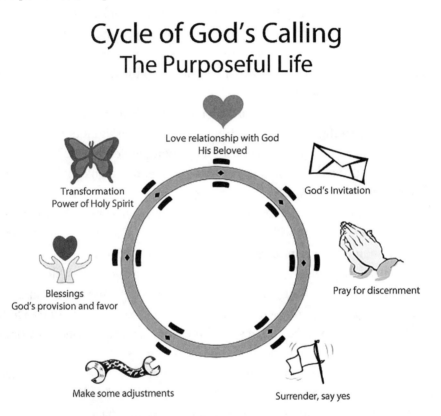

I am reminded how my husband, Paul, often says, "The enemy of the best is often not the bad things in our lives, but the *good things* that fill up our lives." We sometimes have to let go of other good things in order to say yes to the best—which is keeping God first and responding to his invitation in our lives today. We may need to dump some old baggage to enter into God's call for our life in this season.

There are times in our lives when we feel God is calling or nudging our hearts to follow, but we hesitate. Our voice, lives, gifts, talents, and leadership skills are all important to the larger plan. When God invited me to write this book, I initially had so many concerns and reservations. I am not a writer. How will the story of my rape, being public, affect our lives? Could this really help others heal? After praying, I knew my answer was yes. There have been many adjustments and much to learn, but God has blessed me through intimacy with the Spirit as we wrote together each day.

If I spread out on a table a thousand-piece puzzle and asked you to put it together, it would be pretty hard. But if I showed you the box top, it would make it much easier. Jesus came to show us the box top of what the Kingdom of love and forgiveness would look like. God invites each of us to be part of that bigger puzzle.

Ask, "What do you want to birth in me, Lord?" The good news is: 1. Our gifts, vision, strength, and passion will match our assignment from God; 2. His plan is a good plan—the best for living a fulfilled life; 3. This can be accomplished through God's power, not ours alone. Think for a moment, "What is my real passion?"

I sometimes ask my students to write down the answer to this question, "What do you think you will be doing in five years?" Then I ask them to start over and begin to dream bigger about their future. "I want you to imagine what you really would like to be doing in five years and write it down. I believe in you. You can do anything!" The students are excited and are amazed at the enlarged scope of their vision for their future. Over the entrance to the barracks at Virginia Military Institute are Stonewall Jackson's words, "You can be whatever you resolve to be."

Many of the stories in this book are about courageous women who have soared as eagles to overcome difficult challenges, and they have found new passion, vision, and purpose. These inspiring women have faced fears and are now helping others. Be encouraged. You too can soar over your circumstances to live in joy, fulfillment, and freedom.

God is having a Freedom Party and you are invited to join Him!

The first response deals with what fear you would like to surrender to God in order to take a major step in your healing journey. Name it, claim it, and lay it down. Second, who is one person you would like to forgive? Third, what do you perceive as God's purpose and vision for your life? What is something you believe God is inviting you to join him in doing at this season of your life that will make you come alive?

Welcome to God's
FREEDOM PARTY
You are invited to:
Surrender some fear
Forgive someone who has hurt you
Join God in fulfilling his purpose for your life
RSVP: To the Holy Spirit

I hope you will respond to God's invitation today. He will travel down any road to invite us to heal from fear and unforgiveness.

RSVP Card
As an act of faith I will
Surrender the fear of_____
Intend to forgive_____
Walk in God's purpose for my life to_____
Love, _____

We can then respond to his call to walk in freedom, serve others, and live the abundant life. Listen for that stirring in your heart. Turn away from the lies of this world that would have you believe you will never be free from fear. Be open to hear the whisper of God's love. You will always be God's beloved, but you must receive that transforming love, begin to love yourself, and live in a relationship with Jesus through the Spirit.

St. Benedict prayed for this kind of intimate relationship when he said, "O gracious and Holy Father, give us wisdom to perceive you, diligence to seek you, patience to wait for you, eyes to behold you, a heart to meditate on you and a life to proclaim you through the power of the Spirit of Jesus Christ our Lord."[5]

Fear to Freedom

This book is interwoven with a number of images of the dance. I wanted to close by sharing a dream that happened three specific times in my life. This dream and its dance ignited my heart and brought me great comfort. The first time I had this dream was after I surrendered my fear to God following the break-in at our house in Alexandria; the second time was after I forgave the man who raped me; and the third time was after my near-life experience. Here is my dream:

> I was a little girl about four years old and I was walking through a field of tall yellow wheat. I had thick brown curly hair and I was wearing a pale blue dress with flowers on the sash. I saw a man with a wonderful, warm smile walk toward me. He said not a word, but put out his hands as if to ask me to dance. He took me into his arms and I trusted him completely. Then he began to twirl me around and I let my head fly back as we laughed. My feet could feel the wheat blowing past me as we twirled and I gave myself fully to the music. Finally we stopped and he rested his back against a huge oak tree. I sat next to him and felt content and happy as I fell into a deep sleep.

There is a little child within each of us that still dreams of being free to dance. God's music of creation and love is always playing, but we are often too busy to listen for the music. I pose this last question: "When are you going to believe God loves you?" My prayer for you is that you walk in freedom and find your peace and fulfillment in God's presence and promises.

What manner of love is this whose joy is so full, whose whisper so sweet as he invites us, "Come dance with me, for I am the Lord of the Dance."

May your ashes turn into beauty and may your mourning turn into dancing. Now, start the dance!

Dance as Though No One Is Watching

Dance like no one is watching
Laugh like you have never been hurt
Sing like no one is listening
And live as though heaven is on earth.[6]

Devotional Guide

Chapter 1: Will I Ever Dance Again?

Scripture: "You turned my wailing into dancing; . . . and clothed me with joy" (Ps. 30:11).

Pause and Reflect:

- What is stealing your peace and joy?
- How does our culture and media enhance a sense of fear in our world today?
- Are there moments in your life when you feel overwhelmed by anxiety and a lack of well-being?
- Have you experienced a time of suffering or anxiety when you saw God bring something beautiful from that difficult time? Describe what this was like.
- What might freedom from fear look like in your life?

Practical Process:

- Go through some magazines or newspapers and cut out some words that represent to you the brokenness and fear in the world—famine, war, economic problems, etc.
- Now cut out words that represent fear to you—sickness, loneliness, rejection, joblessness, public speaking, etc.
- Paste these words on an 8x10 piece of paper like a collage. What emotions do these words trigger? Share with another person what this process meant to you.
- Now cut out words that represent love, joy, peace, and other life-affirming attitudes. Compare the sheets and notice the changes in your experience and mood from choosing positive rather than negative words.

Chapter 2: Redeeming Love

Scripture: "My lips will shout for joy when I sing praise to you—I whom you have redeemed" (Ps. 71:23).

Pause and Reflect:

- What was the influence of your family on your life?
- Has there been a time when you felt you weren't enough?
- Describe one situation that may have caused you anxiety as a child and how you coped with this. What messages did you get from your family about your self-worth?
- Have you experienced a time of healing in a hurtful relationship from your childhood?

Chapter 3: A Reconciled Heart

Scripture: "A new commandment I give you: Love one another. As I have loved you . . ." (John 13:34).

Pause and Reflect:

- Who most influenced your life when you were a young person? How did this bless you?
- Was there a particular experience that molded you for good or bad and shaped who you are today?
- How have you been hurt or have you ever felt someone took advantage of you?
- Is there a place in your life where you can identify the need for God's redeeming love? How might you reach out in forgiveness?
- Reflect on the strongest love relationships in your life.

Chapter 4: Fear Steals My Joy

Scripture: "Say to those with fearful hearts, 'Be strong, do not fear; your God will come'" (Isa. 35:4).

Pause and Reflect:

- Share a time when you experienced fear.
- Have you known of friends who have been sexually or emotionally abused, or have you faced abuse yourself? If so, how did it make you feel?
- In the midst of challenging circumstances in your life, how have you dealt with pain and fear?

- Was there a time when you were able to put your trust in God even in the midst of great difficulties?

Chapter 5: Will I Ever Feel Normal Again?

Scripture: "I sought the Lord and he heard me and he delivered me from all my fears" (Ps. 34:4).

Pause and Reflect:
- Describe a time you felt you were on an emotional rollercoaster.
- Has there been a time when you wondered if you would ever feel "normal" again? Explain.
- What were some coping mechanisms that were helpful to you?
- When you are fearful, do you want to run away from the situation?
- How have you overcome fear?

Chapter 6: Our Congressional Life Begins

Scripture: "Call on me and I will answer you and tell you great and unsearchable things you do not know" (Jer. 33:3).

Pause and Reflect:
- Have you ever pursued an impossible dream? How did this experience stretch you?
- Has a friend come to your rescue when you needed them most?
- Reflect on a moment of pure joy in your life, such as the birth of a child.
- Share an event in your life when your own faith was strengthened.

Chapter 7: A Victim Again!

Scripture: "I will not leave you or forsake you for I have carved you on the palm of my hand" (Isa. 49:15).

Pause and Reflect:
- Was there a turning point in your life? How did this impact your faith?
- Describe what happened, how you felt, and the difference it made.
- Has there been a time when you surrendered to God's power? Share how you were impacted.
- What do you feel about the statement, "God is not about religion—he is about desiring a relationship"?

Chapter 8: Find Your Elephants!

Scripture: "Two are better than one for if one falls who will lift them up . . . But a three bound cord is hardly ever broken" (Eccles. 4:9).

Pause and Reflect:

- Who are your most trusted friends? Describe what their friendship means to you.
- What are the most important qualities you look for in a friend? Who most represents those qualities?
- Describe a situation in your life when having a friend or being a friend made all the difference.
- Do something special for a friend, or just call and let this person know how much they mean to you.

Chapter 9: God, You Want Me To Go Where?

Scripture: "For if you forgive men when they sin against you, your heavenly Father will also forgive you" (Matt. 6:14).

Pause and Reflect:

- Think of someone you would like to forgive. Are there some things about yourself you need to forgive?
- Share your thoughts on forgiveness with someone else. What do you think the Lord's Prayer means when it says, "Forgive me my trespasses as I forgive those who trespass against me"?
- What does it mean that forgiveness is not about our feelings, but a decision to forgive?
- Have you been comforted or aided by someone very different than yourself?
- Consider how open or closed you are about people from diverse backgrounds and cultures . . . and how your response might change.

Chapter 10: A Door Opens To The Senate

Scripture: "Delight yourself in the Lord and he will give you the desires of your heart" (Ps. 37:4).

Pause and Reflect:

- Have there been times when you and your family have been stretched and challenged? Describe how this affected you and others.

- What has been one of your proudest or happiest moments?
- How has having a grateful heart made a difference in your life? What are you most thankful for today?
- In what ways have you been involved in special projects, community service, or faith activities that have blessed your life? Where is your passion today to serve others?
- What does keeping Jesus number one—keeping him first—mean to you?

Chapter 11: Soul Sisters

Scripture: "There is neither Jew nor Greek, slave nor free, male nor female, for you are all one in Christ Jesus" (Gal. 3:28).

Pause and Reflect:

- How have you cared for those in need?
- Would you be willing to consider building a friendship out of your comfort zone, perhaps across racial, cultural, or political lines?
- Describe how you experienced anxiety or unease when you were with someone from a different background.
- How might we begin setting aside labels and judging from our own perspective before walking in another's shoes?
- Have you experienced a difficult relationship that has produced a valued friend?

Practical Process:

May this Ten Commandments of Our Friendship be helpful to you in reaching out to form friendships outside your comfort zone. You may reproduce this for your personal use. (See page 233)

Chapter 12: Expanded Territories

Scripture: "For God so loved the world that he gave his one and only Son, that whoever believes in him shall not perish but have eternal life" (John 3:16).

Pause and Reflect:

- Why does persecution often make religious faith stronger?
- Who has inspired you by their steadfast faith in the midst of difficult circumstances?

- Is there a part of the world you feel particularly called to pray for? Describe why.
- Is there someone who is having a challenging time in his or her life that you might encourage?

Chapter 13: Coming Home

Scripture: "Who of you by worrying can add a single hour to his life? . . . Therefore do not worry about tomorrow, for tomorrow will worry about itself. Each day has enough trouble of his own" (Matt. 6:27, 34).

Pause and Reflect:

- Have you ever given up something that seemed important in order to spend more time with your family?
- What sacrifices have you or your spouse made for family or career? How did you cope with the challenge of balancing home and career?
- Have your children's words sometimes convicted your own heart with truth?
- What are your priorities for your family?
- What are some of your most precious family memories?

Chapter 14: Saturated By Love

Scripture: "I have loved you with an everlasting love; I have drawn you with loving kindness" (Jer. 31:3).

Pause and Reflect:

- Have you experienced a time with God that was difficult but became a true blessing?
- Have you felt fear when someone you love was sick and there was nothing you could do to help? What comforted you in that situation?
- When in your life did you feel most loved? Who did that love come from?
- How did God answer a prayer from years before?

Chapter 15: My Near-Life Experience

Scripture: "So we fix our eyes not on what is seen, but on what is unseen. For what is seen is temporary, but what is unseen is eternal" (2 Cor. 4:18).

Pause and Reflect:

- What does Jesus dying on the cross mean to you?

Devotional Guide

- Have you seen God bring good out of bad situations?
- Have you heard of someone who has had a near-death experience? Discuss this.
- Have you ever taken a leap of faith to trust God?

Chapter 16: Fighting For Life

Scripture: "Death has been swallowed up in victory. Where, O death, is your victory? Where, O death is your sting?" (1 Cor.15:54–55).

Pause and Reflect:

- Discuss the thought I shared that our journey on this earth is like a service project to learn to love God, to love each other, and learn to forgive.
- I discovered that the veil between the visible and invisible worlds is very thin. Does this encourage you about your loved ones who are deceased?
- Is there someone who has deeply hurt you who you might be willing to forgive? What would you need to do to begin that forgiveness process?
- What does it mean to you that "death has been swallowed up in victory"?

Chapter 17: Death Is Not The Final Dance

Scripture: "Even though I walk through the valley of the shadow of death, I will fear no evil, for you are with me . . ." (Ps. 23:4).

Pause and Reflect:

- Consider the thought, "We are spiritual beings having a human experience." What does this mean to your life?
- Share about a loved one who has died who "ran the race and kept the faith."
- What do you think of the quote by Max Lucado, "Never fear death, only the unlived life"?
- "Where have you found joy in your life and where has your life brought joy to others?" (Quote from *The Bucket List*.)
- What does it mean to give your "ashes of yesterday" to God so he may give you the oil of gladness?

Chapter 18: Abiding In God's Presence

Scripture: "You will seek me and find me when you seek me with all your heart" (Jer. 29:13).

Pause and Reflect:

- Consider establishing a time for prayer. If you already have a regular prayer time, see this as a special "Appointment with the King." How could this impact your life?
- When have you done "small things with great love" as Mother Teresa suggested?
- How do you feel about being quiet? Does it make you anxious or do you desire a time to "be still and know that he is God?"
- How do you best seek God's presence?
- Would you consider applying these prayer guidelines and experience centering prayer?

Prayer Guidelines

1. Seek—Set aside time to abide with God in love. Choose a simple word that expresses your desire to be in God's presence. Begin with a repetition of a phrase or psalm to settle you.

2. Surrender—When you become aware of anything distracting, return ever so gently to your special word, repeat it within a few times, and let the thought go.

3. Soak—Dwell in God's presence, rest in peace, and be restored by God's love. End with the Lord's Prayer, then open your eyes when ready.

Do you want to experience more of the presence of God? Would you be willing to commit to practicing Centering Prayer as a way of cultivating the presence of God? Do this ten minutes a day for a week and journal about the difference in how you experience your intimacy with God.

Practical Process: Welcoming Prayer

- Look at the things that cause you to lose your peace. Identify one circumstance or relationship that is the source of your lack of peace. Look at this "peace thief" more closely and see how the Welcoming Prayer might be helpful.
- Consider the situation that is causing anxiety. Now identify the feelings you are experiencing instead of pushing away from them.
- After acknowledging your primary emotion such as anger, disappointment, fear, or failure, allow yourself to simply experience these

222

emotions directly in your body without needing to do anything about it. Simply be with the feelings.

- Embrace and welcome the emotion causing you fear. Welcome fear. Welcome loneliness. Welcome abandonment. Don't try to fix it, analyze it, or change the situation. Identify your emotion. Fully embrace your feelings.

- Surrender and let go. Be aware, welcome, and then release these feelings and entrust them to God. Take some time to journal how the Welcoming Prayer may have affected you.

Chapter 19: Forgiveness Sets You Free

Scripture: "God was reconciling the world to himself in Christ not counting men's sins against them. . . . We are therefore Christ's ambassadors . . ." (2 Cor. 5:19–20).

Pause and Reflect:

- Write your own one- or two-sentence definition of forgiveness. Do you think forgiveness is for you or the other person?
- What is the purpose of forgiveness? How can forgiveness be a powerful tool in your own life?
- Describe the process of forgiving someone who has hurt you or of being forgiven by someone who you hurt.
- Is there some unforgiveness you are carrying?
- Do you find it hard to forgive yourself?
- What would it mean to you to be an Ambassador for Christ?

Practical Process: Forgiveness

- I encourage you to first read through this practical process for forgiveness and then choose a friend or family member to be your partner.
- First, choose some event that caused your hurt. From that situation identify someone you genuinely would like to forgive. Be open and honest in this process. As you begin, choose an event that is not the most traumatic thing that ever happened to you, but still is something that was painful.
- Choose your partner and face one another.
- **Partner A:** Bring to mind a person that has hurt or upset you whom you would like to forgive.

- **Partner B** is going to represent the person you are going to forgive. Describe to Partner B in some detail the person he or she represents, i.e. your mother, a friend, etc.
- **Partner A:** You are going to take three minutes to explain what he or she did that hurt you. Share the suffering that person caused and how it has affected your life. Give details as to how you have felt because of this hurt.
- **Partner B:** You are to listen with great empathy and concern. Don't say a word until Partner A is finished even if he or she falls silent for a time. Then apologize completely to Partner A for the hurt that you caused. Use your own words. Go into some detail and expand on how you now regret and understand how Partner A feels. Ask if Partner A would forgive you. Give no justification (i.e. "I did it because I too have been hurt"). There is no excuse. "I hear your hurt and pain and ask you to forgive me." Forgive like you would like to be forgiven.
- **Partner A:** Be willing to respond by saying, "I forgive you. Thank you for understanding my hurt. Now it is over." Again, go into some detail as to how you are willing to put this behind you and offer assurance that you have heard and received Partner B's words of apology.
- Reverse the process and allow **Partner B** to bring to mind someone they would like to forgive.

After completing the Forgiveness Practical Process consider these questions:

1. How did it make you feel to forgive someone?
2. How did it feel to have someone genuinely apologize to you?
3. What did you experience when you apologized to someone else?
4. What strengths did you see in the person willing to forgive?
5. Would you be willing to forgive yourself for something?

Did you feel that you completely forgave the person? Many times we forgive but later further hurt comes up and the forgiving act might need to be repeated. Just acknowledge yourself for attempting this act of forgiveness and be open to the healing it brings.

Chapter 20: Living Out The Golden Rule

Scripture: "For God did not send his Son into the world to condemn the world, but to save the world through him" (John 3:17).

Pause and Reflect:

- What experiences of faith from your own life have inspired you?
- Do these transformed lives from around the world encourage you to pray for people across the globe?
- Do you know of people who have been persecuted for their faith?
- Would you be willing to choose a country in the world and pray for the needs of its people faithfully? If so, which country would you choose?
- When have you been treated in the spirit of the Golden Rule and when have you treated someone else in that spirit?

Practical Process

Consider accepting this personal challenge and invite one or two friends to join you in living out the Golden Rule for one month.

- Each day do something that lives out the message of the Golden Rule. Discern or name something you would like to receive from someone else, and find a way to give this to another. If you would like encouragement, then you could call and encourage someone; need kindness—perform an act of kindness; desire respect—be respectful of someone's opinion; want forgiveness—forgive someone. Do whatever is meaningful to you. Record these experiences in a journal so you can be reminded of how living the Golden Rule made you feel and what affect this had on other people.
- The second part of the exercise is to record each day a *Thankfulness Moment*—a person, event, or special moment that made you grateful that day. You may have witnessed a beautiful rainbow or experienced a transforming moment of thankfulness.

Each day you will live out the Golden Rule by doing some deed, saying words of encouragement, or blessing someone's day. Also you will step back and recognize with gratitude something, someone, or some act of goodness.

If you have one or two other friends join you, share once a week how you have been touched or seen some blessing occur from living out the Golden Rule. I find I enjoy something more when I can share it with someone. Also, having a friend as an accountability partner helps remind us of our commitment. After completing the month, you might want to continue to make living out the Golden Rule and a *Thankfulness Moment* a part of your life.

Chapter 21: Hope For The Brokenhearted

Scripture: "For God has not given us a spirit of fear, but a spirit of power, of love and of self-discipline" (2 Tim. 1:7).

Pause and Reflect:

- What does the story of Jesus standing up and honoring the woman with the alabaster jar mean for your life?
- What is the heavy thing you personally may be carrying? Have you experienced a time of great personal pain?
- When have you felt God's comfort during some challenging time? Is there a time when God has taken your broken spirit and made something beautiful out of your life?
- What does it mean for you to guard your heart and face your fear? Do you believe you can set your mind to "think differently"?
- What Scripture might you claim regarding fear or anxiety?
  Here are some of my favorites:
  "Cast all your cares on him for he cares for you" (1 Pet. 5:7).
  "There is no fear in love. But perfect love drives out fear . . ." (1 John 4:18).
  "When you pass through the waters, I will be with you; and when you pass through the rivers, they will not sweep over you . . . Since you are precious and honored in my sight, and because I love you . . . Do not be afraid, for I am with you" (Isaiah 43:2–4, 5).
  "A bruised reed he will not break, and a smoldering wick he will not snuff out. In faithfulness he will bring forth justice" (Isaiah 42:3).
- Have you experienced a time when laughter was good medicine for the soul?
- How many things that cause you to be anxious are in the past or in the future instead of the present? Give your interpretation of the statement, "Fear deals mostly with what isn't, rather than what is".
- Describe a time when you felt caught in the Fear Trap Cycle and could not get free.

- What would it take for you to turn your thinking around, put your trust in God, and surrender your pain when the storms of life come?

Practical Process: Breaking Free

We can break free from our old thoughts that keep us captive and develop new possibilities for today. I had lived with the thought that I would always be broken and never get over this fear. I knew logically what happened was in the *past* but it was still controlling my life *today*. I had to ask myself, "Is this the way I want to keep living?" If not, what would it take for me to surrender this victim point of view and claim a new possibility for my life today?

Answer the Breaking Free questions and write a new possibility statement for your life.

Breaking Free Questions

1. What is the hurtful thought I am believing? "Because of _____, I feel_____,_____&_____."
2. Is it truly real for me today or does it deal mostly with my past? _____.
3. Without this hurtful thought my life could be different and I would be more_____,_____&_____. Would I like this?
4. What would it take for me to surrender this thought? Am I willing to do so? _____.
5. I can create a new *possibility statement* for my life today. _____.

For example, here are my answers to the Breaking Free Questions:

- The hurtful thought I believe: "Because I was raped, I feel my life is ruined, broken and I will always live in fear."
- No, I am not in danger now and I don't really have a reason to be afraid.
- I would be more happy, contented, and not always so anxious. Yes, I would like this!
- I would have to make a choice to not let my negative thought control me. I am willing to let it go, release it to God, and live in the present. So be it!
- *Possibility statement*: "Having been raped, I now am a stronger, more

compassionate woman dedicated to helping others move from fear to freedom."

For further study you might consider looking at a secular approach by Byron Katie that is very creative in what she calls "turn around" thinking in her book, *A Thousand Names for Joy, Living in harmony with the Way Things Are.*[1]

Chapter 22: A Hidden Tragedy

Scripture: "The Lord is close to the brokenhearted and saves those who are crushed in spirit" (Ps. 34:17).

Pause and Reflect:

- Have you ever considered that personal information on the Internet could at times make a person vulnerable?
- Does it come as a surprise that around the world and in our communities, our own children are at risk of sexual violence? Discuss.
- What is your emotional response to the stories of Andrea, Theresa, and Meredith?
- Have you ever felt you were rescued from a difficult situation through the grace of God? What were some lessons you learned?

Practical Process:

A journey toward healing means trusting in God's invisible guidance and not just our own agendas. It also means learning to trust others for help and comfort. Consider this practice:

- We can *set our mind* to trust in what is truth. A "trust walk" can help internalize what it feels like to trust when you cannot physically see. Jesus was the visible expression of God's love.
- Have someone blindfold you and preferably walk you around outside. At first they can use their voice to also guide you. Then you must completely trust them as they lead you with no words.
- Trade places and blindfold the other person for the trust process. Share what you experienced. Were you nervous at first? Was it hard for you to blindly trust? How did it feel when someone put their trust in you and you were guiding them?
- Discuss how you might trust Jesus who is the invisible God and how it felt to trust the person guiding you.

Chapter 23: Beloved, Even When We Are Broken

Scripture: "And we know that in all things God works for the good of those who love him, who have been called according to his purpose" (Rom. 8:28).

Scriptures for *taken, blessed, broken* and *given*:

Taken: Isa. 43:1; John 15:19; Gal. 3:13; Eph. 1:4–14.

Blessed: Luke 11:9–13; Gal. 3:14; Eph. 1:3, 2:4–7.

Broken: Isa. 53:4–6; Rom. 8; Phil. 3:7–11; 1 Thess. 5:23; 1 Pet. 4:1–3, 12–19.

Given: John 15; 1 Cor. 12; 2 Cor. 4:10–12; Eph. 4:7–9; Col. 1:24–29;
1 John 4:12–13.

Pause and Reflect:

- Have you experienced a sense of rejection—felt left out, looked over, and not accepted by others? Perhaps you felt the sting of not being chosen for the soccer team, sorority, or for that special promotion?
- Describe a time you felt the fear of being alone, feeling different, or just unloved.
- Have you or anyone you know struggled with an eating disorder?
- Have you ever fallen into some kind of harmful way of coping and trying to control the pain in your life? How did you respond to your feelings during those times?
- Are these ways of coping still useful to you today? What healthy attitudes and approaches would you like to adopt now?
- How have you experienced the awesome unconditional love of the Father through his Son, Jesus?

Pause and Reflect: Declarations

A declaration is a spoken statement that describes the kind of person you intend to be and the actions you intend to take in your life that will move you toward your passion, purpose and peace. Speaking these out loud to someone can be a powerful experience and help you on your healing journey. They also create an atmosphere where others can support you and hold you accountable for fulfilling those intentions. Listed below are some declarations from recent chapters that might be helpful to call your own.

My ashes of yesterday do not have to define me today.

I can live as if I am loved—not for what I do but for who I am—
God's Beloved.

My heart's greatest desire is for God's presence.

Fear to Freedom

As I guard my heart, my negative emotions no longer control me.

I can face my fear with courage and conviction and experience peace.

I choose to live in the present and trust in truth.

When I forgive, I am set free!

By trusting God, I can soar to freedom.

By living out my purpose, I can find fulfillment.

Declarations can be *present statements* using unequivocal language. You can make declarations regarding ways of being and doing. By ways of being I mean inner qualities of character that are *expressed* through behavior, the actions you actually take. For example, you might say, "I am a loving, trusting, courageous woman." The actions I take to support this are "I call my parents every week and tell them something I appreciate about them. I risk by introducing myself to strangers."

This is much more powerful than saying I want to be or I'd like to be. The idea is to make a declaration and begin to act consistent with that declaration *now*. Of course you will get off track, but when you do, just restate your declaration to yourself or someone else. Keep a written copy with you and remind yourself of your declarations each day.

Exercise:

1. Decide the ways of being you want to develop that will support you in moving toward your peace, purpose and freedom. Three or four are probably a manageable number. Write these down in a statement that says, "I am a _____, _____, _____ women (or man)."

2. Decide the tangible actions or behaviors you will take as an expression of your ways of being. Describe these actions in a statement that says, "I (*description of action/behavior*), I (*action/behavior*) and, I (*action/behavior*)."

3. Find a friend or family member to be your partner. It should be someone you trust who will support you in keeping your declarations. Speak your declarations out loud to your partner with as much certainty and power as you can muster and ask them for feedback.

4. End by praying for God's help in keeping these declarations. Always be compassionate with yourself regardless of your success. "I acknowledgement myself for working on being a _____, _____, _____ women."

Chapter 24: Join The Journey To Joy

Scripture: "I have told you this so that my joy may be in you and that your joy may be complete" (John 15:11).

Pause and Reflect:

- Are their times in your life when you felt you were falling and didn't know where to turn?
- When has God renewed your strength "as an eagle"?
- Where is God encouraging you to soar in your life today?
- What do you see as some of your leadership gifts and talents that can be used for God to make a difference in the lives of others? Could the *Cycle of God's Calling* be helpful to you in identifying your purpose?
- How has the Holy Spirit directed and empowered your life?
- Where in your life today do you feel "The Lord of the Dance" is calling you?

Ten Commandments Of Our Friendship

by Barbara Williams-Skinner and Rosemary Trible

Once you make a deliberate and intentional commitment to enter a cross-cultural covenant relationship, the following principles that guide our relationship may be helpful to you.

I. BE UNITED IN GOD'S LOVE

God's love alone causes us to be honest, open, and trusting with one another. God's love is greater than our fear of rejection. "By this all people will know that you are my disciples, if you have love of one another" (John 13:35).

II. HAVE NO OTHER AGENDA THAN LOVING GOD BY LOVING ONE ANOTHER

It is more important to love than to be right about economic, political, or social issues. We must surrender our positions for God's positions. Once trust is built, we will be more open to hearing one another's positions on issues. We must also surrender our calendars so that we are available to one another. "Love the Lord your God with all your heart, and with all your soul, and with all your mind . . . love your neighbor as yourself" (Matt. 22:37, 38).

233

III. MOVE OUT OF YOUR COMFORT ZONES TOWARD ONE ANOTHER

We do not have to look or think alike to love one another. We must be willing to walk in each other's shoes. Be a friend and receive a friend out of your comfort zones. . . . "They devoted themselves to the apostles' teaching and to the fellowship, to the breaking of bread and to prayer. . . . All the believers were together and had everything in common. . . . And the Lord added to their number daily those who were being saved" (Acts 2:42, 44, 47).

IV. ABILITY IS LESS IMPORTANT THAN AVAILABILITY, ACCOUNTABILITY, AND COMMITMENT.

"I can do all things through him who gives me strength" (Phil. 4:13).

V. ENCOURAGE EACH OTHER TO INVEST OUR LIVES IN SERVICE TO OTHERS

Encourage one another to feed God's sheep, to care as Christ cares; to love and forgive as Christ loves and forgives; and to walk our talk. "When they had finished eating, Jesus said to Simon Peter, 'Simon, son of John, do you love me more than these?'...Jesus said then, 'Feed my lambs'" (John 21:15).

VI. MAKE REGULAR PRAYER TOGETHER OUR FOCUS. DO NOTHING WITHOUT PRAYER.

"Pray constantly" (1 Thess. 5:17).

VII. COMMIT THAT LEAVING OR DIVORCE IS NOT AN OPTION

Never let the sun go down on your hurts, feelings of disappointment or anger. Work out your differences and do not let them divide you. Make your commitment to a healed and reconciled relationship more important to you than any differences that arise. "Can a woman forget the baby at her breast, and have no compassion on the child she has born? Though she may forget, I will not forget you! See, I have engraved you on the palms of my hands..." (Isa. 49:15, 16).

VIII. GIVE YOUR FRIENDS AWAY TO ONE ANOTHER

Friendship is the most important gift we can give to one another. Ask the Spirit to guide your relationship. "And I will ask the Father, and he will

Ten Commandments of Our Friendship

give you another Counselor, to be with you forever—the Spirit of truth. The world cannot accept him, because it neither sees him nor knows him. But you know him, for he lives with you and will be in you. I will not leave you as orphans; I will come to you" (John 14:16–18).

IX. LEARN TO EMBRACE ONE ANOTHER'S PAIN

All forms of pain—e.g. racism, family strife—can be tools, which God can use for healing. Forgiveness can also be a tool to set you free. "He said to them, when you pray say, 'Father, hallowed be your name, your kingdom come. Give us each day our daily bread. Forgive us our sins, for we also forgive everyone who sins against us. And lead us not into temptation . . .'" (Luke 11:2–4).

X. WE MUST DECREASE SO CHRIST CAN INCREASE

"He must become greater; I must become less" (John 3:30).

End Notes

CHAPTER 1

1. RAINN; *Statistics on Rape Victims: Rape, Abuse & Incest*, National Network, 2000 L Street, NW, Suite 406, Washington, DC 20036, Hot Line 1-800-656-HOPE, Statistics reference; U.S. Department of Justice. 2005 *National Crime Victimization Study* and The National Institute of Justice & Centers for Disease Control & Prevention. Prevalence: *Incidence and Consequences of Violence Against Women Survey*, 1998.

2. Speech by President George W. Bush addressing the U.N. General Assembly; September 23, 2003. Statistics from 2003 U.S. State Department estimates.

3. Mother Teresa, *Great Quotes From Great Leaders*, Compiled by Peggy Anderson (Successories Publishing, 1990), 101.

CHAPTER 2

1. *The lessons of Saint Francis: How to bring Simplicity and Spirituality into Your Daily Life*, John Michael Talbot, (New York, Penguin Putnam Group, 1998).

2. Author unknown, *Prayer, Matthew, Mark, Luke and John*; English prayer from the 18th century. Opie and P. Opie, The Oxford Dictionary of Nursery Rhymes (Oxford University Press, 1951, 2nd edn., 1997) 303-4 *Wikipedia, The Free Encyclopedia*

CHAPTER 3

1. Boyd Herb, "Little Rock Nine paved the way." Volume 98, Issue 40 *New York Amsterdam News* (September 27, 2007), *Wikipedia, The Free Encyclopedia*, "The Little Rock Nine" (accessed April 2009).

CHAPTER 5

1. Henri Nouwen, *Turn My Mourning into Dancing*, (Nashville: W Publishing Group, 2001), 12.

End Notes

CHAPTER 9

1. Author unknown, *I Was Hungry*, M. Lunn, Collection, *1,500 Inspirational Quotes and Illustrations, www.greenspun.com/bboard/q-and-a-fetch-msg. tcl?msg_id=00CREt* (accessed August 2009).

2. St. Andrew's Potato and Produce Project, newsletter; Gleaning America's fields—Feeding America's Hungry; Rev. Ray Buchanan and Rev. Ken Horne contacts, mailto:vaglean@endhunger.org.

CHAPTER 11

1. Author unknown, *To Those I Love, poem*, www.obriencastle.com/obrien-castle/thetruespirit/poem.html (accessed August 2009).

2. Barbara Skinner and Rosemary Trible, "Ten Commandments of Our Friendship," (Skinner Leadership Institute, 1996).

CHAPTER 12

1. Operation Moses, Airlift of Ethiopian Jews, http://www.iaej.co.il/pages/ history_operation_moses.htm (accessed August 2009).

CHAPTER 13

1. Congressman Guy Vander Jagt; Speech at 1980 National Prayer Breakfast Washington, DC; Quote attributed to Alexis de Tocqueville; Congressional Record, Proceedings and Debates of the 96th Congress; February 27, 1980; Vol. 126, No. 31

CHAPTER 14

1. Mother Teresa, *Great Quotes From Great Leaders*, Compiled by Peggy Anderson (Successories Publishing, 1990), 101.

CHAPTER 17

1. William P. Young, *The Shack*, (Los Angeles: Windblown Media, 2007).

2. Max Lucado, *Grace for the Moment*, (Nashville: Thomas Nelson, 2000). 180

3. William P. Young, *The Shack*, (Los Angeles: Windblown Media, 2007), 126.

CHAPTER 18

1. St. Augustine, *St. Augustine Confessions*, translated by John K. Ryan, (New York: Doubleday, 1960), 43.

2. Billy Graham, Hope for Each Day, (Nashville: Thomas Nelson, 2002). Also *Nuggets of Wisdom*, http://www.savedhealed.com/nuggets.htm (accessed August 2009).

3. Mother Teresa's speech at the National Prayer Breakfast hosted by the president and members of the Congress, February 3,1994.

4. *Mother Teresa: No Greater Love*; Edited by Becky Benenate and Joseph Durepos (Novato: New World Library, 1987), Chapter On Prayer, 4.
5. Raghu Rai and Navun Chawla, *Faith and Compassion: The Life and Work of Mother Teresa*; (Rockport: Element Books Limited, 1996), 158.
6. Cynthia Bourgeault, *Centering Prayer and Inner Awakening* (Cambridge: Cowley Publishing, 2004), 7.
7. St. Teresa of Avila, volume II, *Interior Castle*, (ICS Publications, Institute of Carmelite Studies, Washington DC 1980), 122.
8. Cynthia Bourgeault; *Centering Prayer and Inner Awakening*, Advanced Centering Prayer, 16
9. Thomas Keating, *Intimacy With God* (New York: Crossroad, 1994), 55.
10. Cynthia Bourgeault, *Centering Prayer and Inner Awakening* (Cambridge: Cowley Publishing, 2004), 143.

CHAPTER 19

1. forgive. (2009). In *Merriam-Webster Online Dictionary*. Retrieved September 2, 2009, from http://www.merriam-webster.com/dictionary/forgive
2. Corrie Ten Boom and John Scherrill, *The Hiding Place* (New Jersey, Fleming H. Revell Company, Oct. 1974). 238
3. Martin Luther King, *Strength to Love* (Minneapolis: Fortress Press, 1981), 50.
4. Peggy Naderson, *Great Quotes from Great Leaders* (Lombard: Successories Publishing, 1990), 81.
5. Frederic Luskin, *Forgive For Good* (New York: Harper Collins, 2003).
6. Governor Tim Kaine of Virginia presented this special citation as State Employee of the Year for Innovative Programs to Sue Kennon for her outstanding service to the Commonwealth, 2006.

CHAPTER 20

1. Scarboro Missions, Golden Rule faith comparison, Scarboro Missions Interfaith Desk, 2685 Kingston Rd. Toronto, Ontario M1M 1M4; www.scarboromissions.ca.
2. Marianne Williamson, *Illuminata: A Return to Prayer* (New York: Penguin Putnam, 1994). Back Cover and Chapter 1, *Renaissance*, # 6 Thoughts
3. The Qur'an: Oxford University Press; Chapter 3:42–51, page 37.
4. Norman Rockwell, *The Golden Rule*, permission to reproduce the picture was given by the Norman Rockwell Family Agency LLC John Rockwell; e-mail: jnrockwell@tds.net.

End Notes

CHAPTER 21

1. Marci Shimoff, *Happy for No Reason* (New York: Simon and Shuster, 2008); speech at Christopher Newport University, Aug. 5, 2009.

2. The Serenity Prayer, Commonly attributed to Reinhold Niebuhr who used the prayer in a sermon, perhaps as early as 1934. (From Wikipedia, The free encyclopedia.)

3. Marci Shimoff, *Happy for No Reason* (New York: Simon and Shuster Free Press, 2008); speech giving demonstration at Christopher Newport University, Aug. 5, 2009.

CHAPTER 22

1. Statistics: Trafficking in Persons: U.S. Policy and Issues for Congress Liana Sun Wyler, Analyst in International Crime and Narcotics (lwyler@crs.loc. gov.) Alison Siskin, Specialist in Immigration Policy (asiskin@crs.loc.gov,) Clare Ribando Seelke, Specialist in Latin American Affairs (cseelke@crs. loc.gov.) July 2, 2009 (RL34317)

2. Remarks at Release of the Ninth Annual Trafficking in Persons Report; Secretary of State Hillary Rodham Clinton, Benjamin Franklin Room; Washington, DC, June 16, 2009

3. Christine Dolan, CEO of the International Humanitarian Campaign Against the Exploitation of Children; Story from personal conversations and remarks to U.S. high school students leaving to attend International Internet Safety Conference in London, May 2008.

4. "A new word for prostitute: Victim;" Article in The Columbus Dispatch, by Alan Johnson and Mike Wagner, Sunday, June 28, 2009

5. Statistics from the Congressional Testimony statement of Chris Swecher, Assistant Director of the Criminal Investigative Division of the FBI 2005. Runaway statistics; 2002 National Incidence Studies of Missing, Abducted, Runaway and Throwaway Children.

6. Director of Redeemed, a safe house in Atlanta. This story, "Lessons" was personally relayed by the director about the life of one of the women who has escaped from her life of prostitution. For their protection, the director's name, and identity of Meredith are kept confidential. www.redeemedlove.org.

CHAPTER 23

1. *U.S. News & World Report's America's Best Colleges.* 2009 edition, New York, NY, 2008, 14-15.

2. Henri J.M. Nouwen, *Life of the Beloved* (New York: The Crossroad Publishing Company, 1992).

CHAPTER 24

1. Max Lucado, *Grace for the Moment*, (Published by J Countryman, a division of Thomas Nelson, 2000) First quote: *He Still Moves Stones* (Nashville: Word, 1993), 60.

2. Dick Woodward, *As Eagles: How to Become an Eagle Disciple*, special publication (Hampton: International Cooperating Ministries, 2000).

3. Teresa of Avila, "Christ Has No Body," *Journey With Jesus*, http://journeywithjesus.net/PoemsAndPrayers/Teresa_Of_Avila_Christ_Has_No_Body.shtml (accessed August 2009).

4. Lance Wallnau, speech, Seven Mountains Strategic Leveraging, the National Prayer Breakfast Seminar, Washington Hilton, Washington, D.C., February 2, 2007.

5. St. Benedict (480–547), Evensong Closing Prayer, Westminster Abby, London, England.

6. Dance As Though No One Is Watching," author unknown, Thinkexist.com, http://thinkexist.com/quotation/-dance_as_though_no_one_is_watching_you-love_as/341162.html, (accessed August 2009).

Devotional Guide
[1] Byron Katie: *A Thousand Names for Joy, Living in harmony with the Way Things Are*. (New York: Random House, 2007).

Joyful Dance drawing; Used with permission of artist, Jean Keaton"
keatonprints.com